W9-BND-634

American Civil War

Facts and Fictions

James R. Hedtke

Historical Facts and Fictions

ABC-CLIO™

An Imprint of ABC-CLIO, LLC

Santa Barbara, California • Denver, Colorado

Copyright © 2018 by ABC-CLIO, LLC

All rights reserved. No part of this publication may be reproduced, stored in a retrieval system, or transmitted, in any form or by any means, electronic, mechanical, photocopying, recording, or otherwise, except for the inclusion of brief quotations in a review, without prior permission in writing from the publisher.

Library of Congress Cataloging-in-Publication Data

Names: Hedtke, James R., author.
Title: American Civil War : facts and fictions / James R. Hedtke.
Description: Santa Barbara, California : ABC-CLIO, 2018. | Series: Historical
   facts and fictions | Includes bibliographical references and index.
Identifiers: LCCN 2018018948 (print) | LCCN 2018022589 (ebook) | ISBN
   9781440860744 (eBook) | ISBN 9781440860737 (hardcopy : alk. paper)
Subjects: LCSH: United States—History—Civil War, 1861–1865—Juvenile literature.
Classification: LCC E468 (ebook) | LCC E468 . H447 2018 (print) | DDC 973.7—dc23
LC record available at https://lccn.loc.gov/2018018948

ISBN: 978-1-4408-6073-7 (print)
         978-1-4408-6074-4 (ebook)

22 21 20 19 18   1 2 3 4 5

This book is also available as an eBook.

ABC-CLIO
An Imprint of ABC-CLIO, LLC

ABC-CLIO, LLC
130 Cremona Drive, P.O. Box 1911
Santa Barbara, California 93116-1911
www.abc-clio.com

This book is printed on acid-free paper ∞
Manufactured in the United States of America

To my daughters, Lisa, Kristi, and Lori. Thank you for your boundless love and the immense joy you have brought into my life.

Contents

Preface

Even though the American Civil War ended more than 150 years ago, it still fascinates and intrigues the American public. Authors have written more books about the Civil War than any other event or conflict in American history. Bibliographers estimate that writers have produced over 50,000 books and pamphlets about the struggle between the states. On average, one book on the Civil War has been published every day since the end of the conflict in 1865. The Pew Research Center for the People & the Press conducted a survey in 2011 that revealed that 56 percent of Americans thought the Civil War was still relevant to American politics. Another 36 percent of the respondents believed the war was a histori-cally important event. The Civil War still commands the attention of the American people.

In their works, authors have written about almost every conceivable topic and aspect of the Civil War. The purpose of this work is relatively unique. This book will expose and debunk 10 popular misconceptions related to the Civil War. A misconception is a false or mistaken view, opinion, or idea based on incorrect facts or faulty reasoning. Each chapter will examine the misconceptions through the same analytical lens and separate fact from fiction. The chapter will describe the misconception and explain how it arose and became ensconced in the American popular memory. Primary sources and documents will be used to demonstrate the rise and spread of the misconception. The author will then provide the reader with historical facts, primary sources, and documents that will correct the misconception and establish an accurate account about what happened during the war. Each chapter will conclude with a short bibliography that allows readers to delve deeper into the misconception and search for the historical truth on their own.

The misconceptions examined in this work cover a diverse set of topics, from why the Southern states left the Union to the plot to assassinate Abraham Lincoln. Most of the misconceptions are still widely embraced by Americans and remain controversial topics discussed at venues ranging from Civil War roundtables to the American political arena.

Chapter 1 examines the controversial debate of why Southern states left the Union in 1860–1861. Were lost-cause advocates correct in arguing that states' rights were the most important cause of secession?

The Civil War commenced in April 1861, when Southern forces bombarded Fort Sumter at Charleston, South Carolina. Chapter 2 critically revisits Edmund Ruffin's claim to have fired the first shot of the Civil War from a battery on Morris Island on the morning of April 12, 1861.

Did African American regiments fight for the Confederacy? Were all combat soldiers men? These questions serve as the focus for chapters 3 and 4.

Ask any grade-school student who freed the slaves, and he or she will answer, "Abraham Lincoln." Is this accurate? Chapter 5 provides the answer to this question.

The Gettysburg Address is an iconic American speech that helped to guide and reshape the nation. Did Lincoln really write the speech on the train while traveling to Gettysburg? Chapter 6 tackles this enduring and popular misconception.

Chapter 7 investigates the misconception that General Ulysses S. Grant was a mediocre commander who won battles through the cruel and needless sacrifice of his troops.

Chapter 8 looks at the use and practice of medicine during the Civil War and examines whether it was cruel and barbaric or state of the art for its time.

Did the U.S. government promise "40 acres and a mule" to the freed people during or after the Civil War? Chapter 9 explores the origins and historical facts behind the controversial idea of reparations for slavery.

Was there a grand conspiracy led by Confederate leaders to assassinate Lincoln? Did Union leaders conspire to kill the president? Chapter 10 examines and evaluates the prominent conspiracy theories about Lincoln's death.

The work concludes with a selected, general bibliography that cites important resources that the reader can use for further research on the American Civil War.

Acknowledgments

There are many people I need to thank for their direct or indirect contributions to this book. I never would have completed this work without their help and encouragement.

My wife, Judy, is my best friend and a steadfast supporter of all my endeavors. Her belief in me is as unwavering as her love. She is the inspiration behind everything I do and write. Though I have done extensive research on the American Civil War, the one true thing I know is our love for each other.

My daughter, Lori Bollinger, took on the arduous of reading my handwriting and turning it into a typed manuscript. She undertook this mission while raising two boys and working fulltime. This work would still be words on yellow legal pads without her help.

Jolyon Girard has been a colleague, friend, and mentor for almost 45 years. He is the individual who introduced me to the editorial staff at ABC-CLIO. He is a loyal friend and an outstanding teacher and writer. His counsel, advice, and editorial assistance have been key ingredients in my success as a scholar.

Cabrini University has been my second home for 45 years. I would like to express my appreciation to my colleagues in the History and Political Science Department: Darryl Mace, Courtney Smith, Nancy Watterson, and Joseph Fitzgerald. Their advice, suggestions, and support have been invaluable to me. It is an honor to be a member of the Cabrini University faculty, a group of individuals who have dedicated their lives to providing their students with an education of the heart.

I especially want to thank the late Dr. David Dunbar. Dr. Dunbar was an exceptional teacher and a noted researcher in the field of molecular biology. His brilliant career came to an abrupt end when he died in a tragic automobile accident in May 2016. David was an avid student of the Civil War and always taught the medical segment of my Civil War course. I wrote the chapter on Civil War medicine in his memory.

Anne Schwelm and her talented staff at Cabrini University's Holy Spirit Library provided invaluable help in procuring primary and secondary sources used in this book. Cabrini ITR personnel answered all of my technical questions in a timely and courteous manner.

Several authors have informed my knowledge of the Civil War and have served as models for my writing style. I am indebted to Bruce Catton, Shelby Foote, James McPherson, and Gary Gallagher for their iconic works on this pivotal time in American history. Their passion for the subject matter and ability to craft a compelling narrative about it have served as an inspiration to me.

Michael Millman at ABC-CLIO has provided me with excellent direction and advice on this project. Eswari Maruthu, the editorial project manager, did an outstanding job guiding the manuscript through revisions to final publication.

Finally, I would like to thank the brave soldiers who fought in the Civil War to preserve the United States and set enslaved persons free. There would be no book without their noble service and sacrifices.

Introduction

The Civil War remains the pivotal event in American history. This conflict answered the two great questions that had dominated American politics since the Revolutionary War: slavery and secession. In January 1865, Congress passed the 13th Amendment, prohibiting the institution of slavery in the United States and its territories. The question of secession was definitively answered on the great battlefields of this war. The Northern victory established the Union as permanent and indestructible. The Civil War also launched the quest for equality in American society. The struggle for equality is still a prominent theme in the American political arena in the 21st century.

Abraham Lincoln's election to the presidency in November 1860 served as the spark that lit the fires of Southern secession. The Republican candidate for president embraced his party's antislavery platform. Lincoln and the Republicans would prohibit slavery in American territories but allow it to remain in the places where it already existed. The hope of the Republicans was to contain slavery to where it already existed and to place the institution on "the road to ultimate extinction."

Many Southerners saw the Republican antislavery platform as the last step before abolition. They warned their Northern countrymen that they would leave the Union if a Republican was elected president. For Southerners, a Republican victory would mean that the North controlled the federal government and would have the political power to eventually abolish slavery in the states as well as the territories.

The presidential election of 1860 was a sectional contest. Lincoln's name did not appear on the ballot in 10 Southern states. He received only

1.4 percent of the popular vote and zero electoral votes from the slave states. Southern presidential candidates John Breckenridge (D, KY) and John Bell (Constitutional Union, TN) dominated the slave-state electorate. Lincoln garnered only 39 percent of the national vote but won 180 electoral votes, all from the free states. Lincoln won the majority of the votes in the electoral college and became the 16th president of the United States.

After Lincoln's election, many Southern state legislatures called conventions to consider secession. Slaveholders feared that the election of a Republican president coupled with Northern control of the federal government would spell doom for the institution of slavery. The South Carolina Convention voted unanimously on December 20, 1860, to enact an ordinance to secede from the Union. Mississippi, Florida, Alabama, Georgia, Louisiana, and Texas followed the lead of South Carolina. By February 1, 1861, seven slaveholding states from the Deep South had left the United States.

In February 1861, the seceded states met in Montgomery, Alabama. The delegates to the convention created a new government, the Confederate States of America. They also elected Jefferson Davis of Mississippi as the first and only president of the C.S.A. The new constitution of the C.S.A provided protection for the institution of slavery.

President Buchanan was a lame-duck president and made no military effort to keep the seceded states in the Union. His relative inaction was a calculated attempt to allow politicians the opportunity to develop compromises to preserve the Union. Buchanan also believed that secession was Lincoln's problem, and the incoming president should have a clean slate so he could deal with the issue unencumbered by previous commitments. All attempts at compromise failed because Lincoln and the Republicans would not allow slavery into the territories. Lincoln believed that any compromise that allowed slavery in the territories would be a betrayal of Republican campaign promises and make a mockery of the democratic election process.

Lincoln's inauguration took place on March 4, 1861, under heavy security in Washington, D.C. The Confederacy seized federal forts, installations, and buildings in the seceded states. By March 5, only Fort Sumter in Charleston, South Carolina, and three coastal forts in Florida remained in Union hands. Fort Sumter was the most important of these forts because it controlled the entrance to one of the most important ports in the Confederacy.

The commander of Fort Sumter, Maj. Robert Anderson, informed Lincoln that he could only hold the fort if the government reinforced it with men, weapons, ammunition, and other supplies. Lincoln was faced with a dilemma. If he evacuated Sumter, he would recognize the legitimacy of the Confederacy, and the Union would be dissolved. If Lincoln sent reinforcements and military supplies to the fort, he would appear as the aggressor and risk a Southern attack that would lead to civil war.

Lincoln followed neither course of action. Instead, he informed Governor Pickins of South Carolina of the U.S. government's peaceful intention to send only humanitarian provisions to the fort. If the Confederacy fired on unarmed Union ships, that would start a civil war and incite Northern public opinion against the South. If the Confederates allowed the fort to be resupplied, it would be a symbolic Northern victory and perhaps a gesture that the Confederacy wanted to negotiate a settlement with the North.

The Confederates made their decision on the morning of April 12, 1861. At 4:30 a.m., Confederate batteries stationed on James Island opened fire on Fort Sumter. After 33 hours of bombardment by almost 4,000 projectiles, Major Anderson surrendered the battered fort to the Confederates. In an ironic twist of fate, there were no fatalities in the battle that commenced the deadliest war in American history. Two American soldiers, however, died after the battle when a cannon imploded during the ceremony to retire the American colors flying over Fort Sumter.

On April 15, Lincoln called 75,000 state militiamen into federal service for 90 days to suppress the rebellion in the Southern states. Instead of 90 days, the war to restore the Union lasted four years. During the Civil War, almost 2,100,000 men served in the Union army. Nearly 190,000 African Americans fought for the Union. Over 800,000 men fought for the Confederacy. Confederate regulations prohibited black men from serving in the Southern army until March 1865. Despite claims to the contrary, no organized black regiment fought on the battlefield for the C.S.A. Regulations of both armies prohibited females from joining the military. Despite these regulations, almost 400 women fought as combat soldiers during the Civil War. More people died in the Civil War than in any other war in American history. According to the official records, the war claimed 620,000 lives (360,000 Northerners and 260,000 Confederates). Today, demographers believe the number of fatalities in the war was 10 percent to 15 percent higher than official numbers, putting the death toll at over 700,000.

The goals of the Confederacy remained constant during the Civil War. The South sought their independence from the United States in order to preserve their institution of slavery. To accomplish their goals, the Confederacy employed several strategies. The South fought a defensive war. This strategy allowed the South to equalize the Northern manpower advantage through shorter lines of supply, communication, and troop reinforcement. The Confederacy did take the offensive when they believed they had the military advantage or could deal a severe blow to Union morale. These offensives, such as the Maryland (1862) and Gettysburg (1863) campaigns, generally ended with disastrous results for the South. The South also attempted to lure England and France into the war by withholding cotton from them. This strategy, known as "King Cotton," was a failure. The British and the French did not diplomatically recognize the Confederacy, and they did not intervene militarily into this war on behalf of the South. The lack of overt European support reduced the South's chances of defeating the North.

The primary goal of the North was to preserve the Union. When Lincoln and other Northern leaders realized that the Union could not be restored as half free and half slave, the abolition of slavery became another important Union goal.

The Union used multiple strategies to defeat the South and preserve the Union. The North blockaded the South to hurt the Confederate military effort and to cause deprivation on the home front. The Union hoped to split the Confederacy in half by seizing the Mississippi River. The North made a concerted effort to capture the Confederate capital at Richmond. The seizure of the capital would be a severe blow to Confederate morale and would figuratively decapitate Southern political leadership. The North also employed a strategy of hard war. By 1864, Union armies destroyed anything that could be used by the Confederacy to sustain their war effort. Hard war not only hurt Confederate armies in the field but also broke the will to resist on the Southern home front. Sherman's "March to the Sea" in 1864 is the classic example of the Union application of hard-war strategy.

In 1862, Confederate and Union troops clashed along the Mississippi, Tennessee, and Cumberland Rivers as well as in Virginia. By the summer, Congress and Lincoln abolished slavery in Washington, D.C., and in the territories. In July, Lincoln made up his mind to emancipate enslaved peoples in the Confederacy. Members of his cabinet, however, urged Lincoln to postpone emancipation until it could be supported by a Union victory.

On September 17, Union forces defeated General Robert E. Lee's army at the battle of Antietam. On September 22, Lincoln issued the preliminary proclamation that the slaves in states still in rebellion on January 1, 1863, would be "forever free." Lincoln's proclamation justified emancipation solely on the grounds of military necessity. The proclamation also deprived the South of an important segment of their workforce, lessened the possibility of European intervention, encouraged blacks to join the Union army, and injected new morale into Northern troops.

The year 1863 proved to be pivotal in the war. On January 1, Lincoln issued the Emancipation Proclamation. This document provided freedom for enslaved persons in the states and areas of states still in the rebellion against the United States. The Union won critical victories at Gettysburg, Vicksburg, and Chattanooga that severely crippled the Confederate war effort. In November, President Lincoln gave an address at Gettysburg that attempted to put the two and a half years of carnage into perspective. His speech, although controversial in its origin, honored the men who died to preserve the Union and put the nation on a new road toward freedom.

In 1864, Lincoln and General Ulysses S. Grant employed a concentration in time strategy to defeat the Confederates. In the spring, Grant issued orders to the five major Union armies to begin coordinated attacks against all Confederate forces. This strategy would deprive Southerners of the ability to reinforce their attacked troops and allow the North to use their manpower advantage to their greatest benefit. Grant took personal command of the Overland Campaign that led to the siege of Petersburg and endangered the Confederate capital at Richmond. General William T. Sherman's Atlanta Campaign ended with Union forces capturing the city on September 2. Sherman then prepared plans for his famous "March to the Sea."

The reelection of Lincoln in 1864 sealed the fate of the Confederacy. Lincoln won 55 percent of the popular vote and defeated the Democratic candidate George McClellan 212 to 21 in the electoral college. On the road to victory, Lincoln captured 78 percent of the votes of Union soldiers. The message behind Lincoln's victory was clear to both the North and South: the Civil War would continue until the Union defeated the Confederacy.

In January 1865, Congress passed the 13th Amendment and ended slavery everywhere in the United States. Union forces continued to attack beleaguered Confederate forces on all fronts. On April 3, Richmond fell to Union troops, and the Confederate government fled from the capital. On April 9, General Lee surrendered his Army of Northern Virginia to General Grant at Appomattox Court House. General Johnston surrendered the remnants of the Army of the Tennessee to General Sherman on April 26. Union cavalry captured Jefferson Davis in Georgia on May 10. General Edmund Kirby Smith surrendered the last Confederate troops on May 26. The war was definitely over, and the Union had prevailed in the contest.

President Lincoln did not live to witness the final capitulation of Confederate troops. On the night of April 14, Lincoln attended a comedy at Ford's Theater. During the performance, John Wilkes Booth entered the president's box and shot Lincoln. Lincoln died the next morning in a boarding house across the street from the theater. Lincoln was the first American president to be killed by an assassin.

There are many myths and misconceptions that have developed about this pivotal event in American history. This work seeks to separate myth from reality and to provide the reader with a factual account of what really happened in the American version of the *Iliad*.

1

The Main Reason the Southern States Seceded from the Union Was States' Rights

What People Think Happened

The antislavery North dominated the election of 1860. Abraham Lincoln, a Republican from Illinois, was elected president of the United States without winning a single electoral college vote from a slave state. The North controlled both the Congress and the presidency and now technically possessed the power to put the institution of slavery on the ultimate road to extinction.

The results of the election of 1860 were not lost on Southern politicians, newspaper editors, and slaveholders. They believed that Northern, antislave control of the central government threatened the existence of their peculiar institution of slavery. Southerners, who favored secession, argued that the best way to protect slavery was to secede from the Union and create a new government dedicated to the protection of that institution. On December 20, 1860, South Carolina was the first state to leave the Union. By March 1861, six more Southern states had seceded from the United States, and these states formed the Confederate States of America. What each of these seceded states shared in common was that they were all from the Deep South, where slavery was the strongest.

After four years of horrific war, the North defeated the South, preserved the Union, and ended slavery. Former Confederates faced a world of loss, devastation, and humiliation. The North had completely defeated the Confederacy on the battlefield and had ended Southern hopes of establishing a slaveholding republic. In the wake of their loss, Southerners searched for reasons for their defeat, a justification for the war, and a way to reestablish Southern honor. Southerners found answers to their questions and purpose for their sacrifice in a set of beliefs known as the lost cause.

Edward A. Pollard, a Virginia journalist and Confederate sympathizer, was the first person to use the term "lost cause." It appeared in the title of his work, *The Lost Cause: A New Southern History of the War of the Confederate States* (1866). He used the term again in another book published in 1868, *The Lost Cause Regained.* In his writings, Pollard developed the two central themes of the lost cause. First, the Confederates lost the war because of the superior resources and manpower of the North and not because of any deficiency in the fighting prowess, honor, or courage of the Southern soldier. The second theme was that the primary reason Southern states left the Union was to protect states' rights rather than to protect the institution of slavery. The misconception that the primary reason for Southern secession was states' rights rather than slavery originated in Pollard's writings and became a basic tenet of the lost cause paradigm.

Pollard and future lost cause writers wanted to construct their own version of secession that would vindicate the Southern cause and favorably position the defeated Confederacy in history. Pollard understood that slavery was an anachronism out of line with contemporary economics and morality. Any acknowledgment that Southern states seceded from the Union to preserve slavery would eternally place the Confederacy on the wrong side of history. Pollard rewrote history by removing slavery as the primary cause of secession and replacing it with states' rights. Through the juxtaposition of cause, future students of the war might view Southerners as the champions of constitutional rights and the rightful heirs to the American revolutionary tradition rather than the villains who fought to perpetuate chattel slavery.

How the Story Became Popular

While Edward Pollard coined the term "lost cause," it was later writers who popularized its themes. It was through the writings and lectures of iconic Confederate leaders, such as Jubal Early, Alexander Stephens, and Jefferson Davis, that the themes of the lost cause became embedded in Southern history and identity. Specifically, these three individuals stressed that states' rights, not slavery, was the primary reason for secession and for the establishment of the Confederate States of America. These individuals also argued that states had a constitutional right to secede from the Union.

Jubal Early was born in Virginia and graduated from the United States Military Academy. After brief service in the U.S. Army, he resigned his commission and practiced law. He joined the Confederate army in 1861 and served in the Eastern Theater under the command of Robert E. Lee. Early rose to the rank of lieutenant general and became a corps commander. He became a household name in both the North and South after his daring raid on Washington, D.C., in July 1864. After the surrender of the Army of Northern Virginia in April 1865, Early fled to Texas, where he hoped to join Confederate forces fighting the North. President Johnson pardoned Early in 1868, and the former general returned to Virginia to practice law.

Early used his pen to commemorate Confederate resistance to Northern aggression. In his memoirs and his writings for the Southern Historical Society, he championed the themes of the lost cause and cemented them into the Southern memory of the Civil War. In his work, *Lieutenant General Jubal Anderson Early C.S.A. Autobiographical Sketch and Narrative of the War between the States*, Early argued that "the struggle made by the people of the South was not for the institution of slavery, but for the inestimable right of self-government against the domination of a fanatical faction at the North." Early concluded that with the Northern victory, "the right to self-govern has been lost." A Southern military hero's testimony provided credence to Pollard's lost cause claim that states' rights was the primary cause of secession.

Jefferson Davis was the first and only president of the Confederate States of America. He was born in Kentucky and raised in Mississippi. He graduated from the United States Military Academy and served the United States as a soldier, a member of the House of Representatives, a senator, and a secretary of war. As a plantation owner, Davis firmly believed in the importance and value of slavery for the South. In February 1861, the Confederate Congress selected Jefferson Davis as the provisional president of the Confederacy.

On April 29, 1861, Davis delivered his first message to the Congress of the Confederate States of America. In his message, he decried the antislavery activities of the North and expressed displeasure with the Republican Party for "rendering the property in slaves so insecure as to be comparatively worthless." Davis argued that the potential Republican policies could annihilate "in effect property worth thousands of millions of dollars." President Davis reached the conclusion that Northern threats to slavery left slaveholding states with no choice but to secede from the Union.

After the collapse of the Confederacy, the U.S. government captured Davis and imprisoned him in Fort Monroe for two years. A decade later, Davis began writing his version of the events preceding the Civil War and the struggle for Southern independence. In his two-volume work, *Rise and Fall of the Confederate Government*, Davis reversed his position on the primary cause of secession. He argued in his book that slavery was "far from being the cause of the conflict." In fact, Davis maintained that Southerners would have eventually ended the institution on their own. Davis repeatedly argued that the Northern denial of Southern states' rights led to the legal, constitutional secession of the slaveholding states. The success of *Rise and Fall of the Confederate Government* in the South and the prominence of its author popularized and continued the states' rights misconception.

Alexander Stephens was born in Georgia and served in the U.S. House of Representatives from 1843 to 1859. He was the only vice president of the Confederate States of America. Stephens was an ardent supporter of slavery. On March 21, 1861, Vice President Stephens delivered an oration at the Athenaeum in Savannah, Georgia. In his address, commonly known as the cornerstone speech, Stephens declared that the immediate cause of secession was the sectional disagreements over the enslavement of Africans. To protect slavery, Southern states seceded from the Union and established a government and a constitution to protect their peculiar institution.

Less than five years after the war ended, Stephens penned his two-volume apology for the Confederacy, *A Constitutional View of the Late War between the States*. In it, Stephens reversed his position from the cornerstone speech that slavery was the immediate cause of secession. The former vice president concluded that Southern states left the union over the issue of states' rights and the right to self-government. Stephens argued that the conflict that ignited the Civil War was the collision between the two antagonistic principles of centralism and states' rights. Stephens claimed that slavery was merely the question that brought this clash to the forefront of American politics. Once again, another prominent Southern politician revised his position on the cause of secession and reinforced the postwar Southern conception that states' rights was the primary reason slaveholding states left the Union.

The lost cause tenet that states' rights was the primary cause of the Civil War is still a vibrant topic among Southern revisionists and apologists today. James and Walter Kennedy's *The South Was Right!* is in its 14th edition. In this work, originally published in 1991, the Kennedys argue that defense of states' rights, not slavery, was the reason for secession. They also claim that secession was a justifiable response to Northern aggression against the states' right to self-government. The same theme appears in Lochlainn Seabrook's *Everything You Were Taught about the Civil War Is Wrong. Ask a Southerner* (2010) and John Tiley's *Facts the Historians Leave Out: A Confederate Primer* (1951, reprinted in 2015).

In 2010, the Texas Board of Education adopted a revised social studies curriculum that provided new state standards for teaching about the Civil War. The standards placed states' rights as the primary cause of the Civil War and relegated slavery to a secondary role as a reason for the conflict. In 2015, new Texas textbooks reflected the 2010 standards and downplayed the role of slavery in the Civil War. The state of Texas continues to socialize a new generation of students into the misconceptions of the lost cause.

In 2011, the Pew Research Center for the People and the Press conducted a study to see if the Civil War was still relevant to Americans. One of the questions researchers asked participants was about what they believed was the main cause of the Civil War. Though there was no majority consensus, 40 percent of the respondents said that states' rights was the primary cause while 39 percent stated it was slavery. Another 9 percent claimed that slavery and states' rights were equal causes of the conflict. Americans younger than 30 believed that states' rights was the main cause, while respondents over 65 were the only group that embraced slavery as the primary reason. The Pew Center study demonstrates the depth and breadth of the impact that Confederate revisionists and apologists have had on the historical interpretation of the cause of the Civil War. It also confirms that the misconception of states' rights as the primary cause of the Civil War endures into the 21st century.

PRIMARY SOURCE DOCUMENTS

JUBAL EARLY, *AUTOBIOGRAPHICAL SKETCH AND NARRATIVE OF THE LATE WAR BETWEEN THE STATES* (1912)

Lt. Gen. Jubal Anderson Early was a lawyer and a Confederate general. The Virginian fought in the Eastern Theater throughout the Civil War. He was a corps commander in Lee's Army of Northern Virginia and launched a daring raid on Washington, D.C., in the summer of 1864. Early escaped to Texas after the war and then traveled to Mexico, Cuba, and Canada. He returned to Virginia after President Johnson pardoned him in 1868. He was an outspoken believer in white supremacy and disliked abolitionists. His memoirs were an unabashed ode to the nobility of the Southern soldier and the valiant causes he fought for: states' rights and resistance to a tyrannical central government. Early was a regular contributor to the Southern Historical Society. He advanced lost cause themes more than any other Confederate officer. The following is an excerpt from his work Lieutenant General Jubal Anderson Early C.S.A. Autobiographical Sketch and Narrative of War between the States, *in which Early writes about the cause of secession and the war.*

During the war, slavery was used as a catch-word to arouse the passions of a fanatical mob, and to some extent the prejudices of the civilized world were excited against us; but the war was not made on our part for slavery. High dignitaries in both church and state in Old England, and puritans in New England, had participated in the profits of a trade by which the ignorant and barbarous natives of Africa were brought from that country and sold into slavery in the American colonies. The generation in the Southern States which defended their country in the late war, found amongst them, in a civilized and Christianized condition, 4,000,000 of the descendants of those degraded Africans. The Creator of the Universe had stamped them, indelibly, with a different color and an inferior physical and mental organization. He had not done this from mere caprice or whim, but for wise purposes. An amalgamation of the races was in contravention of His designs or He would not have made them so different. This immense number of people could not have been transported back to the wilds from which their ancestors were taken, or, if they could have been, it would have resulted in their relapse into barbarism. Reason, common sense, true humanity to the black, as well as the safety of the white race, required that the inferior race should be kept in a state of subordination. The conditions of domestic slavery, as it existed in the South, had not only resulted in a great improvement in the moral and physical condition of the negro race, but had furnished a class of laborers as happy and contented as any in the world, if not more so. Their labor had not only developed the immense resources of the immediate country in which they were located, but was the main source of the great prosperity of the United States, and furnished the means for the employment of millions of the working classes in other countries. Nevertheless, the struggle made by the people of the South was not for the institution of slavery, but for the inestimable right of self-government, against the domination of a fanatical faction at the North; and slavery was the mere occasion of the development of the antagonism between the two sections. That right of self-government has been lost, and slavery violently abolished.

When the passions and infatuations of the day shall have been dissipated by time, and all the results of the late war shall have passed into irrevocable history, the future chronicler of that history will have a most important duty to perform, and posterity, while poring over its pages, will be lost in wonder at the follies and crimes committed in this generation.

Each generation of men owes the debt to posterity to hand down to it correct history of the more important events that have transpired in its day. The history of every people is the common inheritance of mankind, because of the lessons it teaches.

For the purpose of history, the people of the late Confederate States were a separate people from the people of the North during the four years of conflict which they maintained against them.

No people loving the truth of history can have any object or motive in suppressing or mutilating any fact which may be material to its proper elucidation.

Source: Early, Jubal. 1912. *Lieutenant Jubal Anderson Early, C.S.A.: Autobiographical Sketch and Narrative of the War between the States.* Philadelphia: J. B. Lippincott, ix–x.

JEFFERSON DAVIS, *RISE AND FALL OF THE CONFEDERATE GOVERNMENT* (1881)

Jefferson Davis spent over three years researching and writing his monumental work on the history of the Confederacy. Davis's book also served as an apology for the cause that he thought justified Southern secession. Davis argued that states' rights, not slavery, was the primary cause for slaveholding states to leave the Union. The book was published in 1881, and readers had purchased more than 22,000 copies by 1890. In the following excerpt from volume 1 of Rise and Fall of the Confederate Government, *Davis discusses the impact of states' rights on secession and the war that followed.*

The attentive reader of the preceding chapters—especially if he has compared their statements with contemporaneous records and other original sources of information—will already have found evidence enough to enable him to discern the falsehood of these representations, and to perceive that, to whatever extent the question of slavery may have served as an *occasion*, it was far from being the *cause* of the conflict.

I have not attempted, and shall not permit myself to be drawn into any discussion of the merits or demerits of slavery as an ethical or even as a political question. It would be foreign to my purpose, irrelevant to my subject and would only serve—as it has invariably served in the hands of its agitators—to "darken counsel" and divert attention from the genuine issues involved.

As a mere historical fact, we have seen that African servitude among us—confessedly the mildest and most humane of all institutions to which the name "slavery" has ever been applied—existed in all the original states, and that it was recognized and protected in the fourth article of the Constitution. Subsequently, for climatic, industrial, and economical—not moral or sentimental—reasons, it was abolished in the Northern, while it continued to exist in the Southern states. Men differed in their views as to the abstract question of its right or wrong, but for two generations after the Revolution there was no geographical line of demarcation for such differences. The African slave trade was carried on almost exclusively by New England merchants and Northern ships. Jefferson—a Southern man, the founder of the Democratic Party, and the vindicator of states' rights—was in theory a consistent enemy to every form of slavery. The Southern states took the lead in prohibiting the slave trade, and, as we have seen, one of them (Georgia) was the first state to incorporate such a prohibition in her organic Constitution. Eleven years after the agitation on the Missouri question, when the subject first took a sectional shape, the abolition of slavery was proposed and earnestly debated in the Virginia legislature, and its advocates were so near the accomplishment of their purpose, that a declaration in its favor was defeated by only a small majority, and that on the ground of expediency. At a still later period, abolitionist lecturers and teachers were mobbed, assaulted, and threatened with tar and feathers in New York, Pennsylvania, Massachusetts, New Hampshire, Connecticut, and other states. One of them (Lovejoy) was actually killed by a mob in Illinois as late as 1837.

These facts prove incontestably that the sectional hostility, which exhibited itself in 1820, on the application of Missouri for admission into the Union, which again broke out on the proposition for the annexation of Texas in 1844, and which reappeared after the Mexican war, never again to be suppressed until its fell results have been fully accomplished, was not the consequence of any difference on the abstract question of slavery. It was the offspring of sectional rivalry and political ambition. It would have manifested itself just as certainly if slavery had existed in all the states, or if there had not been a Negro in America. No such pretension was made in

1803 or 1811, when the Louisiana Purchase, and afterward the admission into the Union of the state of that name, elicited threats of disunion from the representatives of New England. The complaint was not of slavery, but of the "acquisition of more weight at the other extremity" of the Union. It was not slavery that threatened a rupture in 1832, but the unjust and unequal operation of a protective tariff.

It happened, however, on all these occasions, that the line of demarcation of sectional interests coincided exactly or very nearly with that dividing the states in which Negro servitude existed from those in which it had been abolished. It corresponded with the prediction of Mr. Pickering, in 1803, that, in the separation certainly to come, "the white and black population would mark the boundary"—a prediction made without any reference to slavery as a source of dissension.

Of course, the diversity of institutions contributed, in some minor degree, to the conflict of any general statement of a political truth. I am stating general principles—not defining modifications and exceptions with the precision of mathematical proposition or a bill in chancery. The truth remains intact and incontrovertible that the existence of African servitude was in no wise the cause of the conflict, but only an incident. In the later controversies that arose, however, its effect in operating as a lever upon the passions, prejudices, or sympathies of mankind was so potent that it has spread like a thick cloud over the whole horizon of historic truth.

As for the institution of Negro servitude, it was a matter entirely subject to the control of the states. No power was ever given to the general government to interfere with it, but an obligation was imposed to protect it. Its existence and validity were distinctly recognized by the Constitution in at least three places.

Source: Davis, Jefferson. 1881. *The Rise and Fall of the Confederate Government.* Vol. 1. New York: D. Appleton, 65–68.

ALEXANDER STEPHENS, *A CONSTITUTIONAL VIEW OF THE LATE WAR BETWEEN THE STATES* (1868)

Alexander Stephens was the only vice president of the Confederate States of America. After the Civil War, the U.S. government imprisoned Stephens for five months at Fort Warren in Boston. In 1866, the citizens of Georgia elected him to the U.S. Senate, but radical Republicans in the chamber refused to seat him. Stephens then began to write his two-volume work on the Confederacy,

A Constitutional View of the Late War between the States. He concluded Volume 1 by writing that the right of self-government was the major source of the conflict between the North and South and the primary reason for secession and the war itself. The following is an excerpt from Volume 1 of Stephens's work.

In the prosecution of the design of the writer, it has not been his purpose to treat, at all, of men or their actions, civil or military, further than they relate to, or bear upon, those principles which are involved in the subject under consideration. Principles constitute the subject-matter of his work. Times change, and men often change with them, but principles never! These, like truths, are eternal, unchangeable and immutable!

Most of the diseases with which the human system is afflicted, proceed, as natural and inevitable consequences, from the violation or neglect of some one or more of the vital laws of its organization. All violent fevers and convulsions have their origins in this, though the real cause may be too occult to be ascertained by the most skillful pathologist. So with political organizations, whether simple or complex, single or Federal. No great disorders ever occur in them without some similar real cause.

It is a postulate, with many writers of this day, that the late War was the result of two opposing ideas, or principles, upon the subject of African Slavery. Between these, according to their theory, sprung the "irrepressible conflict," in principle, which ended in the terrible conflict of arms. Those who assume this postulate, and so theorize upon it, are but superficial observers.

That the war had its origin in *opposing principles*, which in their action upon the *conduct of men,* produced the ultimate collision of arms, may be assumed as an unquestionable fact. But the opposing principles which produced these results in physical action were of a very different character from those assumed in the postulate. They lay in the organic Structure of the Government of the States. The conflict in principle arose from different and opposing ideas as to the nature of what is known as the General Government. The contest was between those who held it to be strictly Federal in its character, and those who maintained that it was thoroughly national. It was a strife between the principles of Federation on the one side, and Centralism, or Consolidation, on the other.

Slavery, so called, was but *the question* on which these antagonistic principles, which had been in conflict, from the beginning, on divers *other questions*, were finally brought into actual and active collision with each other on the field of battle.

Some of the strongest Anti-slavery men who ever lived were on the side of those who opposed the Centralizing principles which led to the War. Mr. Jefferson was a striking illustration of this, and a prominent example of a very large class of both sections of the country, who were, most unfortunately, brought into hostile array against each other. No more earnest or ardent devotee to the emancipation of the Black race, upon humane, rational and Constitutional principles, ever lived than he was. Not even Wilberforce himself was more devoted to the cause than Mr. Jefferson was. And yet Mr. Jefferson, though in private life at the time, is well known to have been utterly opposed to the Centralizing principle, when *first* presented, on *this question*, in the attempt to impose conditions and restrictions on the State of Missouri, when she applied for admission into the Union, under the Constitution. He looked upon the movement as a political maneuver to bring this delicate subject (and one that lay so near his heart) into the Federal Councils, with a view, by its agitation in a forum where it did not properly belong, to strengthen the Centralists in their efforts to revive their doctrines, which had been so signally defeated on so many other questions. The first sound of their movements on this question fell upon his ear as a "fire bell at night." The same is true of many others. Several of the ablest opponents of that State Restriction, in Congress, were equally well known to be as decidedly in favor of emancipation as Mr. Jefferson was. Amongst these, may be named Mr. Pinkney and Mr. Clay, from the South, to say nothing of those men from the North, who opposed that measure with equal firmness and integrity.

Source: Stephens, Alexander. 1868. *A Constitutional View of the Late War between the States.* Philadelphia: National Publishing Company, 9–10.

What Really Happened

Slavery was not the only cause of Southern secession, but it was the primary reason why slave states left the Union and formed the Confederate States of America. The actions and testimony of Confederate leaders from 1850 to the end of the Civil War in 1865 make it clear that slavery was the primary motivation for secession. The key to ascertaining what motivated Southerners to leave the United States is to examine what they said and did at the time of secession rather than accepting as fact their revisionist statements and apologies for the Confederacy after their defeat in the war.

A decade before the Civil War, Southern politicians advocated for the central government to provide stringent protection for their slave property. Southerners asked the federal government for a stricter fugitive slave law and a slave code to open and protect slavery in American territories. In both instances, Southern leaders sought federal protection for slavery against the intrusion of antislave Northerners. This Southern request for federal protection for slave interests appears to contradict the postwar claim that Southern states seceded to protect their rights.

Southern lawmakers successfully shepherded the Fugitive Slave Act (1850) through Congress. This federal law allowed slave owners to come north and regain enslaved persons who had attempted to gain their freedom by escaping to Northern states. The clauses of the Fugitive Slave Act favored the slave owner and made it easier to return runaways back into bondage in the South. For example, the law denied the fugitive slave the right to testify on his or her behalf. Northern state legislatures passed acts known as personal liberty laws to protect fugitive slaves and to prevent free blacks from being kidnapped back into slavery. Personal liberty laws virtually nullified the federal Fugitive Slave Act. Ironically, Southerners viewed this exercise of states' rights by Northern legislatures as an unconstitutional interference into the federal mandate to protect property, including enslaved persons.

At the Democratic National Convention in Charleston, South Carolina, in 1860, Southern Democrats pushed the delegates to accept a slave code plank to the party platform. The slave code plank called for a federal law to guarantee the protection of slavery in all U.S. territories. Southern Democrats walked out of the convention when Northern delegates defeated the plank. The Southern dissidents eventually held their own convention and added a slave code plank to their platform. Though the slave code never became law, this is another example of Southern politicians attempting to use the power of the central government to protect slaveholding interests.

When delegates from the seceded states wrote the Confederate Constitution, they designed clauses to allow the central government to protect slavery. The framers inserted the slave code plank in article IV, section 3, clause 3 of the Confederate Constitution. In this clause, it was the function of the central government to protect slavery in all the future territories conquered or acquired by the Confederacy. Article IV, section 2 of the constitution allowed the central government to protect the rights of persons to travel with their slaves in any state, and the right to own slaves and travel with them could not be impaired by the states. In the Confederacy, the constitution clearly invested the power to protect slavery in the central government and not the states.

The secession statements of Mississippi, Texas, South Carolina, and Georgia clearly established slavery as a primary cause for secession. Each of the secessionist statements contained several common elements: First, the federal government had not established or enforced laws to protect slavery. Second, Southerners opposed the states' right of Northern states not to support slavery. Third, slavery was a positive good. Finally, Lincoln, the Republican Party, and the North were dedicated to the extinction of slavery, and the only means to maintain the Southern way of life was to secede from the Union and establish a government that protected slavery.

The Georgia secessionist declaration states that it was leaving the Union because the North's "avowed purpose is to subvert our society and subject us not only to the loss of our property but the destruction of ourselves." The South Carolina statement directly attacked states' rights when it claimed: "States should not have the right to let their citizens assemble and speak freely when their statement threatened slavery." The Texas declaration states that the election of Lincoln by the 17 nonslaveholding states would result in "schemes for the ruin of the slave-holding states." The Mississippi statement proclaimed that their secessionist position "is thoroughly identified with the institution of slavery—the greatest material interest of the world." Clearly, the secessionists of 1860–1861 saw the threats to slavery as a primary reason to leave the Union.

The editors of Southern newspapers warned of the dangers that Lincoln's election posed to slavery. They also extolled the virtues of secession to protect the South's peculiar institution. In November 1860, editors of the *Charleston Mercury* warned their readers that Lincoln's election lifted the abolitionists to power and that "the existence of slavery is at stake." The editors called for South Carolina to call for a convention to consider secession because it was the only way to protect slavery. Also in November, the *Richmond Examiner* exclaimed that a party founded on the single sentiment "of the hatred of African Slavery, is now the controlling power." The editors contended that this reality threatened the Union. Newspaper editorials helped to shape the ideas of the secessionist movement and the declarations that justified their action.

Leaders of the Confederate States of America also cemented slavery as the primary reason for secession. Vice President Alexander Stephens delivered his famous cornerstone speech in Savannah, Georgia, less than three weeks after Lincoln was inaugurated president of the United States. In his speech, Stephens asserted that the new Confederate government was founded on slavery. He said that the Confederate government's "cornerstone rests on the great truth that the Negro is not equal to the white man; that slavery, subordination to the superior race, is his natural and normal condition." Stephens concluded that the Confederate government "is the first in the history of the world, based upon this great physical, philosophical and moral truth." In his postwar writings, the former Confederate vice president pushed slavery into the background and suggested to his readers that states' rights was the central issue in leaving the Union and forming the Confederacy.

President Davis, in his first address to the Confederate Congress, made it clear that Lincoln and the Republican Party posed a direct threat to the interests of slaveholders. He stated that Republican policies would render "the property in slaves so insecure as to be comparatively worthless." He concluded that "with the interests of such overwhelming magnitude imperiled, the people of the Southern states were driven by conduct of the North to the adoption of some course to avert the danger." The central message in Davis's address is that Southern states left the Union to form a central government that would protect slavery. Davis, like Stephens, in his postwar writings, disavowed slavery as the cause for secession and focused in on states' rights as the primary reason.

In conclusion, while there were many reasons for secession, slavery was the primary cause. Southerners prior to the Civil War advocated for the central government to protect slavery. They were against any attempt by Northern state legislatures to exert states' rights to subvert federal laws protecting slavery. When Southerners perceived that Lincoln's election endangered slavery, they seceded from the Union to create a central government to protect their peculiar institution. After the Civil War, lost cause writers, in their quest to be on the right side of history, ignored the discredited institution of slavery as the primary cause of secession and substituted the more noble states' rights reason in its place.

PRIMARY SOURCE DOCUMENTS

JEFFERSON DAVIS, FIRST MESSAGE OF JEFFERSON DAVIS TO THE PROVISIONAL CONGRESS OF THE CONFEDERATE STATES OF AMERICA (APRIL 29, 1861)

President Jefferson Davis delivered his first message to the Provisional Congress of the Confederate States of America on April 29, 1861, in Montgomery, Alabama. Davis gave his address two weeks after Abraham Lincoln called for 75,000 volunteers to suppress the rebellion in the South. In his address, Davis

called on Congress to devise the measures necessary for the defense of the Con-
federacy. He also reviewed the historical relationship between the Northern
and Southern states that drove them into conflict. In this excerpt from Davis's
speech, the president talked about how the Republican threat to slave property
imperiled the interests of the South and pushed them toward secession.

Finally a great party was organized for the purpose of obtaining the administration of the Government, with the avowed object of using its power for the total exclusion of the slave States from all participation in the benefits of the public domain acquired by all the States in common, whether by conquest or purchase; of surrounding them entirely by States in which slavery should be prohibited; of thus rendering the property in slaves so insecure as to be comparatively worthless, and thereby annihilating in effect property worth thousands of millions of dollars. This party, thus organized, succeeded in the month of November last in the election of its candidate for the Presidency of the United States.

In the meantime, under the mild and genial climate of the Southern States and the increasing care and attention for the well-being and comfort of the laboring class, dictated alike by interest and humanity, the African slaves had augmented in number from about 600,000 at the date of the adoption of the constitutional compact, to upward of 4,000,000. In moral and social condition they had been elevated from brutal savages into docile, intelligent, and civilized agricultural laborers, and supplied not only with bodily comforts but with careful religious instruction. Under the supervision of a superior race their labor had been so directed as not only to allow gradual and marked amelioration of their own condition, but to convert hundreds of thousands of square miles of wilderness into cultivated lands covered with a prosperous people; towns and cities had sprung into existence, and had rapidly increased in wealth and population under the social system of the South; the white population of the Southern slaveholding States had augmented from about 1,250,00 at the date of the adoption of the Constitution to more than 8,500,000 in 1860; and the productions of the South in cotton, rice, sugar, and tobacco, for the full development and continuance of which the labor of African slaves was and is indispensable, had swollen to an amount which formed nearly three-fourths of the exports of the whole United States and had become absolutely necessary to the wants of civilized man. With interests of such overwhelming magnitude imperiled, the people of the Southern states were driven by the conduct of the North to the adoption of some course of action to avert the danger with which they were openly menaced. With this view the Legislatures of the several States invited the people to select delegates to conventions to be held for the purpose of determining for themselves what measures were best adapted to meet so alarming a crisis in their history.

Source: Richardson, J. D. 1906. *Messages and Papers of Jefferson Davis and the Confederacy Including Diplomatic Correspondence, 1861–1865.* Nashville: United States Publishing Company.

ALEXANDER STEPHENS: CORNERSTONE SPEECH, SAVANNAH, GEORGIA (MARCH 21, 1861)

Alexander Stephens, vice president of the Confederate States of America, extemporaneously delivered the cornerstone speech on March 21, 1861, at the Athenaeum in Savannah, Georgia. In his address, Stephens stated that the cornerstone of the new Confederate government rested on white superiority and the perpetuation of slavery. Afterward, politicians, editors, and writers commonly referred to Stephens's address as the cornerstone speech because of the cornerstone metaphor he employed to explain Southern secession and the formation of the new government. The following is an excerpt from Stephens's speech.

But not to be tedious in enumerating the numerous changes for the better, allow me to allude to one other though last, not least. The new constitution has put at rest, forever, all the agitating questions relating to our peculiar institution African slavery as it exists amongst us the proper status of the negro in our form of civilization. This was the immediate cause of the late rupture and present revolution. Jefferson in his forecast, had anticipated this, as the "rock upon which the old Union would split." He was right. What was conjecture with him, is now a realized fact. But whether he fully comprehended the great truth upon which that rock stood and stands, may be doubted. The prevailing ideas entertained by him and most of the leading statesmen at the time of the formation of the old constitution, were that the enslavement of the African was in violation of the laws of nature: that it was wrong in principle, socially, morally, and politically. It was an evil they knew not well how to deal with, but the general opinion of the men of that day was that, somehow or other in the order of Providence, the institution would be evanescent and pass away. This idea, though not incorporated in the new constitution, was the prevailing idea at that time. The constitution, it is true, secured every essential guarantee to the institution while it should last, and hence no argument can be justly urged against the constitutional guarantees thus secured, because of the common sentiment of the day. Those ideas, however, were fundamentally wrong. They rested upon the assumption of the equality of races. This was an error. It was a sandy foundation, and the government built upon it fell when the "storm came and the wind blew."

Our new government is founded upon exactly the opposite idea; its foundations are laid, its corner-stone rests, upon the great truth that the negro is not equal to the white man; that slavery subordination to the superior race is his natural and normal condition. This, our new government, is the first, in the history of the world, based upon this great physical, philosophical, and moral truth. This truth has been slow in the process of its development, like all other truths in the various departments of science. It has been so even amongst us. Many who hear me, perhaps, can recollect well, that this truth was not generally admitted, even within their day. The errors of the past generation still clung to many as late as twenty years ago. Those at the North, who still cling to these errors, with a zeal above knowledge, we justly denominate fanatics. All fanaticism springs from an aberration of the mind from a defect in reasoning. It is a species of insanity. One of the most striking characteristics of insanity, in many instances, is forming correct conclusions from fancied or erroneous premises; so with the anti-slavery fanatics. Their conclusions are right if their premises were. They assume that the negro is equal, and hence conclude that he is entitled to equal privileges and rights with the white man. If their premises were correct, their conclusions would be logical and just but their premise being wrong, their whole argument fails. I recollect once of having heard a gentleman from one of the northern States, of great power and ability, announce in the House of Representatives, with imposing effect, that we of the South would be compelled, ultimately, to yield upon this subject of slavery, that it was as impossible to war successfully against a principle in politics, as it was in physics or mechanics. That the principle would ultimately prevail. That we, in maintaining slavery as it exists with us, were warring against a principle, a principle founded in nature, the principle of the equality of men. The reply I made to him was, that upon his own grounds, we should, ultimately, succeed, and that he and his associates, in this crusade against our institutions, would ultimately fail. The truth announced, that it was as impossible to war successfully against a principle in politics as it was in physics and mechanics, I admitted; but told him that it was he, and those acting with him, who were warring against a principle. They were attempting to make things equal which the Creator had made unequal.

In the conflict thus far, success has been on our side, complete throughout the length and breadth of the Confederate States. It is upon this, as I have stated, our social fabric is firmly planted; and I cannot permit myself to doubt the ultimate success of a full recognition of this principle throughout the civilized and enlightened world.

Source: Cleveland, Henry. 1886. *Alexander Stephens in Public and Private with Letters and Speeches, Before, During and Since the War.* Philadelphia: National Publishing Company, 717–29.

A DECLARATION OF THE IMMEDIATE CAUSES WHICH INDUCE AND JUSTIFY THE SECESSION OF THE STATE OF MISSISSIPPI FROM THE FEDERAL UNION (JANUARY 1861)

Mississippi was the second state to leave the Union when it seceded from the United States on January 9, 1861. The Mississippi State Convention then issued "A Declaration of the Immediate Causes Which Induce and Justify the Secession of the State of Mississippi from the Federal Union." This document explained in detail the state's reasons for secession. The Mississippi declaration echoed the themes of Stephens's cornerstone speech: white supremacy and the Northern threat to slavery. The conclusion of the declaration is clear: Mississippians must secede from the Union to preserve slavery and their way of life.

In the momentous step which our State has taken of dissolving its connection with the government of which we so long formed a part, it is but just that we should declare the prominent reasons which have induced our course.

Our position is thoroughly identified with the institution of slavery— the greatest material interest of the world. Its labor supplies the product which constitutes by far the largest and most important portions of commerce of the earth. These products are peculiar to the climate verging on the tropical regions, and by an imperious law of nature, none but the black race can bear exposure to the tropical sun. These products have become necessities of the world, and a blow at slavery is a blow at commerce and civilization. That blow has been long aimed at the institution, and was at the point of reaching its consummation. There was no choice left us but submission to the mandates of abolition, or a dissolution of the Union, whose principles had been subverted to work out our ruin. That we do not overstate the dangers to our institution, a reference to a few facts will sufficiently prove.

The hostility to this institution commenced before the adoption of the Constitution, and was manifested in the well-known Ordinance of 1787, in regard to the Northwestern Territory.

The feeling increased, until, in 1819–20, it deprived the South of more than half the vast territory acquired from France.

The same hostility dismembered Texas and seized upon all the territory acquired from Mexico.

It has grown until it denies the right of property in slaves, and refuses protection to that right on the high seas, in the Territories, and wherever the government of the United States had jurisdiction.

It refuses the admission of new slave States into the Union, and seeks to extinguish it by confining it within its present limits, denying the power of expansion.

It tramples the original equality of the South under foot.

It has nullified the Fugitive Slave Law in almost every free State in the Union, and has utterly broken the compact which our fathers pledged their faith to maintain.

It advocates negro equality, socially and politically, and promotes insurrection and incendiarism in our midst.

It has enlisted its press, its pulpit and its schools against us, until the whole popular mind of the North is excited and inflamed with prejudice.

It has made combinations and formed associations to carry out its schemes of emancipation in the States and wherever else slavery exists.

It seeks not to elevate or to support the slave, but to destroy his present condition without providing a better.

It has invaded a State, and invested with the honors of martyrdom the wretch whose purpose was to apply flames to our dwellings, and the weapons of destruction to our lives.

It has broken every compact into which it has entered for our security.

It has given indubitable evidence of its design to ruin our agriculture, to prostrate our industrial pursuits and to destroy our social system.

It knows no relenting or hesitation in its purposes; it stops not in its march of aggression, and leaves us no room to hope for cessation or for pause.

It has recently obtained control of the Government, by the prosecution of its unhallowed schemes, and destroyed the last expectation of living together in friendship and brotherhood.

Utter subjugation awaits us in the Union, if we should consent longer to remain in it. It is not a matter of choice, but of necessity. We must either submit to degradation, and to the loss of property worth four billions of money, or we must secede from the Union framed by our fathers, to secure this as well as every other species of property. For far less cause than this, our fathers separated from the Crown of England.

Our decision is made. We follow their footsteps. We embrace the alternative of separation; and for the reasons here stated, we resolve to maintain our rights with the full consciousness of the justice of our course, and the undoubting belief of our ability to maintain it.

Source: *Journal of the State Convention.*1861. Jackson: E. Barksdale, State Printer, 86–88.

Further Reading

Bonekemper, Edward H., III. 2015. *The Myth of the Lost Cause: Why the South Fought the Civil War and Why the North Won.* Washington, D.C.: Regnery History.

Civil War Trust. n.d. "The Declaration of Causes of Seceding States; Georgia, Mississippi, South Carolina, Texas and Virginia War Trust." Accessed May 3, 2017. https:www.civilwar.org/learn/primary-sources /declaration-causes-seceding-states.

Cleveland, Henry. 1866. *Alexander Stephens in Public and Private: With Letters and Speeches, Before, During and Since the War.* Philadelphia: National Publishing Company.

Davis, Jefferson. 1881. *The Rise and Fall of the Confederate Government.* Vol. 1. New York: D. Appleton.

Davis, William C. 1996. *The Cause Lost: Myths and Realities of the Confederacy.* Lawrence: University Press of Kansas.

Early, Jubal C. S. A. 1912. *Autobiographical Sketch and Narrative of the War between the States.* Philadelphia: J. B. Lippincott.

Foster, Gaines M. 1987. *Ghosts of the Confederacy: Defeat, the Lost Cause, and the Emergence of the New South, 1865–1913.* New York: Oxford University Press.

Gallagher, Gary W. 2008. *Causes Won, Lost, Forgotten: How Hollywood and Popular Art Shape What We Know about the Civil War.* Chapel Hill: University of North Carolina Press.

Gallagher, Gary W., and Allan T. Nolan, eds. 2010. *The Myth of the Lost Cause and Civil War History.* Bloomington: Indiana University Press.

Graf, Rebecca Simmons. 2015. "Origins of the Lost Cause: Pollard to the Present." *Saber and Scroll* 4, no. 2: article 7.

Johnson, Bethany L. 2010. "The Southern Historical Association: Seventy-Five Years of History 'In the South' and 'Of the South.'" *Journal of Southern History* 76, no. 3: 655–82.

Kennedy, James R., and Walter D. Kennedy. 1994. *The South Was Right!* Gretna, LA: Pelican.

Loewn, James W., and Edward H. Sebesra, eds. 2010. *The Confederate and Neo-Confederate Reader: The "Great Truth" about the "Lost Cause."* Jackson: University Press of Mississippi.

Maddex, Jack P., Jr. 1974. "Pollard's *The Lost Cause Regained*: A Mask for Southern Accommodation." *Journal of Southern History* 40, no. 4: 595–612.

Osterweis, Rollin G. 1973. *The Myth of the Loss Cause: 1865–1900.* Hamden, CT: Anchor Books.

Pew Research Center for the People and the Press. 2011. *Civil War at 150: Still Relevant, Still Divisive.* Washington, D.C.: Pew Research Center for the People and the Press.

Pollard, Edward A. 1866. *The Lost Cause: A New Southern History of the War of the Confederates.* New York: E. B. Treat.

Pollard, Edward A. 1868. *The Lost Cause Regained.* New York: G. W. Carleton.

Seabrook, Lochlainn. 2010. *Everything You Were Taught about the Civil War Is Wrong. Ask a Southerner!* Nashville: Sea Raven.

Stampp, Kenneth. 1991. *The Causes of the Civil War.* 3rd ed. New York: Simon and Schuster.

Stephens, Alexander. 1868. *A Constitutional View of the Late War between the States.* Philadelphia: National Publishing Company.

Tiley, John S. 1951. *Facts the Historians Leave Out: A Confederate Primer.* Montgomery: Paragon.

2

Edmund Ruffin Fired the First Shot at Fort Sumter

What People Think Happened

In April 1861, only four forts remained under Union control in the Confederate States of America. The most important of these Union-occupied forts was Fort Sumter in Charleston, South Carolina. This island fort controlled one of the most valuable ports in the Confederacy. Fort Sumter became a focal point of contention between the Union and the Confederacy. If the Union abandoned Fort Sumter to the Confederacy, this action would be tantamount to recognition of the Confederate government. If the Confederates left Sumter under Union control, questions would arise about the viability of the Confederate government. On April 6, Lincoln informed Governor Pickens of South Carolina that he intended to peacefully resupply the fort "with provisions only." On April 9, the Confederate cabinet made the fateful decision to attack Sumter before the supply flotilla reached the fort.

At exactly 4:30 a.m. on April 12, 1861, Confederate batteries opened fire on Sumter. Over the next 33 hours, approximately 4,000 Confederate projectiles rained down on the fort. On April 14, Maj. Robert Anderson surrendered the battered compound to Gen. P. G. T. Beauregard. Civil War scholars generally agree that the Confederates fired the opening salvos of the Civil War. There is, however, disagreement about which Confederate fired the first shot at Fort Sumter.

The popular misconception is that Virginia secessionist Edmund Ruffin fired the first shot at Fort Sumter on the morning of April 12 from the

Iron Battery stationed on Morris Island. The source of this information was Edmund Ruffin himself. He recorded his alleged historic first shot in his diary. The next day, April 13, *The Charleston Mercury* provided credibility to Ruffin's assertion by printing his version of the initial bombardment of Sumter on the front page of the newspaper. The attachment of a popular secessionist's name to the start of sectional hostilities personalized this momentous occasion for many Southerners.

Edmund Ruffin was a staunch supporter of slavery and an ardent secessionist. He was a Virginia planter known for his keen interest in scientific agriculture. Ruffin was an advocate for agricultural reform in the South and wrote many articles as well as a book on the subject. In the 1850s, Ruffin's interests turned to politics. His writings defended slavery and urged Southern states to secede in order to protect their economic and social institutions. John Brown's failed raid on Harpers Ferry deeply irritated Ruffin. He saw the raid as an overt act of aggression against the South and became determined to witness Brown's execution. Since only military personnel were allowed to be present at Brown's hanging, Ruffin temporarily joined the Virginia Military Institute (VMI) corps of cadets. In his VMI uniform, Ruffin watched Brown die. Ruffin later obtained the pikes Brown's men seized in the raid and sent them to Southern governors as a reminder of the intentions of the North.

Ruffin applauded Southern secession and the establishment of the Confederacy. He strongly advocated for the secession of his native state of Virginia. Ruffin rushed to Charleston when Fort Sumter became the flash point in the North/South conflict. He vowed to remain in Charleston until Virginia joined the Confederacy. Ruffin inspected Confederate positions in Charleston harbor and conversed daily with high-ranking political and military officials. He dutifully recorded his observations and conversations in his diary.

Ruffin was determined to play a leading role in any action that might precipitate a civil war. On April 8, 1861, the 67-year-old fiery secessionist boarded a steamer for the harbor forts, hoping the ship would draw the first fire from Sumter. In his diary entry for that day, Ruffin recorded his desire to make history. He wrote, "I greatly coveted the distinction and éclat which I might have acquired if the steamer had been fired upon."

On April 9, 1861, Ruffin joined the Palmetto Guard on Morris Island. In his diary, Ruffin recorded that on the night of April 11, Captain Cuthbert informed him that the first shot at Fort Sumter would be fired from the Iron Battery on Morris Island. He also told Ruffin that the men of the Iron Battery wanted Ruffin to have the honor of firing the first shot. The next day, April 12, at 4:30 a.m., Ruffin claimed he had fired the opening shot at Fort Sumter, igniting the Civil War. Ruffin's diary entry for April 12 states that he was "highly gratified by the compliment and delighted to perform the service—which I did." Through the power of his own words, Ruffin now had the "distinction and éclat" he desired for himself.

How the Story Became Popular

If journalism is the first rough draft of history, then it was the journalists and editors who gave credence to Ruffin's assertion that he fired the first shot at Fort Sumter. Early accounts of the battle in the press popularized Ruffin's version of what transpired on the morning of April 12, 1861. Ruffin's flamboyant persona, his strident Southern nationalism, and his audacious desire to be at the forefront of the struggle for Confederate independence provided the press with the perfect person to fire the opening salvo at Sumter. The 67-year-old, white-haired volunteer from Virginia symbolized the heart and soul of the secessionist movement and the struggle for independence.

On April 13, *The Charleston Mercury* covered the first day of the attack in an article entitled "Bombardment of Fort Sumter." The article provided a narrative of the artillery duel between Confederate batteries and Sumter on April 12 from 4:30 a.m. to about 9:00 p.m. The article stated that Steven's Battery on Morris Island did conspicuous damage to the southeast portion of the fort. It also stated that "the honor of firing the first shot was accorded to the venerable Edmund Ruffin of Virginia."

Other Southern papers published accounts of the attack on Fort Sumter and Ruffin's role in firing the first shot. *The Charleston Courier* wrote that as soon as Ruffin knew a battle was inevitable, he rushed to Morris Island and joined the Palmetto Guard. The article stated that Ruffin "fired the first gun from Steven's Iron Battery." The author of the article went on to write, "May he live many years to wear the fadeless wreath that honor place upon his brow on our glorious Friday." A Mobile, Alabama, newspaper, *The Daily Mercury*, stated "that it was his hand [Ruffin's] that pointed and fired the first gun at Sumter." The author of the article predicted the notoriety that would be accorded Ruffin when he wrote, "The conduct of Cincinnatus was no more patriotic than that of Edward Ruffin, and side by side in the niche of fame will their names be recorded by every patriotic heart."

Northern papers also acknowledged that Ruffin fired the first shot at Fort Sumter. The Charleston correspondent for the *New York Tribune* wrote, "The first shot from Steven's Battery was fired by the venerable Edmund Ruffin of Virginia." *The New York Post* also reported that Ruffin fired the first shot as a member of Steven's Battery on Morris Island. In an article printed on June 22, 1865, covering the death of Edmund Ruffin, *The New York Times* stated that Ruffin "fired the first gun at Sumter, an act which he always spoke with pride and exultation."

After the capture of Fort Sumter, Ruffin returned to Richmond and championed the cause of secession in his home state. He rejoined the Palmetto Guard and fought with them at the First Battle of Bull Run. He witnessed the Peninsula Campaign in 1862 from one of his family estates near Richmond. Poor health kept Ruffin from further battles, and he spent much of the remainder of the war on his estate near Danville, Virginia. At the conclusion of the Civil War, a distraught Ruffin took his own life on June 18, 1865. His final diary entry provided the reason for his suicide. He wrote, "And now with my latest writing and with what will near to my latest breath, I here repeat and would willing proclaim, my unmitigated hatred to Yankee rule, to all political, social and business connections with Yankees, and to the perfidious, malignant, and vile Yankee race."

Ruffin's deep-rooted Southern nationalism, his passion for the Southern cause, and his tragic suicide secured his place in Confederate history and lore. His willingness to take his own life rather than submit to Northern oppression invested his legacy with a credibility that Southerners were unwilling to question.

One of the first public challenges to Ruffin's claim appeared in the *Southern Historical Society Papers* in 1883. Confederate major general Dabney Herndon Maury founded the Southern Historical Society in 1869 to document Southern military and civilian viewpoints about the war. Gen. Stephen D. Lee wrote a letter to the society in which he claimed that Edmund Ruffin did not fire the first shot at Sumter. The Southern Historical Society published Lee's letter in its papers as well as a rebuttal by Julian Meade Ruffin.

Julian Meade Ruffin was the grandson of Edmund Ruffin. Julian Ruffin's father, Julian Calx Ruffin, was Edmund Ruffin's son and was killed in action at Drewry's Bluff on May 16, 1864. Ruffin's rebuttal to Lee's letter served as the classic defense of his grandfather's legacy and helped propel the elder Ruffin's claims into the 20th century. In his rebuttal, Julian Ruffin used his grandfather's diary entry for April 12, 1861, as well as numerous newspaper stories to buttress his argument. The younger Ruffin concluded his defense by writing that Lee was the first person to cast aspersions on his grandfather's claim and that throughout his diary, his grandfather spoke of firing the first shot at Sumter "as fact." Julian Ruffin believed that his grandfather was an honorable man and his word should be taken as the truth.

Historians and writers popularized the Ruffin story and helped to transmit it into the 21st century. Ben Ames Williams, editor of Mary Boykin Chestnut's diary, said in his comments on Fort Sumter that Ruffin "is usually accorded the distinction of firing the first shot." E. Merton Coulter in his *Confederate States of America, 1861–1865* wrote that "tradition early in the making awarded Ruffin the honor of firing the first gun." The preeminent Southern historian Shelby Foote wrote in his work *The Civil War: A Narrative* that Roger Pryor was offered the honor of firing the first shot at Fort Sumter but refused. Foote then wrote, "Another Virginian Could and Would—White-Haired Edmund Ruffin." Historynet.com's online segment on Fort Sumter states that "Virginia fire-eater Edmund Ruffin who had campaigned relentlessly through the 1850's for states' rights, slavery and secession was given the honor of firing the first shot at Fort Sumter." The Ruffin version of events still has its supporters 155 years after Confederate forces fired the first shot at Fort Sumter.

PRIMARY SOURCE DOCUMENTS

EDMUND RUFFIN'S ACCOUNT OF THE BOMBARDMENT OF FORT SUMTER IN HIS DIARY (APRIL 12, 1861)

Edmund Ruffin was a Virginia planter, writer, and prominent secessionist. He maintained a diary from October 1856 until his death in June 1865. His diary serves as an important chronicle of Southern political attitudes, ideas, and motives during this crucial era in American history. In his diary, Ruffin commented on important events, such as John Brown's raid, Lincoln's election, and secession. In his entry for April 12, 1861, Ruffin described the initial bombardment of Fort Sumter and the leading role he played in this event. The misconception that Ruffin fired the first shot at Sumter started with this account.

April 12. Before 4 a.m. the drums beat for parade, & our company was speedily on the march to the batteries which they were to man.

At 4:30, a signal shell was thrown from a mortar battery at Fort Johnson. Which had been before ordered to be taken as the command for immediate attack—& the firing from all the batteries bearing on Fort Sumter next began in the order arranged—which was that the discharges should be two minutes apart, & the round of all the pieces & batteries to be completed in 32 minutes, & then to begin again. The night before, when expecting to engage, Capt. Cuthbert had notified me that his company requested of me to discharge the first cannon to be fired, which was their 64 lb. Columbiad, loaded with shell. By order of Gen. Beauregard, made known the afternoon of the 11th, the attack was to be commenced by the first shot at the fort being fired by the Palmetto Guard, & from the Iron Battery. In accepting & acting upon this highly appreciated compliment, that company had made me its instrument. . . . Of course I was highly gratified by the compliment, & delighted to perform the service—which I did. The shell struck the fort, at the north-east angle of the parapet. The firing then preceded, as stated, from 14 different batteries, including Fort Moultrie & the floating Sullivan's Island. Most of both shot & shells, at first, missed the fort. But many struck, & the proportion of effective balls & shells increased with the practice. To all the firing, not a gun was fired in return; for two hours or more—& I was fearful that Major Anderson, relying on the security of his men in the covered casemates, proof against shells, & in the strength of the walls against breaching by balls—& in the impossibility of successful storming of the strong fortress, surrounded by water, did not intend to fire at all. It would have cheapened our conquest of the fort, if effected, if no hostile defense had been made—& still more increased the disgrace of failure. So it was gratifying to all of us when Major Anderson opened his fire. He seemed to distribute his shot mostly between our two batteries, Fort Moultrie & the floating battery. Through the forenoon he fired mostly at our two batteries, & especially at the Point—& with 42 lb. round shot, if all were like a few that we then recovered. But later in the day, (about noon), he directed most of his fire on Fort Moultrie—& for an hour before closing his firing at night, he did not send a shot to our side. A battery (the Trapier) of three large mortars, next below or eastward of our iron battery, fired regularly & well, but received but few of Anderson's balls, compared to others.

Source: Ruffin, Edmund. 1915, 1967. *Edmund Ruffin Diaries.* Manuscript Division of the Library of Congress, Box 4, Reel 2. Washington, D.C.

"BOMBARDMENT OF FORT SUMTER!" *CHARLESTON MERCURY* (APRIL 13, 1861)

Henry L. Pinckney started The Charleston Mercury *in 1819. The paper published editions three times a week during the Civil War until it shut down operations under Union occupation in 1865. The paper resumed publication in 1866 until it permanently shut down its presses in 1868. The editors favored secession and slavery as well as seizing Fort Sumter. In its April 13, 1861, edition,* The Charleston Mercury *was one of the first papers to cover the Confederate attack on Fort Sumter. It also anointed Ruffin as the individual who fired the first shot on the fort.*

As may have been anticipated from our notice of the military movements in our city yesterday, the bombardment of Fort Sumter, so long and anxiously expected, has at length become a fact accomplished. The restless activity of the night before was gradually worn down, the citizens who had thronged the battery through the night, anxious and weary, had sought their homes, the Mounted Guard which had kept watch and ward over the city, with the first grey streak of morning were preparing to retire, when two guns in quick succession from Fort Johnson announced the opening of the drama.

Upon that signal, the circle of batteries with which the grim fortress of Fort Sumter is beleaguered opened fire. The outline of this great volcanic crater was illuminated with a line of twinkling lights; the clustering shells illuminated the sky above it; the balls clattered thick as hail upon its sides; our citizens, aroused to a forgetfulness of their fatigue through many weary hours, rushed again to the points of observation; and so, at the break of day, amidst the bursting of bombs, and the roaring of ordinance, and before thousands of spectators, whose homes, and liberties, and lives were at stake, was enacted this first great scene in the opening drama of what, it is presumed, will be a most momentous military act. It may be a drama of but a single act. The madness which inspires it may depart with this single paroxysm. It is certain that the people of the North have rankling at their hearts no sense of wrong to be avenged; and exhibiting to those who expect power to reconstruct the shattered Union, its utter inadequacy to accomplish a single step in that direction, the Administration of the old Government may abandon at once and forever its vain and visionary hope of forcible control over the Confederate States. But it may not be so; they may persist still longer in assertions of their power, and if so, they will arouse an independent spirit in the South, which will exact a merciless and fearful retribution.

But to return to our report. The act which we have undertaken to record was so unique as might be supposed there were few incidents to mark it. Below we have presented the reports as they successively arrived from the different batteries, and which when placed on our bulletin board, were received with the most eager interest by the mass of anxious friends who at every instant of the day came crowding to our office.

There were several circumstances, however, developed by the day experience which it is important to notice.

It affords us infinite pleasure to record that Fort Moultrie has fully sustained the prestige of its glorious name. It fired very nearly gun for gun with Fort Sumter. We counted guns from eleven to twelve, and found them to be 42 to 46, while the advantage was unquestionably upon the side of Fort Moultrie. In that fort not a gun was dismounted, not a wound received, not the slightest permanent injury sustained by any of its defences, while every ball from Fort Moultrie left its mark upon Fort Sumter. Many of its shells were dropped into that fort, and Lieut. JOHN MITCHELL, the worthy son of that patriot sire, who has so nobly vindicated the cause of the South, has the honor of dismounting two of its parapet guns by a single shot from one of the Columbiads, which at the time he had the office of directing.

The famous iron batteries—the one at Cummings' Point—named for Mr. C.H. STEVENS, the inventor, and the celebrated Floating Battery, constructed under the direction of Capt. HAMILTON, have fully vindicated the correctness of their conception. Shot after shot fell upon them and glanced harmless away, while their favorable position their shots fell with effect upon Fort Sumter, and the southeast pancopee, under the fire of the STEVENS' battery, at nightfall, if not actually breached, was badly damaged. At this battery the honor of firing the first gun was accorded to the venerable EDMUND RUFFIN, of Virginia, who marched to the rendezvous at the sound of the alarm on Monday night, and who, when asked by some person who did not know him, to what company he belonged, replied, that in which there is a vacancy.

Source: "Bombardment of Fort Sumter!" *Charleston Mercury*, April 13, 1861.

JULIAN RUFFIN, LETTER IN REPLY TO STEPHEN D. LEE'S CONTENTION OF WHO FIRED THE FIRST GUN AT FORT SUMTER, *SOUTHERN SOCIETY HISTORICAL PAPERS* (1883)

Julian Meade Ruffin was the grandson of Edmund Ruffin. His father, Julian Calx Ruffin, died in action at Drewry's Bluff in May 1864. Julian Meade

Ruffin was the defender of the Ruffin legacy in the Civil War. In a letter pub-
lished in the Southern Historical Society Papers *in 1883, Ruffin defended*
his grandfather's story of firing the first shot at Fort Sumter against Gen. Ste-
phen Lee's allegation that the elder Ruffin's account was inaccurate. In his
letter, Julian Ruffin cited his grandfather's diary entry for April 12, 1861, as
proof that the elder Ruffin fired the first shot at Fort Sumter (see Ruffin's diary
entry above). He then bolstered his argument with quotes from contempo-
rary newspaper reports on Edmund Ruffin's role in the bombardment of Fort
Sumter. The following excerpt from Julian Ruffin's letter provides the reader
with the historiographical sources of the misconception.

The above, as written at that very time, would fully establish the fact that
the first shot was fired by Edmund Ruffin, and it will be observed that the
signal shot which he refers to at Fort Johnson at 4:30 A. M., is the same
that S. D. Lee claims as the first shot at Fort Sumter at the same time
(4:30 A. M.). Now the two might easily be confounded, and to prove that
the one from the iron battery, fired by Edmund Ruffin, was actually the
first gun on Fort Sumter. I will give comments of the press of that date.

The Charleston *Courier* said: "The venerable Edmund Ruffin, who as
soon as it was known as battle was inevitable, hastened over to Morris
Island, and was elected a member of the Palmetto Guard, fired the first
gun from Steven's iron battery. All honor to the chivalric Virginian! May
he live many years to wear the fadeless wreath that honor placed upon his
brow on our glorious Friday!"

From the Charleston correspondent of New York *Tribune:*

"The first shot from Steven's battery was fired by the venerable Edmund
Ruffin, of Virginia. The ball will do more for the cause of secession in the
Old Dominion than volumes of stump speeches."

The Charleston *Mercury* says the first gun fired from the iron battery
off Cumming's Point was discharged by the venerable Edmund Ruffin. He
subsequently shot from all the guns and mortars used during the action.

A Mobile paper had the following:

"A *Sublime Spectacle*—The mother of the Gracchi, when asked for her
jewels, pointed to her children and said, 'There they are.' With the same
propriety can the 'Mother of States' point to her children as the brightest jewels she possesses. At the call of patriotism they are not laggard in
responding to it, and Virginia blood has enriched every battle-field upon
American soil. And we thank God the spirit has not departed from her,
but burns as brightly in the breasts of her children as in the days of her
Washington and her Henry. But of the many bright examples that she has

furnished of patriotism the most sublime is the conduct of the venerable Edmund Ruffin, whose head is silvered over by more than eighty winters, who, when the war-cloud lowered over the gallant city of Charleston, volunteered as a private, and with his knapsack on his back and musket on his shoulder tendered his services to South Carolina to fight against the aggression upon her rights. *It was his hand that pointed and fired the FIRST gun at Fort Sumter.* The world has pointed to the conduct of Cincinnatus, who, when his country was invaded by a hostile foe, left his plow in the furrow to take command of her forces, and after he had driven out the invader and restored his country to peace and prosperity resigned his position and returned to his plow. By this one act he embalmed his memory in the breasts of his countrymen and of all patriots throughout the world. The conduct of Cincinnatus was not more patriotic than that of Edmund Ruffin, and side by side in the niche of fame will their names be recorded by every patriotic heart."

From the New York *Post:*

"*Shot and Hemp*—A Charleston dispatch states that the 'first shot from Steven's battery was fired by the venerable Edmund Ruffin, of Virginia.' A piece of the first hemp that is stretch in South Carolina should be kept for the neck of this venerable and bloodthirsty *Ruffian.*"

From the above quoted expressions it would indeed be impossible to conclude otherwise than that the first gun on Fort Sumter was shot by Edmund Ruffin, and that such should be retorted as an historical fact. In fact, the above from S. D. Lee is the first intimation of a doubt on this subject that has ever been brought to the notice of any of the descendants of Edmund Ruffin. To all who knew Edmund Ruffin it would have been useless to say more than that throughout his manuscript he speaks of it as a fact. To those to whom he was a stranger I would say that many more comments of the press of that date establish the same fact: those of the South being loud in his praise, and those of the North being still more vindictive.

Source: Ruffin, Julian M. 1883. "Reply of Julian M. Ruffin." *Southern Historical Society Papers* 11: 502–05.

What Really Happened

There is no doubt that Edmund Ruffin was present on Morris Island on the morning of April 12, 1861, and fired one of the first shots at Fort Sumter. The question is, did Ruffin fire the first shot as he claimed in his diary? To answer this question, scholars and students need to examine the testimony and writings of those who were present that morning and participated in the bombardment of the island fortress. An evaluation of the eyewitness testimony and evidence provided by Confederates present at the bombardment suggests that someone other than Ruffin fired the first shot at Sumter.

Confederate general Pierre Gustave Toutant Beauregard provided one of the first challenges to Ruffin's story. General Beauregard was a creole from Louisiana. In April 1861, he commanded the defenses at Charleston. Beauregard demanded that Major Anderson surrender Fort Sumter before the planned Union expedition to provision the garrison arrived at its destination. When negotiations between Anderson's and Beauregard's aides broke down in the early hours of April 12, Beauregard ordered the battery at Fort Johnson on James Island to open the assault on Sumter.

In 1883, Alfred Roman wrote a two-volume biographical work about Beauregard entitled *The Military Operations of General Beauregard in the War between the States.* In the preface of Roman's book, Beauregard wrote that Roman penned the work "from my notes and it is authenticated by me as a correct account of my military service and conduct." In recounting the initial attack on Fort Sumter, Beauregard informed Roman that the mortar battery at Fort Johnson fired the first shot. Beauregard continued on about the first shot and told Roman, "It was fired, not by Mr. Edmund Ruffin, of Virginia, as has been erroneously believed, but by Captain George S. James of South Carolina, to whom Stephen D. Lee issued the order." In his authorized biography, the commander of the Confederate forces at Charleston provided a substantial challenge to the veracity of Ruffin's claim.

In 1883, the *Southern Historical Society Papers* published a letter written by former Confederate lieutenant general Stephen D. Lee. In his letter, Lee confirmed Beauregard's version of the initial shots fired at Fort Sumter. In April 1861, Lee was a captain in the regular Confederate States of America Artillery and an aide-de-camp to General Beauregard. On the morning of April 12, Lee was one of the four individuals who delivered Beauregard's final demand to Major Anderson to surrender Sumter. When Anderson refused Beauregard's surrender offer, Lee informed the Union major that Confederate forces would commence fire in about an hour.

Captain Lee then proceeded from Fort Sumter to James Island and delivered the order to fire on the fort to Capt. George S. James, commander of the mortar battery at Fort Johnson. At 4:30 a.m., Captain James offered the honor of firing the first shot to Roger Pryor of Virginia.

Pryor declined the honor. According to Lee, another officer offered to fire the first shot but James replied, "No! I will fire it myself." Lee then notes in his letter that James did fire the shot. He also wrote that "one thing is certain he [Ruffin] never fired the first gun against Fort Sumter. George S. James did. Nor did he fire the second gun." Lee's letter called into question Ruffin's assertions and reinforced Beauregard's recollections of the initial salvo against Sumter.

In 1893, Dr. Robert Lebby wrote a paper in commemoration of the 32nd anniversary of the Battle of Fort Sumter. The Charleston physician, who was present at Fort Johnson on James Island on April 12, 1861, wanted to set the record straight about who fired the first shot that morning. In his paper, Lebby cited many eyewitnesses to the bombardment, including himself, and concluded that Edmund Ruffin did not fire the first shot.

Dr. Lebby cited the testimony of both General Beauregard and Captain Lee that the batteries at Fort Johnson, and not those on Morris Island, fired the opening salvo. Lebby also quoted the eyewitness accounts of Edward Barnwell and Dr. W. H. Prioleau, who were present on James Island on April 12. Barnwell reported that "the first shell fired at Sumter was from the James Island east battery (or the beach battery); the second was from the west (or hill battery)." Dr. Prioleau, the post surgeon, stated that Captain James gave the order to fire the first shot and that Lt. Henry S. Farley was directly in charge of this gun. In a letter he wrote to Dr. Lebby, Henry Farley stated that "Captain James stood on my right with watch in hand, and at the designated moment gave me the order to fire. I pulled the lanyard."

Lebby was a resident of James Island, and Captain James had asked the physician to be available in case hostilities erupted over Sumter. Lebby wrote that he was in position on the morning of April 12 to see the James Battery fire the first shot at 4:30 a.m. The doctor stated that the Wade Hampton Gibbes Battery fired the second shot from the hill battery above the beach. Lebby concluded that the overwhelming preponderance of evidence was that the James Battery fired the first shot at Sumter, not Ruffin's battery stationed on Morris Island. Lebby also reasoned that Lieutenant Farley fired the first shot on the order of Captain James.

The evidence points to three conclusions. First, the initial shot on Fort Sumter originated from James Island. Since Edmund Ruffin was stationed on Morris Island, he could not have fired the first shot. Second, the first shot came from James Battery at Fort Johnson. The most likely scenario is that Captain James gave the order to fire the first shot, and Lieutenant

Farley executed the command when he pulled the lanyard. Finally, it is extremely probable that Ruffin fired the first shot from the batteries stationed on Morris Island, and this is the origin of the misconception about who fired the first shot on Fort Sumter.

PRIMARY SOURCE DOCUMENTS

STEPHEN D. LEE, "WHO FIRED THE FIRST GUN AT SUMTER" (1883)

Stephen D. Lee was no relation to the famous Confederate general Robert E. Lee. Stephen Lee was a graduate of the U.S. Military Academy and an officer in the U.S. Army. Lee resigned his commission when his native state, South Carolina, left the Union. On the morning of April 12, 1861, he was present on James Island and relayed Beauregard's order to commence firing on Sumter to the batteries at Fort Johnson. In a letter to the Southern Historical Society Papers, *he was one of the first individuals to state that Edmund Ruffin had not fired the first shot at Fort Sumter.*

I wish to correct an error which has almost passed into an historical fact. It is this: That Edmund Ruffin, of Virginia, did not fire the first gun at Fort Sumter, but that Captain George S. James, of South Carolina, afterward killed when a Lieutenant-Colonel at Boonsboro', Md., did fire it.

The writer was a captain of the South Carolina army at the time, and an Aide-de-Camp on the staff of General Beauregard. He now has before him a diary written at the time, and there can be no mistake as to the fact.

The summon for the surrender or evacuation was carried by Colonel Chestnut, of South Carolina, and Captain S. D. Lee. They arrived at Sumter at 2:20 P. M. April 11th.

Major Anderson declined to surrender, but remarked "he would be starved out in a few days if he was not knocked to pieces by General Beauregard's batteries." This remark was repeated to General Beauregard, who informed President Davis. The result was, a second message was sent to Major Anderson by the same officers, accompanied by Roger A. Pryor, of Virginia, and Colonel Chisholm, of South Carolina. The messengers arrived at Sumter at 12:25 A.M. April 12th. Major Anderson was informed that if he would say that he would surrender on April 15th, and in the meantime would not fire on General Beauregard's batteries, unless he was fired on, he would be allowed that time; also that he would not be allowed to receive provisions from the United States authorities. The Major declined to accede to this arrangement, saying he would not open fire unless a hostile act was committed against his fort or his flag, but that if he could be supplied with provisions before the 15th of April, he would receive them, and in that event, he would not surrender. This reply being unsatisfactory, Colonel James Chesnut and Captain S. D. Lee gave the Major a written communication, dated "Fort Sumter, S. C., April 12, 1861, 3:20 A. M.," informing him, by authority of General Beauregard, that the batteries of General Beauregard would open fire on the fort in one hour from that time.

The party, as designates, then proceeded in their boats to Fort Johnson, on James Island and delivered the order to Captain George S. James commanding the mortar battery, to open fire on Fort Sumter. At 4:30 A. M. the first gun was fired at Fort Sumter and at 4:40 the second gun was fired from the same battery. Captain James offered the honor of firing the first shot to Roger A. Pryor, of Virginia. He declined, saying he could not fire the first gun. Another officer then offered to take Pryor's place. James replied: "No! I will fire it myself." And he did fire it. At 4:45 A. M. nearly all the batteries in harbor were firing on Sumter. Mr. Edward Ruffin (who was much beloved and respected) was at the iron battery on Morris Island. I always understood he fired the first gun from the iron battery, but one thing is certain—he never fired the first gun from Fort Sumter, George S. James did. Nor did he fire the second gun. He may have fired the third gun, or first gun from the iron battery on Morris Island. Yours respectfully, S. D. Lee

Source: Lee, Stephen D. 1883. "Who Fired the First Gun at Sumter?" *Southern Historical Society Papers* 11: 501–02.

HENRY S. FARLEY, LETTER TO DR. LEBBY (1893)

Lt. Henry S. Farley was a member of Capt. George James's east battery on James Island on April 12, 1861. At 4:30 a.m., Captain James ordered Farley to fire on Fort Sumter. Farley discharged his mortar, which signaled the other batteries to commence firing on the fort. Farley provided this information to Dr. Robert Lebby, who was working on a paper about who fired the first shot at Sumter in commemoration of the 32nd anniversary of the Confederate attack on the fort. Lebby used the following excerpt from Farley's letter in his paper.

The circumstances attending the firing of the first gun at Sumter are quite fresh in my memory. Captain James stood on my right, with watch in hand, and at the designated moment gave me the order to fire. I pulled the lanyard, having already carefully inserted a friction tube, and discharged a thirteen-inch mortar shell, which was the right of battery. In one of the issues of a Charleston evening paper, which appeared shortly after the reduction of Fort Sumter, you will find it stated that Lieutenant Farley fired the first gun, and Lieutenant Gibbes the second.

Source: Lebby, Robert. 1911. "The First Shot on Fort Sumter." *South Carolina Historical and Genealogical Magazine* 12, no. 3 (July): 141–45.

DR. ROBERT LEBBY, "THE FIRST SHOT ON SUMTER" (1893)

Robert Lebby was a physician and resident of James Island. Confederate officers requested his presence at Fort Johnson to treat casualties when hostilities appeared imminent with the garrison at Fort Sumter. Lebby was present on James Island when Captain James's batteries initiated the conflict. After the war, Lebby served as the quarantine officer of the state of South Carolina at the Port of Charleston. In 1893, in commemoration of the 32nd anniversary of the bombardment of Sumter, Lebby prepared a paper about the first shot on Fort Sumter. News and Courier *published the paper on September 3, 1906, and* South Carolina Historical and Genealogical Magazine *published it again in July 1911, shortly after Lebby's death. The following excerpt is Lebby's account of the morning of April 12 and who he believed fired the first shot on Fort Sumter.*

I will now give my personal recollections of the affair. I am a native, and was a resident and practicing physician of James' Island at the time the first gun was fired, and consequently was perfectly conversant with the topography of the location, and having been a college acquaintance of Captain James, was invited by him the previous day, April 11, to be on hand if anything transpired to require my services. I accepted his invitation and remained to witness the first, and last, gun fired at Sumter at that time.

My recollection of the matter is that on the morning of April 12, 1861, about ten minutes before 4 A.M., Captain S. D. Lee, with two other gentlemen, having just returned from Sumter, passed a group of four gentlemen, I among the number, and inquired for Captain James's quarters, and when directed to the house occupied by Captain James, remarked on passing, that the ball would soon be opened.

A short time elapsed, when Captain James and others passed to the beach, or east, battery, and Captain Lee and his party went on down to the wharf. I was midway between the houses on a bridge that connected the beach and the hill, where I could see the fire of either battery, and at 4:30, A.M., a shell was fired from the beach, or east, battery, commanded by Captain James.

The second report heard was the blowing up of Greer's house, contiguous to the hill battery, commanded by Lieutenant W. H. Gibbes, and the second shell was fired from this battery under Lieutenant Gibbes. The firing then became general around the harbor batteries bearing on Sumter.

We have, therefore, the concurrent testimony of General Beauregard, who ordered the fire to commence; of Captain Stephen D. Lee, the officer extending the order; of Lieutenant Farley, who was in the battery when the gun was fired, and of the medical officer, Dr. W. H. Prioleau, who was on duty in the battery: also of Lieutenant Edward H. Barnwell, who was present at the hill, or Gibbes, battery, and of myself, who all bear witness to the fact that the shell was fired from Captain James's battery on the beach. How, then, can anyone claim that the shell was fired from any other point with this weight of evidence against it?

As to the question of who pulled the lanyard of the mortar from which issued the first shell, there are only two living witnesses that I am cognizant of who were in the battery at the time of the fire, viz.: Colonel Henry S. Farley and Dr. W. H. Prioleau. Colonel Henry S. Farley asserts in a letter to me that he pulled the lanyard by Captain James's order, and Dr. Prioleau asserts that Lieutenant Farley had charge of the right gun of the battery, and that the first fire was from that gun, Captain James giving the order to fire, and it is reasonable to conclude, therefore, that Farley pulled the lanyard. Certain it is that either James or Farley fired it, but, as Captain James gave the order to fire, it must have been Farley, as James would never have given himself the order to fire. The order, therefore, must have been given to Farley. I, therefore, conclude that Lieutenant Henry S. Farley fired the first gun at Sumter by Captain James's order.

Source: Lebby, Robert. 1911. "The First Shot on Fort Sumter." *South Carolina Historical and Genealogical Magazine* 12, no. 3 (July): 141–45.

Further Reading

Abrahamson, James L. 2000. *The Men of Secession and Civil War, 1859–1861*. Wilmington, DE: Scholarly Resources.

Basso, Hamilton. 1933. *Beauregard: The Great Creole*. New York: Charles Scribner's Sons.

"Bombardment of Fort Sumter." 1861. *Charleston Mercury* (Newspapers on Microfilm, South Carolina Library, University of South Carolina), April 13.

Bordewich, M. Fergus. 2011. "Fort Sumter: The Civil War Begins." *Smithsonian Magazine*, April. http://www.smithsonian.com/history /fort-sumter-the-civil-war-begins-1018791/.

Bostick, Douglas W. 2009. *The Union Is Dissolved: Charleston and Fort Sumter in the Civil War*. Charleston, SC: History Press.

Civil War Trust. Accessed June 2, 2017. https://www.civilwar.org/learn /civil-war/battles/fortsumter.

Cooper, William J. 2012. *We Have War upon Us: The Onset of the Civil War, November 1860–1861*. New York: Vintage.

Coulter, E. Merton. 1950. *The Confederate States of America, 1861–1865*. Baton Rouge: Louisiana State University Press.

Detzer, David. 2001. *Brother Against Brother*. New York: Harcourt.

Doubleday, Abner. 2000. *Reminiscences of Fort Sumter and Moutrie: In 1860–61*. Scituate, MA: Digital Scanning.

"The First Shot on Fort Sumter." 1911. *South Carolina Historical and Genealogical Magazine* 12, no. 3: 141–45.

Foote, Shelby Dade, Jr. 1958. *The Civil War: A Narrative*. Vol. 1. New York: Random House.

Hatcher, Richard W. 2017. *Thunder in the Harbor: Fort Sumter, Charleston and the American Civil War*. El Dorado Hills, CA: Savas Beatie.

Hattaway, Herman. 1976. *General Stephen D. Lee*. Jackson: University Press of Mississippi.

Hendrickson, Robert. 1996. *Sumter, the First Day of the Civil War*. New York: Promentory.

Hendrix, M. Patrick. 2014. *A History of Fort Sumter: Building a Civil War Landmark*. Charleston, SC: History Press.

History Net. "Battle of Fort Sumter: Facts about Battle of Fort Sumter, the First Civil War Battle of the American Civil War." Accessed July 6, 2017. https://www.historynet.com/battle-of-fort-sumter.

Klein, Maury. 1997. *Days of Defiance: Sumter, Secession, and the Coming of the War*. New York: Alfred A. Knopf.

Mathew, William M. 1988. *Edmund Ruffin and the Crisis of Slavery in the Old South: The Failure of Agricultural Reform.* Athens: University of Georgia Press.

Meredith, Roy. 1957. *Storm over Sumter: The Opening Engagement of the Civil War.* New York: Simon and Schuster.

Mitchell, Betty L. 1981. *Edmund Ruffin: A Biography.* Bloomington: Indiana University Press.

Roman, Alfred. 1883. *The Military Operations of General Beauregard in the War between the States.* Vol. I. New York: Harper and Brothers, Franklin Square.

Ruffin, Edmund. 1972. *The Diary of Edmund Ruffin.* Vol. I. Baton Rouge: Louisiana State University Press.

Ruffin, Edmund. 2015. *The Political Economy of Slavery: Or the Institution Considered in Regard to Its Influence on Public Wealth and the General Welfare.* London: Forgotten Books.

Swanberg, W. A. 1990. *First Blood: The Story of Fort Sumter.* New York: Dorset House.

Williams, T. Harry. 1955. *P. G. T. Beauregard: Napoleon in Gray.* Baton Rouge: Louisiana State University Press.

3

Black Regiments Fought in Combat for the Confederate States of America

What People Think Happened

In the Civil War, over 2,100,000 men fought for the Union. Nearly 180,000 of these individuals were African Americans. About 179,000 blacks were in the army, and another 10,000 were sailors. African Americans comprised around 9 percent of the Union's fighting force. Regulations for the Army of the Confederate States of America barred black men from military service until March 1865. Though individual black men may have fired shots at Union soldiers, there is no evidence that black regiments engaged in combat for the Confederacy. During the Civil War, the misconception developed that large numbers of Southern blacks fought in organized units for the Confederacy. Lost cause advocates and neo-Confederates have advanced this misconception into the 21st century.

The misconception started with the formation of the First Louisiana Native Guard in New Orleans in May 1861. A committee of 10 important black men from Crescent City called for a meeting to pledge their loyalty to the Confederacy and to form a militia unit. Approximately 2,000 individuals attended the meeting held at the Catholic Institute in New Orleans. At the conclusion of the meeting, about 1,500 free blacks signed the muster roll for a new militia regiment.

On May 2, 1861, Gov. Thomas D. Moore accepted the First Louisiana Native Guard into the state militia. Later in the month, the governor appointed three white officers to lead the regiment, but the remaining 33 officers were black. The 731 enlisted men came from all walks of life and included doctors, architects, carpenters, bricklayers, clerks, and laborers. Louisiana did not provide the regiment with any uniforms or weapons. The volunteers did this themselves out of their own pockets.

The First Louisiana Native Guard saw pomp and circumstance but no combat. They participated in the grand review of troops in New Orleans on November 23, 1861, and paraded through the city streets once again on January 8, 1862. Both Confederate and Louisiana officials, however, were uncomfortable with the idea of black and white troops fighting together in combat. The Native Guard provided the Confederacy with a great propaganda tool: loyal black men who were willing to fight and die for Confederate independence. Confederate politicians and military officers remained doubtful, though, about the courage and prowess of black men under fire.

In January 1862, the Louisiana state legislature revised its militia regulations to meet Confederate standards. Under the new rules, only white men could be in the Louisiana State Militia. On February 15, 1862, Governor Moore disbanded the Native Guards. Moore quickly reinstated the Native Guards in late March when Union military forces approached New Orleans. Gen. Mansfield Lovell assigned the Native Guards the inconsequential role of defending the eastern end of the French Quarter. On April 25, Union ships arrived in the port of New Orleans. Regular Confederate forces fled the city. After the North captured New Orleans, Gen. John Lewis of the Louisiana Militia ordered the First Native Louisiana Guard to permanently disband. The unit ended its brief service without ever firing a shot in combat. Public displays and newspaper accounts of the existence of the Native Guards provided the impetus for the misconception that the Confederacy was organizing and using regiments of loyal free black men in combat against the Union.

How the Story Became Popular

Newspaper articles and eyewitness reports during the war popularized the misconception that large numbers of free and enslaved African Americans fought for the Confederate army. After the war was over, lost cause advocates and neo-Confederates continued to perpetuate the misconception to demonstrate the benevolent nature of Southern slavery, the loyalty of enslaved persons to their masters and to the Confederate government, and that the cause of the Civil War was states' rights rather than slavery.

The misconception continued into the 21st century and even found its way into a textbook used by Virginia elementary school students in 2010.

During the war, Northerners and Northern newspapers reported that large numbers of African Americans were fighting for the Confederacy. The prominent African American abolitionist Frederick Douglass published an article in *Douglass' Monthly* in September 1861, saying that the Confederacy had used large numbers of black soldiers at the First Battle of Bull Run. In "Fighting Rebels with Only One Hand," Douglass stated that "it is now pretty well established, that there are at the present moment many colored men in the Confederate army doing duty not only as cooks, servants and laborers, but as real soldiers, having muskets on their shoulders, and bullets in their pockets, ready to shoot down loyal troops."

Douglass, who was not present at Bull Run, used hyperbole in this article to gain support for the enlistment of African Americans into the Union army. If enslaved persons could fight to maintain slavery in the Confederacy, then blacks could be used to fight to preserve the Union. Douglass believed that admission of black men into the Union army would advance the cause of abolition. Over time, students and scholars have used Douglass's article as proof of large numbers of blacks in the Confederate army rather than seeing it as a ploy to force Lincoln and Northern politicians to admit African Americans into the Union army.

Another Northerner, Lewis Henry Steiner, provided an account of African Americans in the Confederate army. During the war, the U.S. Sanitary Commission, a private relief agency whose mission was to support sick and wounded soldiers of the Union army, employed Steiner as an inspector. He was present in Frederick, Maryland, when Lee's army passed through the city during the Antietam Campaign. On September 10, Steiner wrote that "over 2,000 negroes" were with Lee's army. He also wrote that "most of the negroes had arms, rifles, muskets, sabers, bowie knives, dirks, etc." Steiner's account gave credence to the report of black Confederate soldiers in Douglass's article.

Throughout the war, Northern newspapers printed articles about large numbers of black Confederate soldiers. On January 23, 1862, the *New York Herald* ran a headline that said, "The Rebel Negro Regiment under A. S. Johnston." The article beneath the headline told of rebel attempts in Kentucky to lure enslaved persons into the Confederate army. *The Indianapolis Daily Evening Gazette* ran a story on March 12, 1863, about a fire fight on March 5 at Thomson's Station, Tennessee. The article stated that the 85th Indiana "was attacked by two negro regiments" and that Indiana soldiers "cut the black regiments to pieces." *The New York Times* and

Chicago Tribune both published stories after the First Battle of Bull Run about black regiments that allegedly fought for the Confederate army.

Reports of black Confederates came from Northern politicians and soldiers. They also appeared in *War of the Rebellion: A Compilation of the Official Records of the Union and Confederate Armies.* Sen. Lyman Trumbull of Illinois made reference to the Confederate use of black troops at the First Battle of Bull Run during a debate in Congress on the confiscation of Southern property. He stated on the Senate floor, "I understand that negroes were in the fight which has recently occurred." In the same debate, Sen. John C. Ten Eyck of New Jersey stated that he was going to vote in favor of confiscating rebel property because the Confederacy used slaves "with arms in their hands to shed the blood of union-loving men."

Some Northern soldiers wrote home about encountering black Confederates. John Bates of the 13th Indiana was involved in the Peninsula Campaign in the spring of 1862. In a letter to his father, he wrote, "I can assure you of certainty that the rebels have negro soldiers in their army." Reports contained in the *Official Records* also mention black Confederate troops. For example, Lieutenant Colonel Parkhurst's account of a Confederate attack on the Ninth Michigan at Murfreesboro, Tennessee, on July 13, 1862, stated that "there were also quite a number of negroes attached to the Texas and Georgia troops."

Southern newspapers also contained articles about black Confederate troops. *The Western Democrat* of Charlotte, North Carolina, printed an article on July 29, 1861, about the First Battle of Bull Run. In the article was an anecdote about the black servant of Captain Langhorn. When a Union officer ordered the servant to surrender, the servant drew his pistol and killed the officer. The article claimed that after the battle, the servant boasted that he had killed at least one of "the stinken Yankees who came here specting to whip us southerners." *The Richmond Enquirer* and *The Western Democrat* both reported an incident where a black servant of an Alabama officer captured a Northern Zouave at Bull Run and turned him over to Confederate officers. Articles of this nature continued to appear in the Southern press throughout the war.

Historians such as Bell Irvin Wiley, Joseph Wilson, Bruce Levin, and James H. Brewer reference the existence of individual black Confederates in their works. In the 1890 U.S. Census, 3,273 blacks claimed to have been either Confederate soldiers or sailors. In the 21st century, neo-Confederates have used the anecdotal evidence of individual Southern blacks in combat to write a narrative where tens of thousands of African Americans eagerly volunteered to defend the Confederacy.

Neo-Confederates use this misconception to bolster their lost cause argument that states' rights, not slavery, was the primary cause of secession. Unfortunately, this fiction has even found its way into the classroom. In 2010, Virginia distributed a social studies textbook, *Our Virginia: Past and Present*, to its fourth-grade students. In the text, author Joy Masoff wrote, "Thousands of southern blacks fought in the Confederate ranks, including two black battalions under the command of Stonewall Jackson." In her research, Masoff primarily relied on the Internet. The publisher removed the inaccurate statement in the next edition of the text.

PRIMARY SOURCE DOCUMENTS

FREDERICK DOUGLASS, "FIGHTING REBELS WITH ONLY ONE HAND" (SEPTEMBER 1861)

Frederick Douglass was born into slavery on the eastern shore of Maryland. He escaped to freedom in 1838 and eventually resided in Rochester, New York. Douglass was an ardent abolitionist who wrote and spoke passionately about the emancipation of enslaved persons. Douglass published Douglass' Monthly *from 1859 to 1863 in Rochester. Articles in the paper advanced the cause of abolition and other social reforms. In the September 1861 edition of the* Douglass' Monthly, *Douglass authored an article entitled "Fighting Rebels with Only One Hand." In this article, Douglass stated that Confederates were using black men in their army to advance their cause. Douglass argued that by not using African Americans in their army, the Union was hurting its chances of victory and alienating blacks from "the national cause." Douglass hoped that if black men served in the Union army, the next logical steps would be emancipation and then citizenship. Supporters of the myth of large numbers of blacks in the Confederate army use the Douglass article to substantiate their claim. Below is an excerpt from Douglass's article.*

What on earth is the matter with the American Government and people? Do they really covet the world's ridicule as well as their own social and political ruin? What are they thinking about, or don't they condescend to think at all? So, indeed, it would seem from their blindness in dealing with the tremendous issue now upon them. Was there ever anything like it before? They are sorely pressed on every hand by a vast army of slaveholding rebels, flushed with success, and infuriated by the darkest inspirations of a deadly hate, bound to rule or ruin. Washington, the seat of Government, after ten thousand assurances to the contrary, is now positively in danger of falling before the rebel army. Maryland, a little while ago considered safe for the Union, is now admitted to be studded with the materials for insurrection, and which may flame forth at any moment.—Every resource of the nation, whether of men or money, whether of wisdom or strength, could be well employed to avert the impending ruin. Yet most evidently the demands of the hour are not comprehended by the Cabinet or the crowd. Our Presidents, Governors, Generals and Secretaries are calling, with almost frantic vehemence, for men.—"Men! men! send us men!" they scream, or the cause of the Union is gone, the life of a great nation is ruthlessly sacrificed, and the hopes of a great nation go out in darkness; and yet these very officers, representing the people and Government, steadily and persistently refuse to receive the very class of men which have a deeper interest in the defeat and humiliation of the rebels, than all others.—Men are wanted in Missouri—wanted in Western Virginia, to hold and defend what has been already gained; they are wanted in Texas, and all along the sea coast, and though the Government has at its command a class in the country deeply interested in suppressing the insurrection, it sternly refuses to summon from among the vast multitude a single man, and degrades and insults the whole class by refusing to allow any of their number to defend with their strong arms and brave hearts the national cause. What a spectacle of blind, unreasoning prejudice and pusillanimity is this! The national edifice is on fire. Every man who can carry a bucket of water, or remove a brick, is wanted; but those who have the care of the building, having a profound respect for the feeling of the national burglars who set the building on fire, are determined that the flames shall only be extinguished by Indo-Caucasian hands, and to have the building burnt rather than save it by means of any other. Such is the pride, the stupid prejudice and folly that rules the hour.

Why does the Government reject the Negro? Is he not a man? Can he not wield a sword, fire a gun, march and countermarch, and obey orders like any other? Is there the least reason to believe that a regiment of well-drilled Negroes would deport themselves less soldier-like on the battlefield than the raw troops gathered up generally from the towns and cities of the State of New York? We do believe that such soldiers, if allowed to take up arms in defence of the Government, and made to feel that they are hereafter to be recognized as persons having rights, would set the highest example of order and general good behavior to their fellow soldiers, and in every way add to the national power.

If persons so humble as we can be allowed to speak to the President of the United States, we should ask him if this dark and terrible hour of the nation's extremity is a time for consulting a mere vulgar and unnatural prejudice? We should ask him if national preservation and necessity were not better guides in this emergency than either the tastes of the rebels, or the pride and prejudices of the vulgar? We would tell him that General Jackson in a slave state fought side by side with Negroes at New Orleans, and like a true man, despising meanness, he bore testimony to their bravery at the close of the war. We would tell him that colored men in Rhode Island and Connecticut performed their full share in the war of the Revolution, and that men of the same color, such as the noble Shields Green, Nathaniel Turner and Denmark Vesey stand ready to peril everything at the command of the Government. We would tell him that this is no time to fight with one hand, when both are needed; that this is no time to fight only with your white hand, and allow your black hand to remain tied.

Whatever may be the folly and absurdity of the North, the South at least is true and wise. The Southern papers no longer indulge in the vulgar expression, "free n———rs." That class of bipeds are now called "colored residents." The Charleston papers say: "The colored residents of this city can challenge comparison with their class, in any city or town, in loyalty or devotion to the cause of the South. Many of them individually, and without ostentation, have been contributing liberally, and on Wednesday evening, the 7th inst., a very large meeting was held by them, and a committee appointed to provide for more efficient aid. The proceedings of the meeting will appear in results hereinafter to be reported."

It is now pretty well established, that there are at the present moment many colored men in the Confederate army doing duty not only as cooks, servants and laborers, but as real soldiers, having muskets on their shoulders, and bullets in their pockets, ready to shoot down loyal troops, and do all that soldiers may to destroy the Federal Government and build up that of the traitors and rebels. There were such soldiers at Manassas, and they are probably there still. There is a Negro in the army as well as in the fence, and our Government is likely to find it out before the war comes to an end. That the Negroes are numerous in the rebel army, and do for that army its heaviest work, is beyond question. They have been the chief laborers upon those temporary defences in which the rebels have been able to mow down our men. Negroes helped to build the batteries at Charleston. They relieve their gentlemanly and military masters from the stiffening drudgery of the camp, and devote them to the nimble and dexterous use of arms. Rising above vulgar prejudice, the slaveholding rebel accepts the aid of the black man as readily as that of any other. If a bad cause can do this, why should a good cause be less wisely conducted? We insist upon it, that one black regiment in such a war as this is, without being any more brave and orderly, would be worth to the Government more than two of any other; and that, while the Government continues to refuse the aid of colored men, thus alienating them from the national cause, and giving the rebels the advantage of them, it will not deserve better fortunes than it has thus far experienced.—Men in earnest don't fight with one hand, when they might fight with two, and a man drowning would not refuse to be saved even by a colored hand.

Source: Douglass, Frederick. 1861. "Fighting Rebels with Only One Hand." *Douglass' Monthly* (Rochester, NY), September.

ACCOUNT OF THE BATTLE OF BULL RUN, *THE WESTERN DEMOCRAT* (JULY 30, 1861, AND AUGUST 6, 1861)

During the Civil War, newspapers in both the North and South ran articles about individual blacks serving in the Confederate army and firing at Union troops. Southern papers published these articles to demonstrate the loyalty of enslaved persons to the Confederacy and the morality of their peculiar institution. Northern editors used these stories to encourage the enlistment of African American soldiers into the Union army and to advance the cause of emancipation. The two articles below from The Western Democrat *(Charlotte, North Carolina) were published after the First Battle of Bull Run and are examples of the anecdotal stories of blacks fighting for the Confederacy.*

July 30, 1861:

Another of the incidents mentioned to us is that a negro servant of Capt. Langhorn's company was moving about over the field, he was ordered to surrender by a federal officer, who rode up to where he was unexpectedly. Nothing daunted however, and not relishing the idea of surrendering to a Yankee, the negro replied "no sir-ree, you are my prisoner", at the same moment drawing a pistol and shooting the officer dead. The sable hero then secured the officer's side-arms, and when the battle was over boasted largely of having given a quietus to one at least of "the stinken Yankees who came her 'spectin to whip us southerners."

August 6:

Had one of them—a gentleman who was at Manassas on Tuesday morning saw a negro man belonging to an Alabama officer march a

Zouave into camp. The negro, a short thick set fellow, had two guns on his shoulder and drove his prisoner before him. The Zouave was a pert looking fellow and wore his arm in a sling in consequence of his wound. As the negro reached the company in which the officer was standing he handed over his prize, saying, "Massa, here one of dese devils who has been shooting us sir!"

Source: "Battle of Bull." 1861. *The Western Democrat* (Charlotte, NC), July 30, August 6.

LEWIS STEINER, DIARY ACCOUNT OF THE MARYLAND CAMPAIGN (SEPTEMBER 1862)

Lewis Steiner, an inspector for the U.S. Sanitary Commission, was present in Frederick, Maryland, while Lee's Army of Northern Virginia occupied the city. In his diary entry for September 13, 1862, Steiner recorded that he saw "over 2,000" uniformed and armed black men attached to Lee's army. What Steiner probably witnessed was the enslaved teamsters, cooks, and laborers of the Army of Northern Virginia. At this time, Confederate army regulations forbade black men in the army, and there are no existing Confederate or Union records to substantiate Steiner's claim.

Wednesday, September 10.—At four o'clock this morning the rebel army began to move from our town, Jackson's force taking the advance. The movement continued until eight o'clock P. M., occupying sixteen hours. The most liberal calculations could not give them more than 64,000 men. Over 3,000 negroes must be included in this number. These were clad in all kinds of uniforms, not only in cast-off or captured United States uniforms, but in coats with Southern buttons, State buttons, etc. These were shabby, but not shabbier or seedier than those worn by white men in the rebel ranks. Most of the negroes had arms, rifles, muskets, sabers, bowie-knives, dirks, etc. They were supplied, in many instances, with knapsacks, haversacks, canteens, etc., and were manifestly an integral portion of the Southern Confederacy Army. They were seen riding on horses and mules, driving wagons, riding on caissons, in ambulances, with the staff of Generals, and promiscuously mixed up with all the rebel horde. The fact was patent, and rather interesting when considered in connection with the horror rebels express at the suggestion of black soldiers being employed for the National defence. Some of the rebel regiments have been reduced to 150 men; none number over 500. The men are stout and ragged, anxious to "kill a Yankee," and firm in their belief that *Confederate notes* are as good as gold. Their marching is generally very loose. They marched by the flank through the streets of Frederick. Some few houses had rebel flags, to which one enthusiastic admirer of secession had added a white cross on a red ground. Some handkerchiefs waved, but all felt there was no genuine enthusiasm. The movement to Frederick had proved a failure. Their friends were anxious to get rid of them and of the penetrating ammoniacal smell they brought with them. Union citizens had become stronger in their faith. Rebel officers were unanimous in declaring that "Frederick was a d- Union hole." The ill-suppressed expressions of delight on the countenances of the citizens could not be interpreted into indications of sympathy with secession. They manifested only profound delight at the prospect of its speedy departure.

Source: Steiner, Lewis H. 1862. *Report of Lewis H. Steiner, Inspector of the Sanitary Commission: Containing a Diary Kept During the Rebel Occupation of Frederick, MD., and an Account of the Operations of the U.S. Sanitary Commission During the Campaign in Maryland.* New York: Anson D. F. Randolph, 19–20.

What Really Happened

The Confederate government did not allow African Americans to legally join the Confederate military until March 13, 1865. Prior to that date, the Regulations for the Army of the Confederate States required all soldiers to be "free white males." Eventually, all Confederate states applied the same rule to their militia recruits. Even after the Confederate Congress passed General Orders 14 allowing blacks in their military, there is no official evidence or documentation that an all-black military unit fought in combat for the Confederacy. The Confederacy did use thousands of enslaved persons as teamsters, cooks, musicians, laborers, and orderlies to support their army. It is also impossible to state that no individual black man discharged a weapon for the Confederacy. The fact is that large numbers of African Americans officially organized into regiments did not fight for the Confederacy.

Northern newspaper accounts of large numbers of blacks in the Confederate army were generally based on reports of individuals who observed the enslaved teamsters, cooks, and laborers who were compelled to do the fatigue work of the Confederate army. The Northern press also provided individual anecdotal accounts of Southern blacks firing weapons on the battlefield. Most of these reports focused on enslaved body servants who were forced to accompany their masters into combat. Body servants often wore old uniforms and could easily be confused for soldiers.

In some instances, they did fire shots at Union troops. Fear, coercion, loyalty, and self-protection motivated the actions of these individuals. Northern papers exaggerated the number of African Americans involved in these incidents. Northern abolitionist editors, such as Frederick Douglass, embellished the numbers of black soldiers to encourage Northern politicians to emancipate enslaved persons so they could fight on behalf of the Union.

Supporters of the misconception of large numbers of African Americans fighting in the Confederate army use the *Official Records* to bolster their arguments. *The War of the Rebellion: A Compilation of the Official Records of the Union and Confederate Armies* is comprised of more than 50 volumes and over 50,000 pages of documents. In this vast work, there are fewer than 10 eyewitness accounts about black Confederate soldiers. Only three reports by Union officers cite seeing black units in the Confederate army. There are, however, records of the Confederate War Department declining the services of black regiments in 1861 and beyond. In the *Official Records*, there are no reports from Confederate officers having black soldiers under their command. Officers did report African American laborers present in their camps. The *Official Records* provides no evidence to support the claim that tens of thousands of blacks fought for the Confederacy.

On January 2, 1864, Maj. Gen. Patrick Cleburne and several of his fellow officers from the Confederate Army of Tennessee proposed a plan to Lt. Gen. Joseph Johnston to arm enslaved persons and use them as soldiers in the Confederate army. Cleburne was an excellent division commander and became known as "the Stonewall of the west." Cleburne saw the Confederacy's chances for victory as dim after the crushing defeats at Gettysburg, Vicksburg, and Chattanooga. He believed that the only hope for the Confederacy was to enlist enslaved persons. His plan would guarantee freedom for enslaved persons who fought for the Confederate States of America. Cleburne argued that independence was more important than slavery and that bringing black men into the army would give the Confederacy numerical superiority over the Union.

General Johnston, commanding general of the Army of Tennessee, thought that Cleburne's proposal would be divisive and catastrophic, so he did not send it on to President Davis. One of Johnston's generals, Patton Anderson, commented to Lieutenant General Polk in a letter that "if this thing is once openly proposed to the army, the total disintegration of the army will follow in a fort night." When Jefferson Davis eventually found out about Cleburne's proposal, he ordered all copies of the letter confiscated because he feared the missive would produce "discouragement, distraction, and dissension." The scholar is left with two questions: If a large number of enslaved blacks were already in the Confederate army, why would Cleburne have to make this proposal, and why would it be "divisive" and "cause the disintegration of the army"?

In early 1865, the Confederacy was in tatters. Its armies were melting away, and Union forces controlled most of its territory. A desperate President Davis reconsidered Cleburne's plan to arm enslaved persons. With the encouragement of Davis and the wholehearted support of Gen. Robert E. Lee, the Confederate Congress reluctantly passed a bill to enlist black men into the army on March 13, 1865. The bill did not require the provision of freedom for enslaved persons who fought for the Confederacy. There are no known muster rolls for companies raised under this act, and the war ended before any black units could see combat. If there were already large numbers of blacks in the Confederate army, why did the Confederate Congress need to pass this bill? Also, why would it be so hotly contested by the Congress?

In conclusion, there is no evidence that all-black units fought in combat for the Confederate States of America. There is ample evidence that the Confederate government coerced enslaved persons to do the fatigue work of its armies. There is some anecdotal evidence that a small number of individual black Southerners fired on Union soldiers. Historians can only guess at the motivation of these individuals because of the lack of primary documents, such as letters, diaries, or oral testimony, in this area.

PRIMARY SOURCE DOCUMENTS

CONFEDERATE ARMY REGULATIONS (1861)

In 1861, the Confederate War Department published the Regulations for the Army of the Confederate States. Confederate regulations were not substantially different from those of the U.S. Army. The Confederate regulations clearly stated that soldiers must be "white males." The regulations also stated that any individual who falsified information about himself would be discharged from the army. The Confederacy refused to legally recruit and admit black soldiers into its ranks until March 1865, when the Confederate Congress changed the regulations. Below are the Confederate regulations that require recruits for the Confederate army to be free white males.

They will not allow any man to be deceived and or inveigled into the service by false representations, but will in person explain the nature of the service, the length of the term, the pay, clothing, rations, and other allowances to which a soldier is entitled by law, to every man before he signs the enlistment.

With the sanction of the superintendents, recruiting officers may insert, in not exceeding two newspapers, brief notices directing attention to the rendezvous for further information.

Any free white male person above the age of 18 and under the age of 85 years, being at least 5 feet 4 ½ inches high, effective, able bodied, sober, free from disease, of good character and habits, and with a competent knowledge of the English language, may be enlisted. This regulation, so far as respect the *height* and *age* of the recruit, shall not extend to musicians or to soldiers who may *"re-enlist,"* or have served honestly and faithfully a pervious enlistment in the army.

No man having a wife and child shall be enlisted in time *of peace* without special authority obtained from the Adjutant-General's office, through the superintendent. This rule does not apply to soldiers who *"re-enlist."*

Source: Regulations for the Army of the Confederate States. 1861. New Orleans: H. P. Lathrop, 298–99.

PATRICK CLEBURNE, LETTER TO JOSEPH JOHNSTON ON TRAINING SLAVES TO FIGHT FOR THE CONFEDERACY (JANUARY 2, 1864)

As 1863 came to an end, the position of Confederate troops seemed extremely bleak. Critical defeats at Gettysburg, Vicksburg, and Chattanooga dimmed Confederate chances for independence. On January 2, 1864, Maj. Gen. Patrick Cleburne and other officers of the Army of Tennessee met with Gen. Joseph Johnston, their new commanding officer. At that meeting, Cleburne made an astonishing and almost treasonable proposal to enlist enslaved men as soldiers in the Confederate army in return for their freedom. Cleburne believed the recruitment of enslaved blacks was the only way to match the Northern manpower advantage. He argued that the use of large numbers of black soldiers was necessary to ensure independence.

General Johnston rejected Cleburne's plan and refused to send it to Jefferson Davis. Maj. Gen. W. H. T. Walker, however, did send a copy to Davis. The Confederate president also rejected the plan and ordered all copies of Cleburne's proposal to be suppressed. Maj. Calhoun Berhan, Cleburne's aide, kept a copy, and in 1898 it was published in the Official Records. *It is clear from Cleburne's proposal that large numbers of African Americans were not in the Confederate army in 1864 and that Confederate leaders did not want their services. Below is an excerpt from Cleburne's letter to General Johnston.*

COMMANDING GENERAL, THE CORPS, DIVISION, BRIGADE, AND REGIMENTAL COMMANDERS OF THE ARMY OF TENNESSEE:

GENERAL: Moved by the exigency in which our country is now placed, we take the liberty of laying before you, unofficially, our views on the present state of affairs. The subject is so grave, and our views so new, we feel it a duty both to you and the cause that before going further we should submit them for your judgment and receive your suggestions in regard to them. We therefore respectfully ask you to give us an expression of your views in the premises. We have now been fighting for nearly three years, have spilled much of our best blood, and lost, consumed, or thrown to the flames an amount of property equal in value to the specie currency of the world. Through some lack in our system the fruits of our struggles and sacrifices have invariably slipped away from us and left us nothing but long lists of dead and mangled. Instead of standing defiantly on the borders of our territory or harassing those of the enemy, we are hemmed in today into less than two-thirds of it, and still the enemy menacingly confronts us at every point with superior forces. Our soldiers can see no end to this state of affairs except in our own exhaustion; hence, instead of rising to the occasion, they are sinking into a fatal apathy, growing weary of hardships and slaughters which promise no results. In this state of things it is easy to understand why there is a growing belief that some black catastrophe is not far ahead of us, and that unless some extraordinary change is soon made in our condition we must overtake it. The consequences of this condition are showing themselves more plainly every day; restlessness of morals spreading everywhere, manifesting itself in the army in a growing disregard for private rights; desertion spreading to a class of soldiers it never dared to tamper with before; military commissions sinking in the estimation of the soldier; our supplies failing; our firesides in ruins. If this state continues much longer we must be subjugated. Every man should endeavor to understand the meaning of subjugation before it is too late. We can give but a faint idea when we say it means the loss of all we now hold most sacred—slaves and all other personal property, lands, homesteads, liberty, justice, safety, pride, manhood. It means that the history of this heroic struggle will be written by the enemy; that our youth will be trained by Northern school teachers; will learn from Northern school books their version of the war; will be impressed by all the influences of history and education to regard our gallant dead as traitors, our maimed veterans as fit objects for derision. It means the crushing of Southern manhood, the hatred of our former slaves, who will, on a spy system, be our secret police. The conqueror's policy is to divide the conquered into factions and stir up animosity among them, and in training an army of negroes the North no doubt holds this thought in perspective. We can see three great causes operating to destroy us: First, the inferiority of our armies to those of the enemy in point of numbers; second, the poverty of our single source of supply in comparison with his several sources; third, the fact that slavery, from being one of our chief sources of strength at the commencement of the war, has now become, in a military point of view, one of our chief sources of weakness.

The enemy already opposes us at every point with superior numbers, and is endeavoring to make the preponderance irresistible. President Davis, in his recent message, says the enemy "has recently ordered a large conscription and made a subsequent call for volunteers, to be followed, if ineffectual, by a still further draft." In addition, the President of the United States announces that "he has already in training an army of 100,000 negroes as good as any troops," and every fresh raid he makes and new slice of territory he wrests from us will add to this force. Every soldier in our army already knows and feels our numerical inferiority to the enemy. Want of men in the field has prevented him from reaping the fruits of his victories, and has prevented him from having the furlough he expected after the last reorganization, and when he turns from the wasting armies in the field to look at the source of supply, he finds nothing in the prospect to encourage him. Our single source of supply is that portion of our white men fit for duty and not now in the ranks. The enemy has three sources of supply: First, his own motley population; secondly, our slaves; and thirdly, Europeans whose hearts are fired into a crusade against us by fictitious pictures of the atrocities of slavery, and who meet no hindrance from their Governments in such enterprise, because these Governments are equally antagonistic to the institution. In touching the third cause, the fact that slavery has become a military weakness, we may rouse prejudice and passion, but the time has come when it would be madness not to look at our danger from every point of view, and to probe it to the bottom. Apart from the assistance that home and foreign prejudice against slavery has given to the North, slavery is a source of great strength to the enemy in a purely military point of view, by supplying him with an army from our granaries; but it is our most vulnerable point, a continued embarrassment, and in some respects an insidious weakness. Wherever slavery is once seriously disturbed, whether by the actual presence or the approach of the enemy, or even by a cavalry raid, the whites can no longer with safety to their property openly sympathize with our cause. The fear of their slaves is continually haunting them, and from silence and apprehension many of these soon learn to wish the war stopped on any terms. The next stage is to take the oath to save property, and they become dead to us, if not open enemies. To prevent raids we are forced to scatter our forces, and are not free to move and strike like the enemy; his vulnerable points are carefully selected and fortified depots. Ours are found in every point where there is a slave to set free. All along the lines slavery is comparatively valueless to us for labor, but of great and increasing worth to the enemy for information. It is an omnipresent spy system, pointing out our valuable men to the enemy, revealing our positions, purposes, and resources, and yet acting so safely and secretly that there is no means to guard against it. Even in the heart of our country, where our hold upon this secret espionage is firmest, it waits but the opening fire of the enemy's battle line to wake it, like a torpid serpent, into venomous activity.

In view of the state of affairs what does our country propose to do? In the words of President Davis "no effort must be spared to add largely to our effective force as promptly as possible. The sources of supply are to be found in restoring to the army all who are improperly absent, putting an end to substitution, modifying the exemption law, restricting details, and placing in the ranks such of the able-bodied men now employed as waggoneers, nurses, cooks, and other employ's, as are doing service for which the negroes may be found competent." Most of the men improperly absent, together with many of the exempts and men having substitutes, are now without the Confederate lines and cannot be calculated on. If all the exempts capable of bearing arms were enrolled, it will give us the boys below eighteen, the men above forty-five, and those persons who are left at home to meet the wants of the country and the army, but this modification of the exemption law will remove from the fields and manufactories most of the skill that directed agricultural and mechanical labor, and, as stated by the President, "details will have to be made to meet the wants of the country," thus sending many of the men to be derived from this source back to their homes again. Independently of this, experience proves that striplings and men above conscript age break down and swell the sick lists more than they do the ranks. The portion now in our lines of the class who have substitutes is not on the whole a hopeful element, for the motives that created it must have been stronger than patriotism, and these motives added to what many of them will call breach of faith, will cause some to be not forthcoming, and others to be unwilling and discontented soldiers. The remaining sources mentioned by the President have been so closely pruned in the Army of Tennessee that they will be found not to yield largely. The supply from all these sources, together with what we now have in the field, will exhaust the white race, and though it should greatly exceed expectations and put us on an equality with the enemy, or even give us temporary advantages, still we have no reserve to meet unexpected disaster or to supply a protracted struggle. Like past years, 1864 will diminish our ranks by the casualties of war, and what source of repair is there left us? We therefore see in the recommendations of the President only a temporary expedient, which at the best will leave us twelve months hence in the same predicament we are in now. The President attempts to meet only one of the depressing causes mentioned; for the other two he has proposed no remedy. They remain to generate lack of confidence in our final success, and to keep us moving down hill as heretofore. Adequately to meet the causes which are now threatening ruin to our country, we propose, in addition to a modification of the President's plans, that we retain in service for the war all troops now in service, and that we immediately commence training a large reserve of the most courageous of our slaves, and further that we guarantee freedom within a reasonable time to every slave in the South who shall remain true to the Confederacy in this war. As between the loss of independence and the loss of slavery, we assume that every patriot will freely give up the latter—give up the negro slave rather than be a slave himself. If we are correct in this assumption it only remains to show how this great national sacrifice is, in all human probabilities, to change the current of success and sweep the invader from our country.

Source: U.S. War Department. 1880–1891. *The War of the Rebellion. A Compilation of the Official Records of the Union and Confederate Armies.* Series 1, Vol. 52. Washington, D.C.: U.S. War Department, 586–89.

GENERAL ORDERS NO. 14, CONFEDERATE LAW AUTHORIZING THE ENLISTMENT OF BLACK SOLDIERS AS PROMULGATES ON A MILITARY ORDER (MARCH 23, 1865)

In March 1865, the Confederacy was in a precarious position. The desperate times called for desperate measures. On March 13, 1865, the Confederate Congress passed an act "to increase the military force of the Confederate States."

General Orders No. 14 authorized President Davis to ask for and accept from slave owners "the services of such number of able-bodied negro men as he may deem expedient." For the first time in the brief history of the Confederacy, this act allowed black men into its army. Unlike Cleburne's proposal, this act did not guarantee freedom to enslaved persons who joined the army. The war ended before any black unit formed under this act could see combat. If large numbers of African Americans were already in the Confederate army, why was this law necessary to change regulations? Below is an excerpt from General Orders No.14.

Richmond, Va., March 23, 1865.
GENERAL ORDERS, No. 14.

I. The following act of Congress and regulations are published for the information and direction of all concerned:

AN ACT to increase the military force of the Confederate States.

The Congress of the Confederate States of America do enact, That, in order to provide additional forces to repel invasion, maintain the rightful possession of the Confederate States, secure their independence, and preserve their institutions, the President be, and he is hereby, authorized to ask for and accept from the owners of slaves, the services of such number of able-bodied negro men as he may deem expedient, for and during the war, to perform military service in whatever capacity he may direct.

SEC 2. That the General-in-Chief be authorized to organize the said slaves into companies, battalions, regiments, and brigades, under such rules and regulations as the Secretary of War may prescribe, and to be commanded by such officers as the President may appoint.

SEC 3. That while employed in the service the said troops shall receive the same rations, clothing, and compensation as are allowed to other troops in the same branch of the service.

SEC 4. That if, under the previous sections of this act, the President shall not be able to raise a sufficient number of troops to prosecute the war successfully and maintain the sovereignty of the States and the independence of the Confederate States, then he is hereby authorized to call on each State, whenever he thinks it expedient, for her quota of 300,000 troops, in addition to those subject to military service under existing laws, or so many thereof as the President may deem necessary to be raised from such classes of the population, irrespective of color, in each State, as the proper authorities thereof may determine: Provided, That not more than twenty-five per cent. of the male slaves between the ages of eighteen and forty-five, in any State, shall be called for under the provisions of this act.

SEC 5. That nothing in this act shall be construed to authorize a change in the relation which the said slaves shall bear toward their owners, except by consent of the owners and of the States in which they may reside, and in pursuance of the laws thereof.

Approved March 13, 1865.

Source: U.S. War Department. 1880–1901. *The War of the Rebellion: A Compilation of the Official Records of the Union and Confederate Armies*, Series 4, Vol. 3. Washington, D.C.: U.S. War Department, 1161–62.

Further Reading

Barlow, Charles Kelly, J. H. Segars, and R. B. Rosenberg, eds. 2004. *Black Confederates*. Gretna, LA: Pelican.

Bergeron, Arthur W., Jr. 1986. "Free Men of Color in Grey." *Civil War History* 32 (September): 247–55.

Berlin, Ira, Joseph Reidy, and Leslie Rowland, eds. 1998. *Freedom Soldiers: The Black Military Experience in the Civil War*. New York: Cambridge University Press.

"Black Confederates." 2011. *Harvard Gazette*, September 1. Accessed May 2, 2018. http://news.harvard.edu/gazette/story/2011/09/black -confederates/.

Blue II, Al W. 2014. *Black Confederates and Other Minority Soldiers: Black Confederates*. North Charleston, SC: CreateSpace.

Brewer, James H. 2007. *The Confederate Negro: Virginia's Craftsmen and Military Laborers, 1861–1865*. Tuscaloosa: University Press of Alabama.

Confederate States of America War Department. 1861. *Regulations for the Army of the Confederate States*. New Orleans: Henry P. Lathrop.

Dewitt, Ann. "Photographs of Slaves/Freedmen in Confederate Uniform." Black Confederate Soldiers. Accessed August 8, 2017. http://blackconfederatesoldiers.com/military-uniform.html.

Hollandsworth, James G. 1955. *The Louisiana Native Guards: The Black Military Experience During the Civil War*. Baton Rouge: Louisiana State University Press.

Levine, Bruce. 2006. *Confederate Emancipation: Southern Plans to Free and Arm Slaves During the Civil War*. New York: Oxford University Press.

"Militia Law of Louisiana." 1862. Baton Rouge: Tom Byrum, State Printer.

Musck, Michael. 2012. "Is There Archival Proof of Black Confederates?" *Civil War Times* 51, no. 1 (February): 35.

Sampson, Myra Chandler, and Kevin M. Levin. 2013. "The Loyalty of Silas Chandler." *Civil War Times* 51, no. 1 (February): 30–34.

Segars, J. H., and Charles Kelly Barlow, eds. 2007. *Black Southerners in Confederate Armies: A Collection of Historical Accounts.* Gretna, LA: Pelican.

Stauffer, John. 2009. *Giants: The Parallel Lives of Frederick Douglass and Abraham Lincoln.* New York: Twelve, Hachette.

Steiner, Lewis H. 1862. *Report of Lewis H. Steiner: Inspector of the Sanitary Commission, Containing a Diary Kept During the Rebel Occupation of Frederick Md., and an Account of the Operations of the U.S. Sanitary Commission During the Campaign on Maryland, 1862.* Ithaca, NY: Cornell University Library.

Steward, Bruce H. 2009. *Invisible Hero: Patrick R. Cleburne.* Macon, GA: Mercer University Press.

Symonds, Craig L. 1997. *The Stonewall of the West: Patrick Cleburne and the Civil War.* Lawrence: University Press of Kansas.

Van Der Linden, Frank. 2007. "Black Soldiers, Southern Victory?" *Civil War Times* 46 (October): 28–35.

Wesley, Charles H. 1919. "The Employment of Negroes as Soldiers in the Confederate Army." *Journal of Negro History* 4, no. 3: 239–53.

Wiley, Bell Irvin. 2008. *The Life of Johnny Reb: The Common Soldier of the Confederacy.* Baton Rouge: Louisiana State University Press.

Wilson, Joseph. 2012. *The Black Phalanx: A History of the Negro Soldiers of the United States in the Wars of 1775–1812, 1861–'65.* Colorado Springs, CO: CreateSpace.

Yacovone, Donald. 1998. *A Voice of Thunder: A Black Soldier's Civil War.* Chicago: University of Illinois Press.

4

There Were No Female Combat
Soldiers in the Civil War

What People Think Happened

It is the common misconception that the Civil War was a man's fight. Textbooks employ masculine nouns and pronouns in their descriptions of Civil War soldiers. Coverage of women is usually limited to their roles as nurses, spies, and laborers in factories or loyal mothers and wives on the home front. Little or no notice is taken of the more than 400 Northern and Southern women who fought in combat during the Civil War. Female combat soldiers were an open secret during and immediately after the war. Their service to country and cause slowly slipped from memory over the next 150 years.

How did this misconception originally develop? One factor is the regulations for the Confederate and Union armies. Both sets of regulations specifically state that only males could enlist in the army. In fact, women were not officially allowed into the military in the United States until World War I and did not receive permanent status in the service until Congress passed the Women's Armed Services Integration Act in 1948. Despite this act, the U.S. government did not permit women in combat until January 2013. Under the regulations of both armies during the Civil War, no women could officially serve in either side's military. As the lives of female combat soldiers faded from the public memory, the regulations served as proof that no women fought in the Civil War.

Another factor was that the U.S. Army itself attempted to deny the role that women played as combat soldiers in the Civil War. Ida Tarbell was a teacher, author, and journalist. She was the leading female muckraker of the progressive era and was best known for her shocking exposé of the Standard Oil Company. She was one of the founders of the *American Magazine* as well as a major contributor to its content. On October 21, 1909, Tarbell wrote a letter to Maj. Gen. Fred Clayton Ainsworth, who was in command of the Adjutant General's Office in Washington, D.C. In her letter, Tarbell asked Ainsworth "whether your department has any record of the number of women who enlisted and served in the Civil War, or has any record of any women who were in the service?"

Ainsworth quickly responded to Tarbell's inquiry. He informed Tarbell that the War Department had no official record of any woman who enlisted or served in the U.S. military during the Civil War. Ainsworth's words as adjutant general held great weight and authority. He also played a prominent role in compiling and publishing the official record of the Civil War. Ainsworth's response to Tarbell called into question the existence of female combat soldiers during the Civil War and began the misconception that the war had solely been a man's fight. Ainsworth's claim was inaccurate. At the time of his response in 1909, the Adjutant General's Office possessed documents for two female soldiers. Ainsworth had either lied to Tarbell or conducted a superficial search. Either way, Ainsworth's reply became the accepted convention about the service of female soldiers in the Civil War.

How the Story Became Popular

Many factors helped to perpetuate the misconception that the Civil War was solely a man's fight. The number of women who served in either the Confederate or Union armies was extremely small because both sides forbade females from enlisting in the military. The true number of women soldiers may never be known because women had to disguise themselves as men. Experts place the number of women in combat at somewhere between 400 and 1,000 individuals. Over 2,850,000 persons served in both armies during the war. If one uses the high end of the estimate, only 0.000045 percent of the combatants were women. Since the number of women in combat was infinitesimally small, their stories did not appear in the mainstream narrative of the war and eventually became buried in the footnotes of history.

The military service of women did not affect the battles, campaigns, and outcome of the Civil War. There was no high-ranking female officer to affect tactics and strategies. Women were ordinary soldiers in an extraordinary war. As a result of women's small numbers and lack of important roles, authors of major works about the war made little or no mention of female soldiers. In his work *The Civil War*, Bruce Catton does not mention female soldiers. The words "female" and "women" do not appear in the index of Shelby Foote's three-volume work, *The Civil War: A Narrative*. The preeminent Civil War historian James McPherson devotes three paragraphs to female soldiers in the third edition of his text *Ordeal by Fire*. In most textbooks, the emphasis is on women as nurses, spies, and participants in home-front activities. In many works, authors have not included female soldiers in the combat narrative, reinforcing the misconception that the Civil War was an all-man's fight.

Women themselves either knowingly or unknowingly helped to perpetuate the misconception. Some women continued to disguise themselves as men after the war. Jennie Irene Hodgers enlisted in the Union army as Albert D. J. Cashier. Cashier served with the 95th Illinois and fought at Vicksburg, Red River, and Guntown. After the war, Cashier maintained her disguise and lived as a man until 1911. Doctors discovered her secret when they treated Cashier for injuries she suffered in a car accident. Women and their families hid their service when popular culture began to depict female soldiers as camp followers and prostitutes. The Southern lost cause apologist Gen. Jubal Early often referred to female soldiers as prostitutes. In her work *Women in the Civil War*, Mary Massey asserted that "probably most of the women soldiers were prostitutes and concubines." The transformation from heroine to woman of the evening kept some women from revealing their combat service.

Women also left very little documentation of their military service. Many of the women who fought in the Civil War were from poor, immigrant, or rural backgrounds. They disguised themselves as men to earn more money through enlistment bounties and the $13-a-month salary for a private. Quite often these women lacked the skills and inclination to write letters home or keep diaries. Other women were afraid that they would be discovered through their writings. Female soldiers have provided scholars with a dearth of information about their military experiences. Only two female soldiers published memoirs of their service: Sarah Emma E. Edmonds and Loreta Velazquez. The letters of Sarah Rosetta Wakeman are the only known collection of letters written by a female soldier in the Civil War.

Of the two memoirs written by female soldiers, only the work of Edmunds has been verified by researchers. Historians have found that Velazquez's work, *The Woman in Battle*, is more fiction than fact. Velazquez wrote the work for money and to advance her own celebrity status. Velazquez dressed as a Confederate soldier and deliberately risked discovery to attract press coverage and to advance her economic situation. Authentic female soldiers feared discovery and went to great lengths to preserve their disguise; Velazquez reveled in her multiple discoveries.

Gen. Jubal Early was one of the first critics to question the veracity of Velazquez's memoirs. Early challenged the accuracy of her work *The Woman in Battle* and pointed out "inconsistencies, absurdities and impossibilities" in Velazquez's narrative. In May 1878, Velazquez wrote a letter to Early and asked him to stop the public criticism of her work. Early did not directly answer Velazquez's letter but sent his criticisms to Congressman William Ferguson Slemons of Arkansas. General Early then sent copies of Velazquez's and Congressman Slemons's letters to John Tucker of Virginia. In his letter to Congressman Slemons, Early wrote that he cherished the Confederate armies and the people of the South, especially the women, and that he would speak out against any book that lacked "authenticity" and was written by a person who was "no true type of southern woman." Unfortunately, Velazquez's exaggerated escapades cast a veil of doubt over the true motives and exploits of women soldiers.

The small number of women in combat, the lack of significant impact on the war, and their absence from major works about the conflict allowed female soldiers to fade from the American memory. These factors coupled with women not telling their own story through letters, diaries, and memoirs helped hide the female soldier from American consciousness and perpetuate the misconception of the Civil War being solely a man's fight.

PRIMARY SOURCE DOCUMENTS

UNITED STATES ARMY REGULATION (1861)

The army regulations for both the United States and the Confederate States of America prohibited the enlistment of women in their armed services. Military authorities discharged women who disguised themselves as male soldiers. Four hundred or more women disregarded the regulations and enrolled in their respective armies. The U.S. Army allowed women to join the military in World War I. In 1948, Congress granted women permanent status in the military. The Pentagon removed the ban on women in combat in 2013 and opened all combat positions to women in 2016. Below is an excerpt from the revised United States Army Regulation of 1861 that explained to recruiters the eligibility requirements to enlist in the army.

Duties of Recruiting Officers.

925. Success in obtaining recruits depends much on the activity and *personal attention* of recruiting officers, and they will not entrust to enlisted men the duties for which themselves are only responsible. They will in no case absent themselves from their stations without authority from the superintendent.

926. They will not allow any man to be deceived or inveigled into the service by false representations, but will in person explain the nature of the service, the length of the term, the pay, clothing, rations, and other allowances to which a soldier is entitled by law, to every man before he signs the enlistment.

927. If minors present themselves, they are to be treated with great candor: the names and residences of their parents or guardians, if they have any, must be ascertained, and these will be informed of the minor's wish to enlist, that they may make their objections or give their consent.

928. With the sanction of superintendents, recruiting officers may insert, in not exceeding two newspapers, brief notices directing attention to the rendezvous for further information.

929. Any free white male person about the age of eighteen and under thirty-five years, being at least five feet three inches high, effective, able-bodied, sober, free from disease, of good character and habits, and with a competent knowledge of the English language, may be enlisted. This regulation, so far as respects the *height* and *age* of the recruit, shall not extend to musicians or to soldiers who may "*re-enlist*" or have served honestly and faithfully a previous enlistment in the army.

930. No man having a wife or child shall be enlisted *in time of peace* without special authority obtained from the Adjutant-General's office, through the superintendent. This rule is not to apply to soldiers who "*re-enlist.*"

Source: United States. 1863. *Revised United States Army Regulations of 1861, with an Appendix Containing the Changed Laws Affecting Army Regulations and Articles of War to June 25th, 1863.* Washington, D.C.: War Department, 180.

MAJ. GEN. FRED CRAYTON AINSWORTH, LETTER TO IDA TARBELL (1909)

Maj. Gen. Fred Crayton Ainsworth was an army surgeon who possessed exceptional organizational and administrative skills. One of his significant achievements was overseeing the publishing of The War of Rebellion: A Compilation of the Official Records of the Union and Confederate Armies. *In 1907, he took command of the Adjutant General's Office (AGO). Among its various tasks, the AGO compiled military service records of soldiers who fought in the Civil War. In 1909, Ida Tarbell, a famous muckraker journalist, requested information about female Civil War soldiers from the AGO. In his reply, Ainsworth claimed that his department housed no records of women soldiers, despite their existence. Ainsworth's reply substantiated the growing misconception that the Civil War was a man's fight. Below is an excerpt from Ainsworth's letter to Tarbell.*

I have the honor to inform you that no official record has been found in the War Department showing specifically that any woman was ever enlisted in the military service of the United States as a member of any organization of the Regular or Volunteer Army at any time during the period of the civil war. It is possible, however, that there may have been a few instances of women having served as soldiers for a short time without their sex having been detected, but no record of such cases is known to exist in the official files.

Source: F. C. Ainsworth, letter to Ida Tarbell. 1909. Records and Pension Office files, documents numbered 158003, file 184934. Washington, D.C.

What Really Happened

Mary Livermore was an associate member of the U.S. Sanitary Commission. In 1889, she completed an autobiographical sketch of her experiences as a nurse and relief worker during the Civil War. In her book *My Story of the War*, Livermore wrote, "Someone has stated that the number of women soldiers known to service as little less than four hundred." She then stated that she believed the number was probably higher than that figure. Historians have used Livermore's estimate of 400 women as a benchmark in their research and publications. The number of female soldiers may have been higher or lower, but there is no doubt that women of both sides fought for their respective militaries.

Women joined the armed services during the Civil War for adventure, patriotism, financial remuneration, vengeance, to stay with a loved one, and to escape the strict social conventions for women in the Victorian age. They were able to enter the service because medical exams were pro forma and rarely involved a thorough physical examination. Women were able to maintain their disguise through loose-fitting male attire, the youthful appearance of many recruits, and mid-19th-century societal standards of modesty. Males were also reluctant to believe that women could function as competent soldiers. Authorities discovered women soldiers when they were hospitalized for disease or wounds, captured, became pregnant, or were killed.

Newspaper reports provided the first evidence of women soldiers in the ranks of both armies. Writers found the women interesting not because of their significant contribution to the war effort but for their presence in the military in defiance of societal norms. Female soldiers made good copy because they broke the stereotype of the midcentury woman as demur, passive, and obedient. *The Richmond Examiner*, *The Chicago Tribune*, and *The New York Times* published stories about female soldiers in which they praised the patriotism and extolled the free spirit of these women. One example is *The Richmond Examiner*'s coverage in the fall of 1864 of two Virginia cousins, Mary and Molly Bell. The pair had served in the Confederate army for two years and fought in several battles, including Chancellorsville and Gettysburg. In October 1864, Confederate officials found out their identity and imprisoned them at Castle Thunder in Richmond. They were released from prison in late November 1864 and sent home to their parents. *The Richmond Examiner* reported that the Bells "seemed perfectly disconsolate at the idea of being separated from their male companions in arms."

Officers of both armies reported discovering women serving under their command. In his memoirs, General Sheridan recounts the story of his men discovering two women under Sheridan's command frolicking in the Stone River. Sheridan interviewed the women the next day and then cashiered them from the army. Maj. Gen. William S. Rosecrans, commander of the Union Army of the Tennessee, was enraged when he discovered that one of his noncommissioned officers had given birth to a baby. General Rosecrans noted that this "is a violation of all military law and of the army regulations." The sergeant was not alone. There were at least five other cases where female soldiers concealed their pregnancies until the baby was born. Gen. Jubal Early also commented on female soldiers in his writings, including the Bell cousins.

The Adjutant General's Office did possess records of women soldiers despite General Ainsworth's claim to the contrary in his response to Ida Tarbell. At the time of Ainsworth's response in 1909, the AGO had meticulously compiled service records for military personnel from the Civil War. These records included documentation of female soldiers. For example, AGO records show that John Williams of the 17th Missouri Infantry was discharged on the grounds that she was a woman. Confederate records show that S. M. Blaylock of the 26th North Carolina was discharged for impersonating a man. Charles Freeman of the 52nd Ohio was discharged when doctors discovered her sexual identity while treating her for a fever. The available government records at the time of Tarbell's request provide ample evidence of women serving in both the Union and Confederate armies.

The diary of Sarah Emma Edmonds and the letters of Sarah Rosetta Wakeman document the Civil War experiences of two female soldiers who fought for the Union. The Canadian-born Edmonds enlisted in the Second Michigan Volunteers as Franklin Thompson on May 25, 1861. She participated in the battles of First Bull Run, Antietam, and Fredericksburg as a regimental nurse and courier. She contracted malaria and deserted in April 1863 rather than being unmasked during a hospital stay. Her memoirs, *Nurse and Spy in the Union Army*, provide an interesting and reliable account of her service despite the fact that she did not reveal to her readers that her exploits occurred while she was disguised as a man. She maintained her secret until 1886, when she applied for and received a pension from the U.S. government for her military service.

Sarah Rosetta Wakeman enlisted in the 153rd New York State Volunteers on August 30, 1862, as Lyons Wakeman. Her letters to her family are the only known collection written by a female combat soldier during the war. From October 1862 to February 1864, Wakeman and her regiment performed guard and provost duty in Alexandria, Virginia. In March 1864, the War Department dispatched her unit to Louisiana to be part of the Red River campaign. She was on the front lines of the Battle of Pleasant Hill and wrote home to her mother, father, and siblings about the experience. Near the end of the campaign, Wakeman developed chronic diarrhea and died on June 19, 1864, after a month of hospitalization. Wakeman's letters provided testimony to the service of females during the Civil War as well as a glimpse into the mind and soul of women soldiers.

In conclusion, a small number of female soldiers fought in the Civil War. Newspaper articles, the testimony of officers, government records, and the evidence that the women themselves provided substantiate their existence in both sides' militaries. Historians continue to search for more documentation and information on female combatants. This research is significant because it demonstrates that there were women who challenged the stereotypes and prejudices women faced in the Victorian age. Women soldiers fought not only for cause and country but also to remove the barriers to gender equality.

PRIMARY SOURCE DOCUMENTS

MARY LIVERMORE, ACCOUNT OF WOMEN IN UNION ARMY FROM *MY STORY OF THE WAR* (1889)

Mary Livermore was an abolitionist, suffragette, and social reformer as well as a nurse and journalist. During the Civil War, she volunteered as a member of the U.S. Sanitary Commission. She raised money for food and supplies for hospitals, organized aid societies, and inspected hospital sites and camps. Livermore became a codirector of the Chicago branch of the Sanitary Commission. In her work with the Sanitary Commission, she encountered female soldiers. In her autobiographical account of the war, My Story of the War, *Livermore documented the exploits of some female soldiers. She also helped to establish the number of female soldiers at 400. This number has served as a benchmark for historians since the publication of Livermore's work. Below is an excerpt from Livermore's account of female soldiers in the Civil War.*

Madame Turchin, the wife of the Colonel of the Nineteenth Illinois, was the daughter of a Russian officer, and was born and reared in foreign camps, a favorite with the men of her father's command. She followed the fortunes of her husband in the War of the Rebellion and accompanied him to the field. I met her at Springfield 111 where her husband's regiment was waiting marching orders. Fine looking but unmistakably foreign in appearance and manner she was intensely loyal to the Union and thoroughly American in her sympathies and interests. She was as popular with the men of her husband's regiment as she had been with the Russian soldiers commanded by her father. They went to her with their illnesses and troubles, and she received them with kindness a good deal of playful badinage, and very careful nursing when it was needed.

In the spring of 1862, when the Nineteenth Illinois was actively engaged in Tennessee, Colonel Turchin was taken seriously ill, and was carried for days in an ambulance. Madame Turchin not only nursed her husband most tenderly, but took his place at the head of the regiment—the men in the ranks, and the subordinate officers, according her implicit and cheerful obedience. She was not one whit behind her husband in courage or military skill. Utterly devoid of fear, and manifesting perfect indifference to shot or shell, or minie-balls even when they fell thickly around her, she led the troops into action, facing the hottest fire, and fought bravely at their head. When her husband was able to resume his command, she gave herself again to the care of the sick and wounded in the field hospital.

An attempt was made to drive Colonel Turchin from the army, and on some pretext, ill or well founded, he was court-martialed. His plucky wife hastened to Washington, and not only obtained an order to set aside the court-martial, but her husband's promotion to the rank of Brigadier-General. Dashing back to Tennessee, she entered the court-room triumphantly, just as her husband was being declared "guilty" with the order to abandon his trial in one hand, and his commission in the other. If the young woman who was mustered into her husband's regiment, disguised as a man, appealed to Madame Turchin for permission to accompany her young soldier husband, I know she was not denied. No captain would be allowed to conduct her out of camp a second time. Madame Turchin's permission for her to serve as a soldier would be as effective as one from the Secretary of War.

The number of women who actually bore arms and served in the ranks during the war was greater than is supposed. Sometimes they followed the army as nurses, and divided their services between the battle-field and hospital. I remember Annie Etheridge, of Michigan, who was with the Third Michigan in every battle in which it was engaged. When their three years' service was ended, the re-enlisted veterans joined the Fifth Michigan, and Annie went with them. Through the whole four years of the war she was found in the field, often in the thickest of the fight, always inspiring the men to deeds of valor, always respected for her correctness of life. Soldiers and officers vied with one another in their devotion to her.

Bridget Devens, known as "Michigan Bridget," went to the field with the First Michigan Cavalry in which her husband was a private, and served through the war. Sometimes when a soldier fell she took his place, fighting in his stead with un-quailing courage. Sometimes she rallied retreating troops—sometimes she brought off the wounded from the field—always fearless and daring, always doing good service as a soldier. Her love of army life continued after the war ended, and with her husband she joined a regiment of the regular army, stationed on the Plains.

Mrs. Kady Brownell was, like Madame Turchin, born in camp, her father being attached to the British army. She accompanied the Fifth

Rhode Island Infantry to the war, of which regiment her husband was a non-commissioned officer. She was the color-bearer of the regiment, and was a skillful sharp-shooter and expert swordsman. She marched with the men, and asked no favors as a woman, but bore the brunt of the battle, on occasion, as fearlessly as her comrades. She was in General Burnside's expedition to Roanoke Island and Newbern, where her husband was severely wounded. When he was pronounced unfit for further service, and discharged, she also sought a discharge, and retired with him to private life and domestic duty.

The Plattville, Wis., Witness, of March, 1864, records, as if it were nothing unusual, "the return from the army of Miss Georgianna Peterman." Says the local paragrapher, "Miss Peterman has been for two years a drummer in the Seventh Wisconsin. She lives in Ellenboro', Wis., is about twenty years old, wears soldier clothes, and is quiet and reserved." Similar paragraphs appeared occasionally in other Western papers all through the war. These half-soldier heroines generally adopted a semi-military dress, and became expert in the use of the rifle, and skillful shots.

Some one has stated the number of women soldiers known to the service as little less than four hundred. I cannot vouch for the correctness of this estimate, but I am convinced that a larger number of women disguised themselves and enlisted in the service, for one cause or other, than was dreamed of. Entrenched in secrecy, and regarded as men, they were sometimes revealed as women, by accident or casualty. Some startling histories of these military women were current in the gossip of army life; and extravagant and unreal as were many of the narrations, one always felt that they had a foundation in fact.

Such service was not the noblest that women rendered the country during its four years' struggle for life, and no one can regret that these soldier women were exceptional and rare. It is better to heal a wound than to make one. And it is to the honor of American women, not that they led hosts to the deadly charge and battled amid contending armies, but that they confronted the horrid aspects of war with mighty love and earnestness. They kept up their own courage and that of their households. They became ministering angels to their countrymen who perilled health and life for the nation. They sent the love and impulses of home into the extended ranks of the army, through the unceasing correspondence they maintained with the "boys in blue." They planned largely, and toiled untiringly, and with steady persistence to the end, that the horrors of the battle-field might be mitigated, and the hospitals abound in needed comforts. The men at the front were sure of sympathy from the homes, and knew that women remembered them with sleepless interest. "This put heroic fibre into their souls," said Dr. Bellows, "and restored us our soldiers with their citizen hearts beating normally under their uniforms, as they dropped them off at the last drum-tap."

Source: Livermore, Mary A. 1889. *My Story of the War: A Woman's Narrative.* Hartford, CT: A. D. Worthington, 116–21.

GEN. PHILIP SHERIDAN'S ENCOUNTER WITH FEMALE SOLDIERS (1889)

Gen. Philip H. Sheridan was a graduate of U.S. Military Academy. During the Civil War, he was an infantry commander in the Army of the Cumberland. In the spring of 1864, Gen. Ulysses S. Grant brought Sheridan to the Eastern Theater to lead the cavalry corps of the Army of the Potomac. By the end of 1864, Sheridan had defeated Confederate forces in the Shenandoah Valley. In April 1865, troops under his command played a key role in encircling the Army of Northern Virginia and forcing Lee's surrender at Appomattox Court House.

While on a foraging expedition in Tennessee in 1862, Colonel Conrad of the 15th Missouri came upon two female Union soldiers frolicking in the Stone River. He turned them over to his commander, General Sheridan. Below is Sheridan's account of the encounter from his personal memoirs.

Colonel Conrad . . . had been mortified greatly by the conduct of *the two females belonging to the detachment and division train at my headquarters.* These women, he said, had given much annoyance by getting drunk, and to some extent demoralizing his men. To say that I was astonished at his statement would be a mild way of putting it, and had I not known him to be a most upright man and of sound sense, I should have doubted not only his veracity, but his sanity. Inquiring who they were and for further details, I was informed that there certainly were in the command two females, that in some mysterious manner had attached themselves to the service as soldiers; that one, an East Tennessee woman, was a teamster in the division wagon-train and the other a private soldier in a cavalry company temporarily attached to my headquarters for escort duty. While out on the foraging expedition these Amazons had secured a supply of "apple-jack" by some means, got very drunk, and on the return had fallen into Stone River and been nearly drowned. After they had been fished from the water, in the process of resuscitation their sex was disclosed, though up to this time it appeared to be known only to each other. The story was straight and the circumstance clear, so, convinced of Conrad's continued sanity. I directed the provost-martial to bring in arrest to my headquarters the two disturbers of Conrad's peace of mind. After some little search the East Tennessee woman was found in camp, somewhat the worse for the experiences of the day before, but awaiting her fate contentedly smoking a cob-pipe. She was brought to me, and put in duress under charge of the division surgeon until her companion could be secured. To the doctor she related that the year before she had "refugeed" from East Tennessee, and on arriving in Louisville assumed men's apparel and south and obtained employment as a teamster in the quartermaster's department. Her features were very large, and so coarse and masculine was her general appearance that she would readily have passed as a man, and in her case the deception was no doubt easily practiced. The next day the "she dragoon" was caught, and proved to be a rather prepossessing young woman, and though necessarily bronzed and hardened by exposure, I doubt if, even with these marks of campaigning, she could have deceived as readily as did her companion. How the two got acquainted I never learned, and though they had joined the army independently of each other, yet an intimacy had sprung up between them long be for [sic] the mishaps of the foraging expedition. They both were forwarded to army headquarters, and, when provided with clothing suited to their sex, sent back to Nashville, and thence beyond our lines to Louisville.

Source: Sheridan, Philip. 1889. *Personal Memoirs of P. H. Sheridan.* New York: Charles L. Webster, 253–55.

GENERAL ROSECRANS, DISCOVERY OF A PREGNANT SERGEANT (APRIL 1863)

General William Rosecrans graduated from U.S. Military Academy in 1842. He left the military to pursue a career in civil engineering. At the start of the Civil War, he served under Gen. George McClellan in the West Virginia Campaign. He took command of the Army of the Cumberland in 1862 and fought Braxton Bragg's Army of Tennessee to draw at the Battle of Stone River. In September 1863, his army suffered a horrific defeat at the Battle of Chickamauga. Lincoln removed Rosecrans from command of the Army of the Cumberland after a humiliating retreat to Chattanooga. After the war, Rosecrans was the U.S. minister to Mexico and then served in the U.S. House of Representatives.

On April 17, 1863, he penned an order to discipline a sergeant under his command who had become pregnant. Contrary to Rosecrans's assertion in the order, there was no prohibition against a soldier becoming pregnant because all soldiers were supposed to be males.

"Headquarters Department of the Cumberland, April 17, 1863.

"General:—The general commanding directs me to call your attention to a flagrant outrage committed in your command—a person having been admitted inside your lines without a pass and in violation of orders. The case is one which calls for your personal attention, and the general commanding directs that you deal with the offending party or parties according to law."

"The medical director reports that an orderly sergeant in Brigadier-General ——'s division *was to-day delivered of a baby*—which is in violation of all military law and of the army regulations. No such case has been known since the days of Jupiter."

"You will apply the proper punishment in the case. And a remedy to prevent a repetition of the act."

Source: Brockett, L. P. 1866. *The Camp, the Battlefield and the Hospital.* Philadelphia: National Publishing, 303.

SUSAN B. ANTHONY, MATILDA GAGE, ELIZABETH CADY STANTON, AND IDA HUSTED HARPER, PROMINENT SUFFRAGETTES ON FEMALE SOLDIERS IN THE CIVIL WAR (1882)

Women suffragettes Elizabeth Cady Stanton, Susan B. Anthony, Matilda Joslyn Gage, and Ida Husted Harper authored History of Woman Suffrage. *This work documented the history of the women's suffrage movement in six volumes containing over 5,700 pages. It was published over a 41-year span from 1881 to 1922. In volume 2, the authors of* History of Woman Suffrage *wrote about the exploits of female Union soldiers during the war. The authors noted the service of women in the Civil War to reinforce their argument that women deserved the right to vote. For the authors, the government's ban on female soldiers in the army corresponded directly to the government's refusal to recognize the rights of women. The following is an excerpt from* History of Woman Suffrage, *Vol. 2.*

Many women fought in the ranks during the war, impelled by the same patriotic motives which led their fathers, husbands, and brothers into the contest. Not alone from one State, or in one regiment, but from various parts of the Union, women were found giving their services and lives to their country among the rank and file of the army. Although the nation gladly summoned their aid in camp and hospital, and on the battle-field with the ambulance corps, it gave them no recognition as soldiers, even denying them the rights of chaplaincy, and by "army regulations" entirely refusing them recognition as part of the fighting forces of the country.

Historians have made no mention of woman's services in the war; scarcely referring to the vast number commissioned in the army, whose sex was discovered through some terrible wound, or by their dead bodies on the battle-field. Even the volumes especially devoted to an account of woman's work in the war, have mostly ignored her as a common soldier, although the files of the newspapers of that heroic period, if carefully examined, would be found to contain many accounts of women who fought on the field of battle.

Gov. Yates, of Illinois, commissioned the wife of Lieut. Reynolds of the 17th, as Major, for service in the field, the document being made out with due formality, having attached to it the great seal of State. President Lincoln, more liberal than the Secretary of War, himself promoted the wife of another Illinois officer, named Gates, to a majorship, for service in the hospital and bravery on the field.

One young girl is referred to who served in seven different regiments, participated in several engagements, was twice severely wounded; had been discovered and mustered out of service eight times, but as many times had re-enlisted, although a Canadian by birth, being determined to fight for the American Union.

Hundreds of women marched steadily up to the mouth of a hundred cannon pouring out fire and smoke, shot and shell, mowing down the advancing hosts like grass; men, horses, and colors going down in confusion, disappearing in clouds of smoke; the only sound, the screaming of shells, the crackling of musketry, the thunder of artillery, through all this women were sustained by the enthusiasm born of love of country and liberty.

Nor was the war without its naval heroines. Among the vessels captured by the pirate cruiser Retribution, was the Union brigantine, J. P. Ellicott, of Bucksport, Maine, the wives of the captain and mate being on board. Her officers and crew were transferred to the pirate vessel and ironed, while a crew from the latter was put on the brigantine; the wife of the mate was left on board the brig with the pirate crew. Having cause to fear bad treatment at the hands of the prize-master and his mate, this woman formed the bold plan of capturing the vessel. She succeeded in getting the officers intoxicated, handcuffed them and took possession of the vessel, persuading the crew, who were mostly colored men from St. Thomas, to aid her. Having studied navigation with her husband on the voyage, she assumed command of the brig, directing its course to St. Thomas, which she reached in safety, placing the vessel in the hands of the United States Consul, who transferred the prize-master, mate, and crew to a United States steamer, as prisoners of war. Her name was not given, but had this bold feat been accomplished by a man or boy, the country would have rung with praises of the daring deed, and history would have borne the echoes down to future generations.

Not alone on the tented field did the war find its patriotic victims. Many women showed their love of country by sacrifices still greater than enlistment in the army. Among these, especially notable for her surroundings and family, was Annie Carter Lee, daughter of Gen. Robert E. Lee, Commander-in-Chief of the rebel army. Her father and three brothers fought against the Union which she loved, and to which she adhered. A young girl, scarcely beyond her teens when the war broke out, she remained firm in her devotion to the National cause, though for this adherence she was banished by her father as an outcast from that elegant home once graced by her presence. She did not live to see the triumph of the cause she loved so well, dying the third year of the war, aged twenty-three, at Jones Springs, North Carolina, homeless, because of her love for the Union, with no relative near her, dependent for care and consolation in her last hours upon the kindly services of an old colored woman. In her veins ran pure the blood of "Light-Horse Harry" and that of her great aunt, Hannah Lee Corbin, who at the time of the Revolution, protested against the denial of representation to taxpaying women, and whose name does much to redeem that of Lee from the infamy, of late so justly adhering to it. When her father, after the war, visited his ancestral home, then turned into a vast national cemetery, it would seem as though the spirit of his Union-loving daughter must have floated over him, whispering of his wrecked hopes, and piercing his heart with a thousand daggers of remorse as he recalled his blind infatuation, and the banishment from her home of that bright young life.

Of the three hundred and twenty-eight thousand Union soldiers who lie buried in national cemeteries, many thousands with headboards marked "Unknown," hundreds are those of women obliged by army regulations to fight in disguise. Official records of the military authorities show that a large number of women recruits were discovered and compelled to leave the army. A much greater number escaped detection, some of them passing entirely through the campaigns, while others were made known by wounds or on being found lifeless upon the battle-field. The history of the war—which has never yet been truly written—is full of heroism in which woman is the central figure.

Source: Anthony, Susan B., Matilda Gage, and Elizabeth Cady Stanton. 1882. *History of Woman Suffrage*. Vol. 2. New York: Fowler and Wells, 21.

Further Reading

Anthony, Susan B., Matilda Gage, Elizabeth Cady Stanton, and Ida Husted Harper. 1882. *History of Woman Suffrage*. 6 vols. New York: Fowler and Wells.

Blanton, DeAnne. 1993. "Women Soldiers in the Civil War." *National Archives* 25. Accessed April 16, 2018. https://www.archives.gov /publications/prologue/1993/spring/women-in-the-civil-war-2.html.

Blanton, DeAnne, and Lauren M. Cook. 2003. *They Fought Like Demons: Women Soldiers in the Civil War*. New York: Vintage.

Burgess, Lauren Cook, ed. 1994. *An Uncommon Soldier: The Civil War Letters of Sarah Rosetta Wakeman, Alias Private Lyons Wakeman, 153rd Regiment, New York State Volunteers, 1862–1864*. New York: Oxford University Press.

Clausius, Gerhard. 1958. "The Little Soldier of the 95th: Albert D. J. Cashier." *Journal of the Illinois State Historical Society* 51: 380–87.

Culpepper, Marilyn Mayer. 1992. *Trials and Triumphs: The Women of the American Civil War*. East Lansing: Michigan State University Press.

Davis, William C. 2016. *Inventing Loreta Velasquez: Confederate Soldier, Impersonator, Media Celebrity, and Con Artist*. Carbondale: Southern Illinois University Press.

Davis, William C. 2017. "Confederate Con Artist." *Civil War Times* 56, no. 8: 52–59.

Edmonds, S. Emma E. 1864. *Unsexed; or, The Female Soldier: The Thrilling Adventures, Experiences and Escapes of a Woman, as Nurse, Spy, Scout, in Hospitals, Camp and Battlefields*. Philadelphia: Philadelphia Publishing.

Gangler, Laura Leedy. 2005. *The Mysterious Private Thompson: The Double Life of Sarah Emma Edmonds, Civil War Soldier*. New York: Free Press.

Hall, Richard H. 1993. *Patriots in Disguise: Women Warriors of the Civil War Era*. New York: Paragon House.

Hall, Richard H. 2006. *Women on the Civil War Battlefront*. Lawrence: University Press of Kansas.

King, Wendy A. 1992. *Clad in Uniform: Women Soldiers of the Civil War*. Haddon Township, NJ: CW Historicals.

Leonard, Elizabeth D. 2001. *All the Daring of the Soldiers: Women of the Civil War Armies*. New York: Penguin.

Livermore, Mary A. 1889. *My Story of the War: A Woman's Narrative*. Hartford, CT: A. D. Worthington.

Massey, Mary Elizabeth. 1966. *Bonnet Brigades*. New York: Knopf.

Massey, Mary Elizabeth. 1994. *Women in the Civil War*. Lincoln: University of Nebraska Press.

Schulte, Brigid. 2013. "Women Soldiers Fought, Bled and Died in the Civil War, Then Were Forgotten." *The Washington Post*, April 29. Accessed April 16, 2018. https://www.washingtonpost.com/local/women-soldiers-fought-bled-and-died-in-the-civil-war-then-were-forgotten.

Sheridan, Philip. 1888. *Personal Memoirs of P. H. Sheridan*. New York: Charles L. Webster.

Sibler, Nina. 2005. *Daughters of the Union: Northern Women Fight the Civil War*. Cambridge, MA: Harvard University Press.

Taylor, Susie King. 1988. *A Black Woman's Civil War Memoirs: Reminiscences of My Life in Camp with the 33rd U.S. Colored Troops, Late 1st South Carolina Volunteers*. New York: Marcus Wiener.

Tsui, Bonnie. 2006. *She Went to the Field: Women Soldiers of the Civil War*. Guilford, CT: Globe Pequot.

Wheelwright, Julie. 1989. *Amazons and Military Maids: Women Who Dressed as Men in the Pursuit of Life, Liberty and Happiness*. London: Pandora.

Wiley, Bell Irving. 1979. *Confederate Women*. Westport, CT: Greenwood.

Worthington, C. J., ed. 1972. *The Women in Battle: A Narrative of the Exploits, Adventures, and Travels of Madame Loreta Janeta Velazquez*. New York: Arno.

Young, Elizabeth. 1999. *Disarming the Nation: Women's Writing and the American Civil War*. Chicago: University of Chicago Press.

Zeinert, Karen. 1998. *Those Courageous Women of the Civil War*. Brookfield, CT: Millbrook.

5

Lincoln Freed the Slaves

What People Think Happened

If one asked the average American who freed the enslaved peoples, invariably the quick, succinct reply would be Abraham Lincoln. Most Americans believe that Lincoln freed all the enslaved peoples with a single stroke of his pen when he issued the Emancipation Proclamation on January 1, 1863. In reality, the Emancipation Proclamation only affected some of the individuals held in bondage in the American South. Lincoln played an important role in the process that ended slavery in the United States, but he was not solely responsible for the demise of the institution.

The misconception that Lincoln freed all the enslaved peoples began with his issuance of the Emancipation Proclamation. In the summer of 1862, Lincoln decided to free the enslaved persons in the areas still in rebellion against the United States. The president made his decision based on moral, political, economic, military, and diplomatic reasons. Lincoln was morally opposed to the institution of slavery and believed the nation could not be reunited half free and half slave. The liberation of enslaved peoples would deny the Confederates a large segment of their workforce. Free blacks could also join the Union army and provide needed manpower in the ranks. The fight to set other people free would establish a new motive for individuals to volunteer for service in the Union military. Finally, emancipation would make it difficult for European countries to recognize and support the Confederacy.

On July 22, 1863, Lincoln revealed his decision to liberate enslaved persons in the rebellious South to his cabinet. Lincoln expressly informed cabinet members that he would countenance no opposition or debate on the matter. Secretary of State William Seward counseled Lincoln that he should wait to issue his emancipation order until the Union won a victory on the battlefield. Lincoln postponed announcing his proclamation until the Union victory at the Battle of Antietam on September 17, 1862.

Lincoln delivered his emancipation edict in two steps. On September 22, 1862, he issued a preliminary proclamation that stated that the president would free enslaved persons on January 1, 1863, in all states and areas of states still in rebellion against the United States. This provided the Confederate states 100 days to rejoin the Union and preserve the institution of slavery. No Confederate state accepted Lincoln's offer.

On New Year's Day, 1863, Lincoln signed the Emancipation Proclamation. After Lincoln affixed his signature to the document, he stated, "I never in my life felt more certain that I am doing right than I do signing this paper." The document itself only freed enslaved peoples in states and areas of states still in rebellion against the United States. The state of Tennessee was mostly under Union control and was exempted from the proclamation. Lincoln also exempted 13 parishes in Louisiana and 48 counties in western Virginia. The Emancipation Proclamation did not affect the loyal border states of Maryland, Missouri, Delaware, and Kentucky. Lincoln believed that his commander-in-chief powers did not legally allow him to end slavery in states within the Union. Emancipation in these states would require action by their legislatures or a constitutional amendment.

Lincoln's proclamation did not free all the enslaved persons. Of the nearly 4 million enslaved persons in the United States, only about 20,000 to 50,000 individuals immediately received their freedom. They lived in areas under the control of Union forces. Approximately 800,000 enslaved persons remained in bondage in the exempted areas and border states. The remainder of the enslaved population awaited the advance of Union forces before escape and freedom became a reality.

How the Story Became Popular

The misconception that Lincoln freed all the enslaved peoples was born on January 1, 1863. Though the Emancipation Proclamation only freed some of the enslaved persons, it became emblematic of the end of slavery in the United States. The Civil War became a crusade to set people free as well as a struggle to restore the Union. Over the next century and a half, writers, abolitionists, African Americans, artists, sculptors, and politicians honored Lincoln as the "Great Emancipator." The misconception that a heroic Lincoln acting alone ended slavery became entrenched in the American memory.

Newspapers in 1863 might disagree on the impact and worth of Lincoln's proclamation, but they agreed that Lincoln had struck a deathblow against the institution of slavery. The influential *Chicago Tribune* stated that Lincoln's order "was the grandest proclamation ever issued by man." Notable literary figures such as John Greenleaf Whittier, William Cullen Bryant, and James Russell Lowell praised Lincoln's actions and saw the proclamation as the end of slavery. Ralph Waldo Emerson claimed that through his proclamation, Lincoln had done "more for America than any other American man." The Italian patriot and advocate of Italian unification wrote a letter to Lincoln on August 6, 1863. In that letter, Giuseppe Garibaldi told Lincoln that "posterity will call you the great emancipator." By the end of 1863, prominent voices were already hailing Lincoln as the man who ended slavery in the United States.

Isaac N. Arnold was a Republican congressman from Illinois and an ardent supporter of both Lincoln and abolition. In February 1864, he introduced a resolution for a constitutional amendment to end slavery everywhere in the United States. Later in 1864, Arnold decided not to run for reelection to the House of Representatives, and Lincoln appointed him an auditor in the Treasury Department. After Lincoln's death, Arnold returned to Chicago to practice law.

In 1866, Arnold published *Abraham Lincoln and the Overthrow of Slavery*. In this biography, he focused on Lincoln as the Great Emancipator. Arnold's main theme throughout his work was that Lincoln was the heroic figure who put an end to the struggle between freedom and slavery with the Emancipation Proclamation. This was one of the first biographies about Lincoln and firmly established Lincoln in the popular memory as the individual who ended slavery.

African Americans hailed the Emancipation Proclamation as the end of slavery. The prominent black abolitionist Frederick Douglass saw the proclamation "as the doom of slavery in all the states." He also said that "we can scarcely conceive of a more complete revolution in the position of a nation." African Americans began to commemorate January 1 as "emancipation day" or "independence day" as early as 1864. On New Year's Day, 1865, many African Americans joined Lincoln at a reception at the White House to commemorate the second anniversary of the proclamation. When Lincoln entered Richmond in April 1865, he was surrounded and cheered by a group of freedmen who saw Lincoln as their liberator.

For over a century, African Americans regarded Lincoln as their Moses, their emancipator. The Emancipation Proclamation was the sacred document that had set them free. The fact that Lincoln was assassinated enhanced his reputation as the Great Emancipator in the black community. He was the martyr who died to set others free. African Americans were among the first individuals who called for a monument to honor Lincoln's legacy. The civil rights movement in the 1960s diminished some of Lincoln's luster but did not completely tarnish his role as emancipator. Lincoln was still seen as having an important role in the liberation of enslaved persons, even though the promise of equality was still unfinished business in American society.

Sculptors and artists indelibly etched Lincoln's image as the Great Emancipator into the hearts and minds of generations of Americans. Thomas Ball sculpted the Freedman's Memorial Monument in tribute to Lincoln emancipating enslaved persons. The 12-foot-high statue mounted on a 10-foot pedestal shows Lincoln standing over an enslaved person crouched on one knee. Lincoln is holding the Emancipation Proclamation in his right hand. The president's left hand is extended over the former enslaved man, bidding him to rise to freedom. President Grant presided over the unveiling ceremony in Washington, D.C., on April 14, 1876. In his speech at the dedication ceremony, Frederick Douglass said that he hoped the monument would capture for all Americans "something of the exalted character and great work of Abraham Lincoln." Generations later, the monument stands as a reminder to all who visit it that Lincoln freed the enslaved persons.

Artists captured the Emancipation Proclamation and the Great Emancipator on canvas. Two of the earliest paintings to embrace this topic were W. T. Carlton's *Watch Meeting: Waiting for the Hour* and Francis Bicknell Carpenter's *First Reading of the Emancipation Proclamation of Abraham Lincoln*. Carlton's 1863 work depicts the immense anticipation of enslaved persons waiting in a cabin for the moment of freedom, midnight January 1, 1863. Photographs of the painting were sold across the country in the form of cartes de visite and captured the imaginations of both whites and blacks. The painting now hangs in the White House.

Carpenter finished *First Reading of the Emancipation Proclamation of Abraham Lincoln* in 1864. This oil-on-canvas painting depicts Lincoln, pen in hand, reading over the proclamation for the first time with his cabinet. The Emancipation Proclamation inspired Carpenter to record for posterity an act that he called "unparalleled for moral grandeur in the history of mankind." Today, the painting is on display in the west staircase in the Senate wing of the Capitol building.

Thomas Nast's illustration *Emancipation* may be the best-known work of art about the proclamation. *Harper's Weekly* first published the illustration in their January 24, 1863, edition. The left side of the illustration depicts the horrors of the institution of slavery. The right side shows the freedmen after Lincoln's proclamation. The center oval provides a look into the future in which three generations of a black family celebrate a good life under a portrait of Lincoln, their emancipator. In 1865, King and Bond of Philadelphia released a revised print of Nast's illustration. The original version contained a small oval where Father Time and the 1863 New Year's baby broke the shackles of the enslaved person. In the 1865 version, Nast removed the original characters and replaced them with a portrait of Lincoln. The updated version ensconced Lincoln in popular culture as the individual who ended slavery.

During the civil rights movement in the 1960s, Martin Luther King Jr., John Kennedy, and Lyndon Johnson all referred to Lincoln as the Great Emancipator and the Emancipation Proclamation as the document that freed enslaved persons. In his "I Have a Dream" speech delivered on the steps of the Lincoln Memorial, Dr. King said that the proclamation "came as a joyous daybreak to end the long night of captivity." On June 11, 1963, President Kennedy delivered a nationally televised speech on civil rights. Kennedy told the audience that "one hundred years of delay have passed since President Lincoln freed the slaves, yet their heirs, their grandsons are not fully free." In a speech in Gettysburg on May 30, 1963, Vice President Lyndon Johnson informed the crowd that "one hundred years ago, the slave was freed." Over the last 155 years, the writings and speeches of prominent Americans coupled with artists' depictions of the Great Emancipator have reinforced the misconception that Lincoln, through his Emancipation Proclamation, freed all the enslaved persons.

PRIMARY SOURCE DOCUMENTS

ABRAHAM LINCOLN, EMANCIPATION PROCLAMATION (JANUARY 1, 1863)

Abraham Lincoln issued the Emancipation Proclamation on January 1, 1863. Lincoln used his war powers as commander in chief to free enslaved persons in states and parts of states still in rebellion against the United States. The document also encouraged and allowed the freedmen to enlist in the armed services of the United States. The Emancipation Proclamation did not free all the enslaved persons in the United States, but it did alter the purpose of the war and the peace that followed it. It laid the groundwork for the 13th Amendment and fostered the image of Lincoln as the Great Emancipator.

By the President of the United States of America:

A Proclamation.

Whereas, on the twenty-second day of September, in the year of our Lord one thousand eight hundred and sixty-two, a proclamation was issued by the President of the United States, containing, among other things, the following, to wit:

"That on the first day of January, in the year of our Lord one thousand eight hundred and sixty-three, all persons held as slaves within any State or designated part of a State, the people whereof shall then be in rebellion against the United States, shall be then, thenceforward, and forever free; and the Executive Government of the United States, including the military and naval authority thereof, will recognize and maintain the freedom of such persons, and will do no act or acts to repress such persons, or any of them, in any efforts they may make for their actual freedom.

"That the Executive will, on the first day of January aforesaid, by proclamation, designate the States and parts of States, if any, in which the people thereof, respectively, shall then be in rebellion against the United States; and the fact that any State, or the people thereof, shall on that day be, in good faith, represented in the Congress of the United States by members chosen thereto at elections wherein a majority of the qualified voters of such State shall have participated, shall, in the absence of strong countervailing testimony, be deemed conclusive evidence that such State, and the people thereof, are not then in rebellion against the United States."

Now, therefore I, Abraham Lincoln, President of the United States, by virtue of the power in me vested as Commander-in-Chief, of the Army and Navy of the United States in time of actual armed rebellion against the authority and government of the United States, and as a fit and necessary war measure for suppressing said rebellion, do, on this first day of January, in the year of our Lord one thousand eight hundred and sixty-three, and in accordance with my purpose so to do publicly proclaimed for the full period of one hundred days, from the day first above mentioned, order and designate as the States and parts of States wherein the people thereof respectively, are this day in rebellion against the United States, the following, to wit:

Arkansas, Texas, Louisiana, (except the Parishes of St. Bernard, Plaquemines, Jefferson, St. John, St. Charles, St. James Ascension, Assumption,

Terrebonne, Lafourche, St. Mary, St. Martin, and Orleans, including the City of New Orleans) Mississippi, Alabama, Florida, Georgia, South Carolina, North Carolina, and Virginia, (except the forty-eight counties designated as West Virginia, and also the counties of Berkley, Accomac, Northampton, Elizabeth City, York, Princess Ann, and Norfolk, including the cities of Norfolk and Portsmouth[)], and which excepted parts, are for the present, left precisely as if this proclamation were not issued.

And by virtue of the power, and for the purpose aforesaid, I do order and declare that all persons held as slaves within said designated States, and parts of States, are, and henceforward shall be free; and that the Executive government of the United States, including the military and naval authorities thereof, will recognize and maintain the freedom of said persons.

And I hereby enjoin upon the people so declared to be free to abstain from all violence, unless in necessary self-defence; and I recommend to them that, in all cases when allowed, they labor faithfully for reasonable wages.

And I further declare and make known, that such persons of suitable condition, will be received into the armed service of the United States to garrison forts, positions, stations, and other places, and to man vessels of all sorts in said service.

And upon this act, sincerely believed to be an act of justice, warranted by the Constitution, upon military necessity, I invoke the considerate judgment of mankind, and the gracious favor of Almighty God.

In witness whereof, I have hereunto set my hand and caused the seal of the United States to be affixed.

Done at the City of Washington, this first day of January, in the year of our Lord one thousand eight hundred and sixty three, and of the Independence of the United States of America the eighty-seventh.

By the President: ABRAHAM LINCOLN
WILLIAM H. SEWARD, Secretary of State.

Source: Lincoln, Abraham. 1863. Emancipation Proclamation, January 1. Presidential Proclamations, 1791–1991, Record Group 11, General Records of the United States Government, National Archives.

FREDERICK DOUGLASS AT THE COPPER INSTITUTE, RESPONDING TO THE EMANCIPATION PROCLAMATION (FEBRUARY 6, 1863)

On February 6, 1863, the famous black abolitionist Frederick Douglass gave a speech to an overflow audience at the Cooper Institute in New York City.

In his speech, Douglass recounted the reactions of friends and acquaintances when they first heard the Emancipation Proclamation. Douglass praised Lincoln for his action and hailed the proclamation "as the doom of slavery in all the states." Douglass also encouraged black men to join the army and strike a blow for freedom. Douglass's speech emphasized the role of President Lincoln and the Emancipation Proclamation in destroying the institution of slavery in the United States. Douglass called the proclamation the "greatest event of our nation's history." Below is an excerpt from Douglass's speech.

I congratulate you, upon what may be called the greatest event of our nation's history, if not the greatest event of the century. In the eye of the Constitution, the supreme law of the land, there is not now, and there has not been, since the 1st day of January, a single slave lawfully deprived of Liberty in any of the States now recognized as in Rebellion against the National Government. In all these States Slavery is now in law, as in fact, a system of lawless violence, against which the slave may lawfully defend himself. [Cheers.] In the hurry and excitement of the moment, it is difficult to grasp the full and complete significance of President Lincoln's proclamation. The change in attitude of the Government is vast and startling. For more than sixty years the Federal Government has been little better than a stupendous engine of Slavery and oppression, through which Slavery has ruled us, as with a rod of iron. The boast that Cotton is King was no empty boast. Assuming that our Government and people will sustain the President and the Proclamation, we can scarcely conceive of a more complete revolution in the position of a nation. England, no longer ruled by a king, the Pope turned Protestant, Austria Republic, would not present a greater revolution. I hail it as the doom of Slavery in all the States. I hail it as the end of all that miserable statesmanship, which has for 60 years juggled and deceived the people, by professing to reconcile what is irreconcilable. No politician need now hope to rise to power, by crooking the pregnant binges of the knee to slavery. We part company with that amphibious animal called a Northern man with Southern principles. Color is no longer a crime or a badge of bondage. At last the out-spread wings of the American Eagle afford shelter and protection to men of all colors, all countries and climes, and the long oppressed black man may honorably fall or gloriously flourish under the star-spangled banner. [Applause.] I stand here tonight not only as a colored man and an American, but by the express decision of the Attorney-General of the United States, as a colored citizen, having, in common with all other citizens, a stake in the safety, prosperity, honor, and glory of a common country. [Cheering.] We are all liberated by this proclamation. Everybody is liberated. The white man is liberated, the black man is liberated, the brave men now fighting the battles of their country against rebels and traitors are now liberated, and may strike with all their might, even if they do hurt the Rebels, at their most sensitive point. [Applause.] I congratulate you upon this amazing change—the amazing approximation toward the sacred truth of human liberty. All the space between man's mind and God's mind, says Parker, is crowded with truths that wait to be discovered and organized into law for the better government of society. Mr. Lincoln has not exactly discovered a new truth, but he has dared, in this dark hour of national peril, to apply an old truth, long ago acknowledged in theory by the nation—a truth which carried the American people safely through the war for independence, and one which will carry us, as I believe, safely through the present terrible and sanguinary conflict for national life, if we shall but faithfully live up to that great truth. [Cheers.] Born and reared as a slave, as I was, and wearing on my back the marks of the slave-driver's lash, as I do, it is natural that I should value the Emancipation Proclamation for what it is destined to do for the slaves. I do value it for that. It is a mighty event for the bondman, but it is a still mightier event for the nation at large, and mighty as it is for the both, the slave and the nation, it is still mightier when viewed in its relation to the cause of truth and justice throughout the world. It is in this last character that I prefer to consider it. There are certain great national acts, which by their relation to universal principles, properly belong to the whole human family, and Abraham Lincoln's Proclamation of the 1st of January, 1863, is one of these acts. Henceforth shall that day take rank with the Fourth of July. [Applause.] Henceforth it becomes the date of a new and glorious era in the history of American liberty. Henceforth it shall stand associated in the minds of men, with all the stately steps of mankind, from the regions of error and oppression, which have lifted the trial by poison and fire to the trial by Jnry [Jury]—from the arbitrary will of a despot to the sacred writ of habeas corpus—from abject serfdom to absolute citizenship. It will stand with Catholic Emancipation, with the British Reform Bill, with the Corn Laws, and with that noble act of Russian liberty, by which twenty millions of serfs, against the clamors of haughty tyrants, have been released from servitude. [Loud cheering.] Aye! It will stand with every distinguished event which marks any advance made by mankind from the thraldom and darkness of error to the glorious liberty of truth. I believe in the millennium—the final perfection of the race, and hail this Proclamation, though wrung out under the goading lash of a stern military necessity, as one reason of the hope that is in me. Men may see in it only a military necessity. To me it has a higher significance. It is a grand moral necessity.

Source: Douglas, Frederick. 1863. "The Proclamation and the Negro Army." Speech at the Copper Institute, New York, February 6. Accessed April 16, 2018. https://www.sethkaller .com/about/educational/douglass/.

What Really Happened

The reality is that Lincoln and his Emancipation Proclamation did not begin the fight against slavery or end the institution in the United States. It was a long, arduous process that freed enslaved persons, not a single individual or document. This process began decades before Lincoln was born and culminated after his death with the ratification of the 13th Amendment to the Constitution. Lincoln played an integral role in the process to end slavery, but it is a popular misconception that he freed enslaved persons by himself.

The emancipation of enslaved persons had already begun by the time Lincoln was elected president in 1860. Beginning in Pennsylvania, Massachusetts, and New Hampshire, the legislatures of 18 Northern states outlawed the institution of slavery before Lincoln's inauguration on March 4, 1861. The legislatures abolished slavery for moral, economic, and political reasons. Also, the number of enslaved persons in the Northern states was never as high as in the South, making it easier for Northern legislatures to abolish the institution.

Not only did state legislatures outlaw slavery but so did the Articles of Confederation Congress. In 1787, Congress passed the final Northwest Ordinance. This act laid out the basis for government in the Northwest Territory and the process of how states from this area would be admitted to the Union. The Northwest Ordinance also stated, "There shall be neither slavery nor involuntary servitude in said territory." This was the first time the central government of the United States outlawed slavery on American soil and effectively kept the institution out of the states of Ohio, Indiana, Illinois, Michigan, and Wisconsin. The Articles of Confederation government and Northern state legislatures initiated the process to free enslaved persons.

Prior to the Emancipation Proclamation, Congress passed several acts that led to the freedom of enslaved persons. At the start of the Civil War, there were more than 3.5 million enslaved persons in the Confederate states. They comprised about 40 percent of the Southern population and over half of the Southern workforce. Enslaved laborers allowed the

Confederates to use a large portion of their white men as combat soldiers. The U.S. Congress passed the Confiscation Act of 1861 to deprive the Confederacy of this advantage. The act authorized Union forces to seize all property, including enslaved persons, used by the Confederacy to aid the rebellion. This act did not legally provide seized enslaved person with their freedom, but, in effect, they became free when they reached Union lines.

In July 1862, Congress passed a second bill, the Confiscation Act of 1862. This act went further than the first law. It allowed Union forces to seize the property of persons who were in rebellion against the United States, including enslaved persons of rebellious masters once they came inside Union lines. The legal caveat to freedom, however, was that their owners had to be engaged in the rebellion against the United States. Freedom hinged on whether the courts believed masters were actually engaged in the rebellion. There was also some question as to whether this act violated the punishment for treason clauses contained in Article III of the Constitution. Despite its shortcomings, this act began to alter the purpose of the war by including emancipation in its provisions.

Congress passed the District of Columbia Emancipation Act, and Lincoln signed it into law on April 16, 1862. This law provided for the immediate emancipation of about 3,100 enslaved persons in the nation's capital. Owners who were loyal to the Union received up to $300 each for their former enslaved persons. The act encouraged colonization of free blacks by providing up to $100 to any freedman who would emigrate from the United States to another country. A three-member emancipation commission administered the law and decided who would be compensated and for what amount. At the completion of the emancipation process, the federal government spent close to $1 million to end slavery in the nation's capital.

In June 1862, Republicans in Congress kept their campaign pledge to outlaw slavery in the territories. Congress passed an emancipation act that forbade slavery or involuntary servitude in any territory in the United States. The law also applied to any territories the United States might acquire in the future. Owners of enslaved persons were not compensated for their lost property. The same month, the Senate gave its consent to a new treaty with Great Britain that provided for a more effective policing of the Atlantic slave trade.

Words alone cannot set people free. Lincoln's Emancipation Proclamation depended on two factors to be effective: the advancement of the Union army and self-liberation of enslaved peoples. The Union army provided the opportunity for enslaved persons to escape to freedom and provided them with some measure of protection from Confederate retribution. The Union army and enslaved persons, working in unison, turned Lincoln's rhetoric into reality.

The 13th Amendment to the Constitution delivered the final blow to slavery. The amendment abolished slavery and involuntary servitude in the United States except as punishment for a crime. The Senate passed the amendment on April 8, 1864. The House of Representatives approved the amendment on January 31, 1865. Congress then sent the amendment to the state legislatures for ratification. The Constitution requires that three-fourths of the states approve an amendment before it can become part of the document. Lincoln's home state of Illinois was the first state to ratify the amendment. Georgia approved the amendment in December and provided the necessary vote to adopt the amendment. On December 6, 1865, the 13th Amendment became the law of the land, and the institution that sparked the Civil War no longer legally existed in the United States. The 13th Amendment finally freed all the slaves.

In conclusion, the emancipation of enslaved persons was a process that began before Lincoln was born. The Civil War accelerated the process of emancipation. Lincoln played an essential but not singular role in the process. Congress, abolitionists, the Union army, state legislators, and the enslaved peoples themselves played key roles in emancipation and the end of slavery. The road to emancipation was a long and complex journey. It is part of human nature to seek simple answers to complicated questions. The misconception that the heroic Lincoln, through a noble document, freed all the slaves with a stroke of his pen fits this need.

PRIMARY SOURCE DOCUMENTS

THE ACT FOR THE RELEASE OF CERTAIN PERSONS HELD TO SERVICE OR LABOR IN THE DISTRICT OF COLUMBIA (APRIL 16, 1862)

In April 1862, Congress passed an act to emancipate enslaved persons in Washington, D.C. This was the first federal law to abolish slavery since the now-defunct Articles of Confederation Congress passed the Northwest Ordinances in 1787. It was the first of a series of laws passed by Congress to end slavery. The act also provided funds for freedmen who wanted to leave the United States and live in another country. The first seven sections of the act are excerpted below.

Be it enacted by the Senate and House of Representatives of the United States of America in Congress assembled, That all persons held to service or labor within the District of Columbia by reason of African descent are hereby discharged and freed of and from all claim to such service or labor; and from and after the passage of this act neither slavery nor involuntary servitude, except for crime, whereof the party shall be duly convicted, shall hereafter exist in said District.

Sec. 2. And be it further enacted, That all persons loyal to the United States, holding claims to service or labor against persons discharged therefrom by this act, may, within ninety days from the passage thereof, but not thereafter, present to the commissioners hereinafter mentioned their respective statements or petitions in writing, verified by oath or affirmation, setting forth the names, ages, and personal description of such persons, the manner in which said petitioners acquired such claim, and any facts touching the value thereof, and declaring his allegiance to the Government of the United States, and that he has not borne arms against the United States during the present rebellion, nor in any way given aid or comfort thereto: Provided, That the oath of the party to the petition shall not be evidence of the facts therein stated.

Sec. 3. And be it further enacted, That the President of the United States, with the advice and consent of the Senate, shall appoint three commissioners, residents of the District of Columbia, any two of whom shall have power to act, who shall receive the petitions above mentioned, and who shall investigate and determine the validity and value of the claims therein presented, as aforesaid, and appraise and apportion, under the proviso hereto annexed, the value in money of the several claims by them found to be valid: Provided, however, That the entire sum so appraised and apportioned shall not exceed in the aggregate an amount equal to three hundred dollars for each person shown to have been so held by lawful claim: And provided, further, That no claim shall be allowed for any slave or slaves brought into said District after the passage of this act, nor for any slave claimed by any person who has borne arms against the Government of the United States in the present rebellion, or in any way given aid or comfort thereto, or which originates in or by virtue of any transfer heretofore made, or which shall hereafter be made by any person who has in any manner aided or sustained the rebellion against the Government of the United States.

Sec. 4. And be it further enacted, That said commissioners shall, within nine months from the passage of this act, make a full and final report of their proceedings, findings, and appraisement, and shall deliver the same to the Secretary of the Treasury, which report shall be deemed and taken to be conclusive in all respects, except as hereinafter provided; and the Secretary of the Treasury shall, with like exception, cause the amounts so apportioned to said claims to be paid from the Treasury of the United States to the parties found by said report to be entitled thereto as aforesaid, and the same shall be received in full and complete compensation: Provided, That in cases where petitions may be filed presenting conflicting claims, or setting up liens, said commissioners shall so specify in said report, and payment shall not be made according to the award of said commissioners until a period of sixty days shall have elapsed, during which time any petitioner claiming an interest in the particular amount may file a bill in equity in the Circuit Court of the District of Columbia, making all other claimants defendants thereto, setting forth the proceedings in such case before said commissioners and their actions therein, and praying that the party to whom payment has been awarded may be enjoined from receiving the same; and if said court shall grant such provisional order, a copy thereof may, on motion of said complainant, be served upon the Secretary of the Treasury, who shall thereupon cause the said amount of money to be paid into said court, subject to its orders and final decree, which payment shall be in full and complete compensation, as in other cases.

Sec. 5. And be it further enacted, That said commissioners shall hold their sessions in the city of Washington, at such place and times as the President of the United States may direct, of which they shall give due and public notice. They shall have power to subpoena and compel the attendance of witnesses, and to receive testimony and enforce its production, as in civil cases before courts of justice, without the exclusion of any witness on account of color; and they may summon before them the persons making claim to service or labor, and examine them under oath; and they may also, for purposes of identification and appraisement, call before them the persons so claimed. Said commissioners shall appoint a clerk, who shall keep files and [a] complete record of all proceedings before them, who shall have power to administer oaths and affirmations in said proceedings, and who shall issue all lawful process by them ordered. The Marshal of the District of Columbia shall personally, or by deputy, attend upon the sessions of said commissioners, and shall execute the process issued by said clerk.

Sec. 6. And be it further enacted, That said commissioners shall receive in compensation for their services the sum of two thousand dollars each, to be paid upon the filing of their report; that said clerk shall receive for his services the sum of two hundred dollars per month; that said marshal shall receive such fees as are allowed by law for similar services performed by him in the Circuit Court of the District of Columbia; that the Secretary of the Treasury shall cause all other reasonable expenses of said commission to be audited and allowed, and that said compensation, fees, and expenses shall be paid from the Treasury of the United States.

Sec. 7. And be it further enacted, That for the purpose of carrying this act into effect there is hereby appropriated, out of any money in the Treasury not otherwise appropriated, a sum not exceeding one million of dollars.

Source: U.S. National Archives and Records Administration, Washington, D.C. Accessed July 12, 2017. https://www.archives.gov/exhibits/featured-documents/dc-emancipation -act/transcription.html.

LAW ENACTING EMANCIPATION IN THE TERRITORIES (JUNE 19, 1862)

In June 1862, Congress passed a bill to outlaw slavery in all American territories. This succinct law prohibited slavery in territories possessed by the United States at the time of the act and any territory acquired thereafter. This law fulfilled a plank in the 1860 Republican platform to end slavery in the territories and put the institution on "the road to ultimate extinction."

CHAP. CXI.–An Act to secure Freedom to all Persons within the Territories of the United States.

Be it enacted by the Senate and House of Representatives of the United States of America in Congress assembled, That from and after the passage of this act there shall be neither slavery nor involuntary servitude in any of the Territories of the United States now existing, or which may at any time hereafter be formed or acquired by the United States, otherwise than in punishment of crimes whereof the party shall have been duly convicted. APPROVED, June 19, 1862.

Source: *U.S. Statutes at Large, Treaties, and Proclamations of the United States.* Vol. 12. Boston: Little, Brown, 1863, 432.

THE SECOND CONFISCATION ACT (JULY 17, 1862)

Abraham Lincoln signed the Second Confiscation Act into law on July 17, 1862. This act strengthened the First Confiscation Act passed in 1861. The purpose of the confiscation acts was to deprive the Confederacy of needed resources to successfully prosecute the war. The Second Confiscation Act allowed Union forces to seize the property of persons in rebellion against the United States. This provision included enslaved persons. Section 9 of the act specified that enslaved persons of rebellious owners who came inside Union lines "shall be deemed captives of war and shall be forever free." Freedom, however, depended on judicial proceedings to determine the loyalty of the owner. This act foreshadowed Lincoln's Emancipation Proclamation. The first nine sections of the act are excerpted below.

CHAP. CXCV.–An Act to suppress Insurrection, to punish Treason and Rebellion, to seize and confiscate the Property of Rebels, and for other Purposes.

Be it enacted by the Senate and House of Representatives of the United States of America in Congress assembled, That every person who shall hereafter commit the crime of treason against the United States, and shall be adjudged guilty thereof, shall suffer death, and all his slaves, if any, shall be declared and made free; or, at the discretion of the court, he shall be imprisoned for not less than five years and fined not less than ten thousand dollars, and all his slaves, if any, shall be declared and made free; said fine shall be levied and collected on any or all of the property, real and personal, excluding slaves, of which the said person so convicted was the owner at the time of committing the said crime, any sale or conveyance to the contrary notwithstanding.

SEC. 2. And be it further enacted, That if any person shall hereafter incite, set on foot, assist, or engage in any rebellion or insurrection against the authority of the United States, or the laws thereof, or shall give aid or comfort thereto, or shall engage in, or give aid and comfort to, any such existing rebellion or insurrection, and be convicted thereof, such person shall be punished by imprisonment for a period not exceeding ten years, or by a fine not exceeding ten thousand dollars, and by the liberation of all his slaves, if any he have; or by both of said punishments, at the discretion of the court.

SEC. 3. And be it further enacted, That every person guilty of either of the offences described in this act shall be forever incapable and disqualified to hold any office under the United States.

SEC. 4. And be it further enacted, That this act shall not be construed in any way to affect or alter the prosecution, conviction, or punishment of any person or persons guilty of treason against the United States before the passage of this act, unless such person is convicted under this act.

SEC. 5. And be it further enacted, That, to insure the speedy termination of the present rebellion, it shall be the duty of the President of the United States to cause the seizure of all the estate and property, money, stocks, credits, and effects of the persons hereinafter named in this section, and to apply and use the same and the proceeds thereof for the support of the army of the United States, that is to say:

First. Of any person hereafter acting as an officer of the army or navy of the rebels in arms against the government of the United States.

Secondly. Of any person hereafter acting as President, Vice-President, member of Congress, judge of any court, cabinet officer, foreign minister, commissioner or consul of the so-called confederate states of America.

Thirdly. Of any person acting as governor of a state, member of a convention or legislature, or judge of any court of any of the so-called confederate states of America.

Fourthly. Of any person who, having held an office of honor, trust, or profit in the United States, shall hereafter hold an office in the so-called confederate states of America.

Fifthly. Of any person hereafter holding any office or agency under the government of the so-called confederate states of America, or under any of the several states of the said confederacy, or the laws thereof, whether such office or agency be national, state, or municipal in its name or character: Provided, That the persons, thirdly, fourthly, and fifthly above described shall have accepted their appointment or election since the date of the pretended ordinance of secession of the state, or shall have taken an oath of allegiance to, or to support the constitution of the so-called confederate states.

Sixthly. Of any person who, owning property in any loyal State or Territory of the United States, or in the District of Columbia, shall hereafter assist and give aid and comfort to such rebellion; and all sales, transfers, or conveyances of any such property shall be null and void; and it shall be a sufficient bar to any suit brought by such person for the possession or the use of such property, or any of it, to allege and prove that he is one of the persons described in this section.

SEC. 6. And be it further enacted, That if any person within any State or Territory of the United States, other than those named as aforesaid, after the passage of this act, being engaged in armed rebellion against the government of the United States, or aiding or abetting such rebellion, shall not, within sixty days after public warning and proclamation duly given and made by the President of the United States, cease to aid, countenance, and abet such rebellion, and return to his allegiance to the United States, all the estate and property, moneys, stocks, and credits of such person shall be liable to seizure as aforesaid, and it shall be the duty of the President to seize and use them as aforesaid or the proceeds thereof. And all sales, transfers, or conveyances, of any such property after the expiration of the said sixty days from the date of such warning and proclamation shall be null and void; and it shall be a sufficient bar to any suit brought by such person for the possession or the use of such property, or any of it, to allege and prove that he is one of the persons described in this section.

SEC. 7. And be it further enacted, That to secure the condemnation and sale of any of such property, after the same shall have been seized, so that it may be made available for the purpose aforesaid, proceedings in rem shall be instituted in the name of the United States in any district court thereof, or in any territorial court, or in the United States district court for the District of Columbia, within which the property above described, or any part thereof, may be found, or into which the same, if movable, may first be brought, which proceedings shall conform as nearly as may be to proceedings in admiralty or revenue cases, and if said property, whether real or personal, shall be found to have belonged to a person engaged in rebellion, or who has given aid or comfort thereto, the same shall be condemned as enemies' property and become the property of the United States, and may be disposed of as the court shall decree and the proceeds thereof paid into the treasury of the United States for the purposes aforesaid.

SEC. 8. And be it further enacted, That the several courts aforesaid shall have power to make such orders, establish such forms of decree and sale, and direct such deeds and conveyances to be executed and delivered by the marshals thereof where real estate shall be the subject of sale, as shall fitly and efficiently effect the purposes of this act, and vest in the purchasers of such property good and valid titles thereto. And the said courts shall have power to allow such fees and charges of their officers as shall be reasonable and proper in the premises.

SEC. 9. And be it further enacted, That all slaves of persons who shall hereafter be engaged in rebellion against the government of the United States, or who shall in any way give aid or comfort thereto, escaping from such persons and taking refuge within the lines of the army; and all slaves captured from such persons or deserted by them and coming under the control of the government of the United States; and all slaves of such person found on [or] being within any place occupied by rebel forces and afterwards occupied by the forces of the United States, shall be deemed captives of war, and shall be forever free of their servitude, and not again held as slaves.

Source: *U.S. Statutes at Large, Treaties and Proclamations of the United States of America.* Vol. 12. Boston: Little, Brown, 1863, 589–92.

THE 13TH AMENDMENT (PASSED JANUARY 31, 1865, RATIFIED DECEMBER 6, 1865)

This amendment ended slavery, except for punishment of a crime, everywhere in the United States. It was the culmination of the emancipation process that included abolitionists, Abraham Lincoln, Congress, state legislatures, and the enslaved persons themselves. The Senate passed the amendment on April 8, 1864, by a vote of 38 to 6. On January 31, 1865, the House of Representatives approved the measure by a vote of 119 to 56. Congress then sent the amendment to the state legislatures for ratification. The necessary three-fourths vote in the states was received in December 1865. Secretary of State William Seward declared the amendment in force on December 18, 1865. Prior to this amendment, each state could determine whether slavery was legal within its borders. The 13th Amendment deprived both the states and the federal government of this power. It completed the work started by the Northern state legislatures almost 90 years prior to the amendment.

Amendment XIII
Section 1.

Neither slavery nor involuntary servitude, except as a punishment for crime whereof the party shall have been duly convicted, shall exist within the United States, or any place subject to their jurisdiction.

Section 2.

Congress shall have power to enforce this article by appropriate legislation.

Source: Charters of Freedom, U.S. National Archives and Record Administration.

Further Reading

Bennett, Lerone, Jr. 2000. *Forced into Glory: Abraham Lincoln's White Dream.* Chicago: Johnson.

Biddle, Daniel R., and Murray Dubin. 2013. "God Is Settling the Accounts: African American Reaction to Lincoln's Emancipation Proclamation." *Pennsylvania Magazine of History and Biography* 137, no. 1: 57–58.

Blair, William A., and Karen Fisher Younger. 2009. *Lincoln's Proclamation: Emancipation Reconsidered.* Chapel Hill: University of North Carolina Press.

Bolden, Tonya. 2013. *Emancipation Proclamation: Lincoln and the Dawn of Liberty.* New York: Harry N. Abrams.

Bolz, Herman. 1978. *Emancipation and Equal Rights: Politics and Constitutionalism in the Civil War Era.* New York: W. W. Norton.

Brewster, Todd. 2014. *Lincoln's Gamble: The Tumultuous Six Months That Gave America the Emancipation Proclamation and Changed the Course of the Civil War.* New York: Scribner.

Carnahan, Burrus M. 2007. *Act of Justice: Lincoln's Emancipation Proclamation and the Law of War.* Lexington: University Press of Kentucky.

Ewan, Christopher. 2005. "The Emancipation Proclamation and British Public Opinion." *Historian* 57, no. 1: 1–19.

Foner, Eric. 2006. *Nothing but Freedom: Emancipation and Its Legacy.* New York: Vintage Books.

Franklin, John Hope. 1993. "The Emancipation Proclamation: An Act of Justice." *Prologue* 25, no. 2: Prologue.

Franklin, John Hope. 1994. *The Emancipation Proclamation.* Hoboken, NJ: Wiley-Blackwell.

Guelzo, Allen C. 2002. "Defending Emancipation: Abraham Lincoln and the Conkling Letter, 1863." *Civil War History* 48, no. 4: 313–37.

Guelzo, Allen C. 2004. *Lincoln's Emancipation Proclamation: The End of Slavery in America.* New York: Simon and Schuster.

Holzer, Harold. 2009. "A Promise Fulfilled." *Civil War Times* 48, no. 6: 28–35.

Holzer, Harold. 2012. *Emancipating Lincoln: The Proclamation in Text, Context, and Memory.* Cambridge, MA: Harvard University Press.

Holzer, Harold, Edna G. Medford, and Frank J. Williams. 2006. *The Emancipation Proclamation: Three Views.* Baton Rouge: Louisiana State University Press.

Jones, Howard. 1999. *Abraham Lincoln and a New Birth of Freedom: The Union and Slavery in the Diplomacy of the Civil War.* Lincoln: University of Nebraska Press.

Kennon, Donald R., and Paul Finkleman, eds. 2016. *Lincoln, Congress and Emancipation*. Athens: Ohio University Press.

Klingsman, William. 2001. *Abraham Lincoln and the Road to Emancipation, 1861–1865*. New York: Viking.

Kolchin, Peter. 2015. "Reexamining Southern Emancipation in Comparative Perspective." *Journal of Southern History* 81, no. 1: 7–40.

Magness, Phillip W., and Sebastian N. Page. 2011. *Colonization after Emancipation: Lincoln and the Movement for Black Resettlement.* Columbia: University of Missouri Press.

Sale, Kirk Patrick. 2015. *Emancipation Hell: The Tragedy Wrought by Lincoln's Proclamation.* Columbia, SC: Shotwell.

Siddell, Silbana R. 2005. *From Property to Person: Slavery and the Confiscation Acts of 1861–1862.* Baton Rouge: Louisiana State University Press.

Striner, Richard. 2006. *Father Abraham: Lincoln's Relentless Struggle to End Slavery.* New York: Oxford University Press.

Syrett, John. 2009. *The Civil War Confiscation Acts: Failing to Reconstruct the South.* New York: Fordham University Press.

Voreneberg, Michael. 2001. *Final Freedom: The Civil War, the Abolition of Slavery, and the Thirteenth Amendment.* New York: Cambridge University Press.

6

The Gettysburg Address Was Written on a Train

What People Think Happened

The Union victory at Gettysburg in early July 1863 left massive carnage in its wake. Nearly 10,000 soldiers from both sides were killed or mortally wounded in three days of battle. David Wills and other prominent area residents supported by Pennsylvania governor Andrew Curtin formed a committee to select a site for a cemetery to properly bury the remains of Union soldiers. The cemetery committee used state-appropriated funds to purchase an area of the battlefield where Union forces repulsed Pickett's Charge. The committee then commenced the reburial process in what became known as Soldiers' National Cemetery.

The committee held the dedication for Soldiers' National Cemetery on November 19, 1863. They invited the famous Massachusetts orator Edward Everett to deliver the main address. The committee also issued an invitation to President Lincoln to deliver "a few appropriate remarks." Lincoln's 272-word oration became the most famous speech in American history. Lincoln's "few appropriate remarks" honored the sacrifice of the men who fought at Gettysburg and linked the struggle to the unfinished ideals of the American Revolution. The speech, destined to be known as the Gettysburg Address, also envisioned remaking a nation without slavery and on the road to equality.

After Lincoln's address, myths and misconceptions abounded about when and where Lincoln wrote the speech. The most persistent of these myths is that Lincoln wrote the Gettysburg Address on November 18, 1863, while traveling by train from Washington, D.C., to Gettysburg. The first mention of this story appeared in Isaac N. Arnold's biography of Lincoln, *The History of Abraham Lincoln and the Overthrow of Slavery*, published in 1866. In his work, Arnold claimed that while Lincoln was on his way from Washington to Gettysburg, he "was notified that he would be expected to make some remarks." Arnold then wrote that Lincoln retired for a short time and wrote his famous address. The fact that the cemetery committee had invited Lincoln to make remarks at the dedication ceremony three weeks prior to his departure to Gettysburg was not mentioned in Arnold's work.

Most historians credit Benjamin Perley Poore with originating the myth that Lincoln penned the Gettysburg Address aboard the train. Poore was a well-known journalist and editor and served for many years as the Washington correspondent to *The Boston Journal*. In *Reminiscences of Lincoln by Distinguished Men of His Time* (1886), Poore claimed that Lincoln wrote his speech on a piece of pasteboard on the train ride to Gettysburg while other travelers on the train talked around him. Poore's story became the standard version of the misconception because he was a respected and trusted journalist. Later, writers and alleged eyewitnesses would embellish Poore's account with their own versions of the story.

How the Story Became Popular

Throughout the postwar 19th century, prominent Americans gave credence to the train myth through their writings and speeches. The testimony of these notable individuals etched the scene of Lincoln composing and writing his famous address on the train to Gettysburg into the memory of American popular culture. Harriet Beecher Stowe, abolitionist and author of *Uncle Tom's Cabin*, was one of these individuals. In 1866, she wrote that Lincoln had composed his famous speech in only a few moments on his way to Gettysburg. Stowe, who had influenced Northern public opinion on the evils of slavery, now helped form American consciousness about Lincoln's momentous address.

Steel magnate and captain of industry Andrew Carnegie claimed to be aboard Lincoln's train bound for Gettysburg on November 18, 1863. At that time, Carnegie was the secretary to the president of the Baltimore and Ohio Railroad. Carnegie claimed that he and his boss boarded Lincoln's train in Baltimore and accompanied the president to Gettysburg. Carnegie asserted that he not only saw Lincoln write the Gettysburg Address aboard the train but also that he personally loaned Lincoln the pencil he used to write his speech. Carnegie became one of the richest and most powerful individuals in the late 19th-century United States. His words carried great weight in society. Besides being rich and powerful, Carnegie must also have been omnipresent. Research shows that Carnegie was in Pittsburg on November 18, 1863, not on his way to Gettysburg with Lincoln.

Gen. Julius Stahel was a Hungarian soldier who migrated to the United States in 1859. He fought for the Union during the Civil War and was promoted to brigadier general in November 1862. Stahel received the Medal of Honor for his gallant service at the Battle of Piedmont (1864). On November 18, General Stahel was in charge of Lincoln's military escort and was aboard the train bound for Gettysburg. In a letter to Isaac Markens in 1911, Stahel wrote that he rode in the same car as Lincoln. On the journey, Stahel said he saw Lincoln write on something placed on his knees, "which I fully believe was the famous address which he delivered at the battle-field."

Lt. Henry Clay Cochrane was a marine stationed in Washington, D.C. He received orders to accompany the marine band to Gettysburg to take part in the dedication ceremonies. Cochrane recalled that it was not until the train was near Hanover Junction that Lincoln excused himself from the traveling party to prepare remarks for the next day's dedication. This assertion by Cochrane provides Lincoln with little time to write his iconic address before he arrived at the station in Gettysburg.

William Osborn Stoddard was an active participant in Lincoln's campaign for president in 1860. In 1861, Lincoln appointed Stoddard as one of his three secretaries, joining John Hay and John Nicolay in that role. Stoddard did not make the journey to Gettysburg with Lincoln. In 1884, Stoddard stated that Lincoln wrote the address on his way to Gettysburg. Despite not being present at the time, Stoddard's statement reinforced the myth because of his close personal relationship to Lincoln as an assistant secretary.

The train myth gained so much acceptance in the public memory that even Lincoln's son, Robert Todd Lincoln, wrote about it. On December 16, 1885, Robert Todd Lincoln wrote a letter to Belle F. Keyes in Boston. In his letter, Lincoln talked about his father's address at Gettysburg. The younger Lincoln told Keyes, "My father's Gettysburg Address was jotted down in pencil, in part at least on his way to the place." Robert Todd Lincoln would eventually discredit the train myth, but at the time he added a powerful voice to its veracity.

Prominent Americans perpetuated the myth that Lincoln wrote the Gettysburg Address on the train, but it was Mary Raymond Shipman

Andrews who popularized the misconception in the 20th century. Andrews published *The Perfect Tribute* in 1906. *The Perfect Tribute* is a fictionalized account about Lincoln and the Gettysburg Address. Andrews's intended audience for her book was schoolchildren. The novel depicts Lincoln writing his speech on the train to Gettysburg and then delivering it on November 19, 1863. In the book, Lincoln concluded that his address at Gettysburg was a complete failure. On his return to Washington, Lincoln visited a prison hospital, where he comforted a Confederate officer who was terminally ill. The officer did not recognize Lincoln but praised the Gettysburg Address as "one of the great speeches in history." The main theme of the work is the reconciliation of North and South.

Andrews's *The Perfect Tribute* sold over 600,000 copies and became one of the most widely read books about Lincoln. Teachers assigned the reading of the book to generations of students. The book became the subject of two movies. MGM released the first version in 1935 as a 20-minute short historical drama starring Charles "Chic" Sale as Lincoln. The second was a 1991 made-for-television movie running 1 hour and 40 minutes with Jason Robards as the president. Over time, fiction turned into fact as readers and viewers accepted as truth the misconception that Lincoln wrote his address on the train.

Even though she wrote a fictional account about the Gettysburg Address, Andrews contended that Lincoln's writing of his speech on the train had some basis in fact. She said that she first heard the story from her son Paul, who had heard the story from his history teacher, Walter Burlingame, who learned the story from his father, American diplomat Anson Burlingame. Allegedly, it was Edward Everett who informed the elder Burlingame that Lincoln wrote his speech on the train in pencil. This circuitous route of information provided the basis for Andrews including the story in her work. Though Andrews did not create the train myth, she is responsible for its persistent existence into the 21st century.

PRIMARY SOURCE DOCUMENTS

ABRAHAM LINCOLN, THE GETTYSBURG ADDRESS (NOVEMBER 19, 1863)

On November 19, 1863, Abraham Lincoln delivered the 272 most famous words in American history. In his Gettysburg Address, Lincoln gave meaning to the great carnage of the Civil War and linked that struggle to the values upon

*which the founders formed the American republic. The president paid homage
to the soldiers who lost their lives to preserve the Union, defend democracy,
and set other people free. This iconic speech spawned many myths, including
the legend that Lincoln composed and wrote his remarks on the train journey
to Gettysburg.*

Four score and seven years ago our fathers brought forth on this conti-
nent, a new nation, conceived in Liberty, and dedicated to the proposition
that all men are created equal.

Now we are engaged in a great civil war, testing whether that nation, or
any nation so conceived and so dedicated, can long endure. We are met on
a great battle-field of that war. We have come to dedicate a portion of that
field, as a final resting place for those who here gave their lives that that
nation might live. It is altogether fitting and proper that we should do this.

But, in a larger sense, we can not dedicate—we can not consecrate—
we can not hallow—this ground. The brave men, living and dead, who
struggled here, have consecrated it, far above our poor power to add or
detract. The world will little note, nor long remember what we say here,
but it can never forget what they did here. It is for us the living, rather,
to be dedicated here to the unfinished work which they who fought here
have thus far so nobly advanced. It is rather for us to be here dedicated
to the great task remaining before us—that from these honored dead we
take increased devotion to that cause for which they gave the last full
measure of devotion—that we here highly resolve that these dead shall not
have died in vain—that this nation, under God, shall have a new birth
of freedom—and that government of the people, by the people, for the
people, shall not perish from the earth.

Abraham Lincoln
November 19, 1863

Source: Bliss, Alexander. 1864. *Autograph Leaves of Our Country's Authors.* Baltimore:
Cushing and Bailey.

BENJAMIN PERLEY POORE, *REMINISCENCES OF LINCOLN
BY DISTINGUISHED MEN OF HIS TIME* (1886)

*Benjamin Perley Poore was born in Newburyport, Massachusetts, in 1820.
He became interested in journalism and edited his father's newspaper in
Athens, Georgia, the* Southern Whig. *He was a foreign correspondent for
the* Boston Atlas. *In 1854, Poore became a Washington correspondent for*

The Boston Journal *and quickly developed a national reputation as a journalist. He served for a short time as an officer in the Eighth Massachusetts in the Union army during the Civil War. After his stint in the military, he covered the war as a correspondent. Poore became acquainted with Lincoln in his role as a reporter. It is Poore's account of the train ride to Gettysburg in* Reminiscences of Lincoln by Distinguished Men of His Time *that helped launch the myth that Lincoln wrote the Gettysburg Address in pencil on the train ride to Gettysburg. Below is Poore's account of the origin of the Gettysburg Address.*

When irate correspondent appealed to Mr. Lincoln, he would good-naturedly declare that he had no control over his secretaries, and would endeavor to mollify their wrath by telling them a story. One morning in the winter of 1862, when two angry journalists had undertaken to explain the annoyances of the censorship, Mr. Lincoln, who had listened in his dreamy way, finally said:

"I don't know much about this censorship, but come down-stairs and I will show you the origin of one of the pet phrases of you newspaper fellows."

Leading the way down into the basement, he opened the door of a larder and solemnly pointed to the hanging carcass of a gigantic sheep.

"There," said he, "now you know what '*Revenons à nos moutons*' means. It was raised by Deacon Buffum at Manchester, up in New Hampshire. Who can say, after looking at it, that New Hampshire's only product is granite?"

Often when Mr. Lincoln was engaged, correspondents would send in their cards, bearing requests for some desired items of news, or for the verification of some rumor. He would either come out and give the coveted information, or he would write it on the back of the card, and send it to the owner. He wrote a legible hand, slowly and laboriously perfecting his sentences before he placed them on paper. The long epistles that he wrote to his generals he copied himself, not wishing anyone else to see them, and these copies were kept in pigeon-holes for reference. His remarks at Gettysburg, which have been compared to the Sermon on the Mount, were written in the car on his way from Washington to the battlefield, upon a piece of pasteboard held on his knee, with persons talking all around him; yet when a few hours afterward he read them, Edward Everett said:

"I would rather be the author of those twenty lines than to have all the fame my oration of to-day will give me."

Source: Poore, Benjamin Perley. 1886. *Reminiscences of Lincoln by Distinguished Men of His Time.* Edited by Allen Thorndike Rice. New York: North American Publishing, 228.

MARY RAYMOND SHIPMAN ANDREWS, *THE PERFECT TRIBUTE* (1908)

Mary Raymond Shipman Andrews was born in Mobile, Alabama. She spent most of her adult life residing in Syracuse, New York, with her husband, William, a New York Court of Appeals judge. She was an author who wrote stories primarily about the outdoor adventures of boys. She also wrote historical fiction, biographies, and poetry. Her best-known work is The Perfect Tribute, *a fictional account of Lincoln's Gettysburg Address.*

In her work, published by Charles Scribner and Sons in 1906, Andrews described where and how Lincoln wrote the Gettysburg Address. The author claimed that she heard the story of Lincoln writing his speech on the train from her son Paul. Paul Andrews said that he learned the story from his history teacher, Walter Burlingame. The Perfect Tribute was immensely popular and sold over 600,000 copies. Generations of schoolchildren read the book and were socialized into believing Lincoln wrote his famous address on the train to Gettysburg. Below is an excerpt from The Perfect Tribute *that describes Lincoln writing his speech on the train.*

Yet the people had a right to the best he could give, and he would give them his best; at least he could see to it that the words were real and were short; at least he would not, so, exhaust their patience. And the work might as well be done now on the leisure of the journey. He put a hand, big, powerful, labor-knotted, into first one sagging pocket and then another, in search of a pencil, and drew out one broken across the end. He glanced about inquiringly—there was nothing to write upon. Across the car the Secretary of State had just opened a package of books and their wrapping of brown paper lay on the floor, torn carelessly in a zigzag. The President stretched a long arm. "Mr. Seward, may I have this to do a little writing?" he asked, and the Secretary protested, insisting on finding better material.

But Lincoln, with few words, had his way, and soon the untidy stump of a pencil was at work and the great head, the deep-lined face, bent over Seward's bit of brown paper, the whole man absorbed in his task.

Earnestly, with that "capacity for taking infinite pains" which has been defined as genius, he labored as the hours flew, building together close-fitted word on word, sentence on sentence. As the sculptor must dream the statue prisoned in the marble, as the artist must dream the picture to come from the brilliant unmeaning of his palette, as the musician dreams a song, so he who writes must have a vision of his finished work before he touches, to begin it, a medium more elastic, more vivid, more powerful than any other—words—prismatic bits of humility, old as the Pharaohs, new as the Arabs of the street, broken, sparkling, alive, from the age-long life of the race. Abraham Lincoln, with the clear thought in his mind of what he would say, found the sentences that came to him colorless, wooden. A wonder flashed over him once or twice of Everett's skill with these symbols which, it seemed to him, were to the Bostonian a key-board facile to make music, to Lincoln tools to do his labor. He put the idea aside, for it hindered him. As he found the sword fitted to his hand he must fight with it; it might be that he, as well as Everett, could say that which should go straight from him to his people, to the nation who struggled at his back towards a goal. At least each syllable he said should be chiseled from the rock of his sincerity. So he cut here and there an adjective, here and there a phrase, baring the heart of his thought, leaving no ribbon or flower of rhetoric to flutter in the eyes of those with whom he would be utterly honest. And when he had done he read the speech and dropped it from his hand to the floor and stared again from the window. It was the best he could do, and it was a failure. So, with the pang of the workman who believes his work done wrong, he lifted and folded the torn bit of paper and put it in his pocket, and put aside the thought of it, as of a bad thing which he might not better, and turned and talked cheerfully with his friends.

Source: Andrews, Mary Raymond Shipman. 1906. *The Perfect Tribute*. New York: Charles Scribner and Sons, 5–8.

GEN. JULIUS STAHEL, LETTER ABOUT LINCOLN'S JOURNEY TO GETTYSBURG (1911)

Maj. Gen. Julius Stahel was born in Szeged, Hungary, and was an officer in the Austrian army. He came to the United States in 1859. Stahel fought in both battles of Bull Run. In November 1863, he was a member of the military escort that accompanied Lincoln on the train to Gettysburg. In a letter Stahel sent to Isaac Markens in 1911, the general claimed he saw Lincoln writing on the train. Below is an excerpt from Stahel's letter that pertains to the Gettysburg Address.

I escorted President Lincoln from Washington to Gettysburg, and was with him in the same car when he wrote something on his knee, which I fully believe was the famous address which he delivered at the battle-field. I was near him when he delivered that world-wide and celebrated dedication address. I will remember that Lincoln seemed to be impressed with the sanctity of the occasion, and delivered the oration in accord with his well-known nature, in an earnest, calm, dignified manner, and that the same was received and listened to by all by-standers with reverence due to the occasion. No one expected the President to deliver an oration, Edward Everett having been assigned for that purpose, and therefore it was but natural that the short address of the President should not have made the impression which it created later on. I do not remember that it was received with plaudit, but I know that it was received with the solemnity due to the occasion, and that the President on stepping forward was received with all honors and hearty applause. It was a memorable moment, and one which inspired each and every person present. To me it is one of the most treasured memories, holy in its influence, and patriotically inspiring.

Source: Markens, Isaac. 1913. *Lincoln's Masterpiece: A Review of the Gettysburg Address New in Treatment and Matter.* New York: Isaac Markens, 16–17.

What Really Happened

It was John Nicolay who exposed the myth that Lincoln wrote the Gettysburg Address on the train. Nicolay was Lincoln's assistant secretary and worked with the president on a daily basis. He screened and received visitors to the White House, wrote and edited letters, and delivered messages for Lincoln. On November 18, 1863, he accompanied Lincoln on the train to Gettysburg. In 1894, he wrote an article for *The Century Magazine* in which he rebutted the contention of many prominent Americans that Lincoln wrote his speech on the train ride to Pennsylvania.

In his article "Lincoln's Gettysburg Address," Nicolay wrote, "There is neither record, evidence, nor well-founded tradition that Mr. Lincoln did any writing, or made any notes, on the journey between Washington and Gettysburg." Nicolay contended that the noise, conversation, and movement of the train created conditions that made it impossible for Lincoln to work on his speech. According to Nicolay, the president had already written part of his speech in Washington and carried it with him to Gettysburg in his coat pocket. Lincoln wrote this portion of the speech on executive mansion stationery, and it comprised the first 19 lines of the Gettysburg Address.

Lincoln composed the final nine and a half lines at David Will's house on the morning of November 19. He wrote the closing lines of his speech in pencil on a piece of bluish-gray foolscap. Nicolay estimated that it took about one hour for Lincoln to compose the epic conclusion to his address. Nicolay then helped transcribe the final copy of the speech that Lincoln delivered that afternoon at the cemetery.

Nicolay provided a facsimile of Lincoln's speech in the president's handwriting to *The Century Magazine* to document his story. The first two-thirds of the address are on executive mansion stationery and demonstrate that Lincoln worked on his speech before leaving Washington. The writing is in perfect penmanship and shows no evidence of being written on a bumpy train ride. The last third of the address is in pencil and written on foolscap, as Nicolay claimed. The end of the speech also appears to be written on a stationary platform rather than a moving train. John Nicolay's article provides a reliable eyewitness account and empirical evidence that Lincoln did not write his remarks while traveling by rail to Gettysburg.

Many other prominent Americans have provided testimony to support Nicolay's account of events. The famous reporter Noah Brooks asked Lincoln on November 8, 1863, if he had already written his remarks for the Gettysburg dedication. Lincoln replied that they were "not finished." He also told Brooks, "I have written it over, two or three times, and I shall have to give it another lick before I am satisfied." Lincoln told James Speed, his attorney general, that he had found time to write at least half the speech before leaving the capital. Ward Hill Lamon, the marshal of the District of Columbia, traveled with Lincoln to Gettysburg. Lamon later claimed that Lincoln read him the entire speech before they left for Gettysburg. The marshal probably only heard the first 19 lines Lincoln composed in Washington. Simon Cameron, the former secretary of war, also said he saw a copy of the speech before Lincoln left for Gettysburg. This testimony seems to confirm Nicolay's claim that Lincoln wrote a large portion of the Gettysburg Address before he departed from Washington.

Nicolay confessed that he did not know exactly when the president commenced writing his remarks. He stated that Lincoln probably followed his usual habit of taking great pains to "arrange his thoughts" and "mold his phrases" before he placed them on paper. It would have been completely out of character for Lincoln to wait until the train ride to Gettysburg to compose his speech. Lincoln even changed the War Department's plan for him to travel to Gettysburg on the same day as the speech to the day before so that he would not miss the dedication. On the night of November 18, a crowd gathered at the Wills House and asked Lincoln to speak. Lincoln declined the offer, stating that he had not prepared remarks to offer the audience. This incident depicts Lincoln's reluctance to improvise speeches. It was not in Lincoln's nature to have left Washington without some proposed remarks for the dedication and then to try to adlib them on a crowded, noisy train.

Many of the individuals who claimed Lincoln wrote the Gettysburg Address on the train ride were not with the president at that time. Isaac Arnold, Harriet Beecher Stowe, William Stoddard, Andrew Carnegie, and Robert Todd Lincoln were not on the train and, therefore, could not have witnessed Lincoln writing the address. Mary Raymond Shipman Andrews fictionalized an account of the writing of the Gettysburg Address based on a story that Edward Everett allegedly told American diplomat Anson Burlingame. Everett could not have seen Lincoln writing the speech because he was on a different train and arrived in Gettysburg before Lincoln.

Gen. James B. Fry contradicted the statements of Lieutenant Cochrane and General Stahel. General Fry fought at the battles of Shiloh and Perryville. The War Department promoted him to provost marshal general of the U.S. Army. He was a member of Lincoln's escort on November 18 and was in Lincoln's railcar throughout the journey. He believed that the assertion that Lincoln wrote the address on the train was false. Fry stated, "I have no recollection of seeing him writing or even reading his speech during the journey. In fact, there was hardly any opportunity for him to read or write."

In conclusion, Lincoln wrote most of the Gettysburg Address in Washington, D.C., and finished it in Gettysburg on the morning of November 19, 1863. He did not write it on the train journey. The individuals who claimed to see Lincoln write the address on the train wanted to have an intimate relationship with the most famous speech in American history. The individuals who perpetuated the myth were motivated by the romantic concept that the noblest of ideas can spring from the most humble of origins. Despite the many myths surrounding its origin, the Gettysburg Address remains Lincoln's most iconic and enduring speech.

PRIMARY SOURCE DOCUMENTS

JOHN NICOLAY, "LINCOLN'S GETTYSBURG ADDRESS" (1894)

John Nicolay was born in Bavaria and immigrated with his family to the United States as a young boy. He was a journalist and editor and served as

Lincoln's private secretary from 1861 to 1865. He became one of Lincoln's most trusted aides and an intimate associate of the president. He rode in Lincoln's railcar to Gettysburg and helped to transcribe the president's address on November 19, 1863. Nicolay decided to set the record straight about the Gettysburg Address after hearing half-truths about the speech for over three decades. In an article he wrote for The Century Magazine *in 1894, Nicolay put to rest the myth that Lincoln composed, and wrote, the address aboard the train bound for Gettysburg. The following is an excerpt from Nicolay's "Lincoln's Gettysburg Address" that discusses where and when Lincoln wrote his speech.*

THERE are three sources of authority for Lincoln's Gettysburg address, or, to speak more concisely, three successive versions of it—all identical in thought, but differing slightly in expression. The last of these is the regular outgrowth of the two which preceded it, and is the perfected product of the President's rhetorical and literary mastery. The three versions are:

1. The original autograph MS. draft, written by Mr. Lincoln partly at Washington and partly at Gettysburg.
2. The version made by the shorthand reporter on the stand at Gettysburg when the President delivered it, which was telegraphed, and was printed in the leading newspapers of the country on the following morning.
3. The revised copy made by the President a few days after his return to Washington, upon a careful comparison of his original draft and the printed newspaper version with his own recollections of the exact form in which he delivered it.

Mr. David Wills, of Gettysburg, first suggested the creation of a national cemetery on the battle-field, and under Governor Curtin's direction and cooperation he purchased the land for Pennsylvania and other States interested, and superintended the improvements. It had been intended to hold the dedication ceremonies on October 23, 1863, but Edward Everett, who was chosen to deliver the oration, had engagements for that time, and at his suggestion the occasion was postponed to November 19.

On November 2 Mr. Wills wrote the President a formal invitation to take part in the dedication.

These grounds [said his letter in part] will be consecrated and set apart to this sacred purpose by appropriate ceremonies on Thursday, the 19th inst. Hon. Edward Everett will deliver the oration. I am authorized by the governors of the different States to invite you to be present, and to participate in these ceremonies, which will doubtless be very imposing and solemnly impressive. It is the desire that, after the oration, you, as Chief Executive of the nation, formally set apart these grounds to their sacred use by a few appropriate remarks.

Accompanying this official invitation was also a private note from Mr. Wills, which said:

As the hotels in our town will be crowded and in confusion at the time referred to in the inclosed invitation, I write to invite you to stop with me. I hope you will feel it your duty to lay aside pressing business for a day to come on here to perform this last sad rite to our brave soldier dead, on the 19th inst. Governor Curtin and Hon. Edward Everett will be my guests at that time, and if you come you will please join them at my house.

From the above date it will be seen that Mr. Lincoln had a little more than two weeks in which to prepare the remarks he might intend to make. It was a time when he was extremely busy, not alone with the important and complicated military affairs in the various armies, but also with the consideration of his annual message to Congress, which was to meet early in December. There was even great uncertainty whether he could take enough time from his pressing official duties to go to Gettysburg at all. Up to the 17th of November, only two days before the ceremonies, no definite arrangements for the journey had been made. The whole cabinet had of course been invited, as well as the President, and on the 17th, which was Tuesday, Mr. Lincoln wrote to Secretary Chase:

I expected to see you here at cabinet meeting, and to say something about going to Gettysburg. There will be a train to take and return us. The time for starting is not yet fixed; but when it shall be I will notify you.

However, Mr. Chase had already written a note to Mr. Wills, expressing his inability to go, and apparently a little later on the same day Secretary Stanton sent the President this "timetable" for the trip:

It is proposed by the Baltimore and Ohio road: First, to leave Washington Thursday morning at 6 A. M. Second, to leave Baltimore at 8 a.m., arriving at Gettysburg at twelve, noon, thus giving two hours to view the ground before the dedication ceremonies commence. Third, to leave Gettysburg at 6 P. M., and arrive at Washington at midnight, thus doing all in one day.

Upon this proposition Mr. Lincoln, with his unfailing common-sense judgment, made this indorsement:

I do not like this arrangement. I do not wish to so go that by the slightest accident we fail entirely; and, at the best, the whole to be a mere breathless running of the gantlet. But any way.

There is no decisive record of when Mr. Lincoln wrote the first sentences of his proposed address. He probably followed his usual habit in such matters, using great deliberation in arranging his thoughts, and molding his phrases mentally, waiting to reduce them to writing until they had taken satisfactory form.

There was much greater necessity for such precaution in this case, because the invitation specified that the address of dedication should only be "a few appropriate remarks." Brevity in speech and writing was one of Lincoln's marked characteristics; but in this instance there existed two other motives calculated to strongly support his natural inclination. One was that Mr. Everett would be quite certain to make a long address; the other, the want of opportunity even to think leisurely about what he might desire to say. All this strongly confirms the correctness of the statement made by the Hon. James Speed, in an interview printed in the "Louisville Commercial" in November, 1879, that the President told him that "the day before he left Washington he found time to write about half of his speech."

The President's criticism of the time-table first suggested must have struck Secretary Stanton as having force, for the arrangement was changed, so that instead of starting on Thursday morning, the day of the ceremonies, the President's special train left Washington at noon of Wednesday the 18th. Three members of the cabinet—Mr. Seward, Secretary of State, Mr. Usher, Secretary of the Interior, and Mr. Blair, Postmaster-General—accompanied the President, as did the Trench minister M. Mercier, the Italian minister M. Bertinatti, and several legation secretaries and attaches. Mr. Lincoln also had with him his private secretary Mr. Nicolay, and his assistant private secretary Colonel John Hay. Captain H. A. Wise of the navy and Mrs. Wise (daughter of Edward Everett) were also of the party; likewise a number of newspaper correspondents from Washington, and a military guard of honor to take part in the Gettysburg procession. Other parties of military officers joined the train on the way.

No accident or delay occurred, and the party arrived in Gettysburg about nightfall. According to invitation Mr. Lincoln went to the house of Mr. Wills, while the members of the cabinet, and other distinguished persons of his party, were entertained elsewhere.

Except during its days of battle the little town of Gettysburg had never been so full of people. After the usual supper hour the streets literally swarmed with visitors, and the stirring music of regimental bands and patriotic glee-clubs sounded in many directions. With material so abundant, and enthusiasm so plentiful, a serenading party soon organized itself to call on prominent personages for impromptu speeches, and of course the President could not escape . . .

The crowd followed the music to seek other notabilities, and had the satisfaction of hearing short speeches from Secretary Seward, Representatives McPherson and McKnight, Judge Shannon, Colonel John W. Forney, Wayne MacVeagh, and perhaps others. These addresses were not altogether perfunctory. A certain political tension existed throughout the entire war period, which rarely failed to color every word of a public speaker, and attune the ear of every public listener to subtle and oracular meanings. Even in this ceremonial gathering there was a keen watchfulness for any sign or omen which might disclose a drift in popular feeling, either on the local Pennsylvania quarrel between Cameron and Curtin, or the final success or failure of the Emancipation Proclamation; or whether the President would or would not succeed himself by a renomination and reelection in the coming campaign of 1864.

There were still here and there ultra-radical newspapers that suspected and questioned Seward's hearty support of the emancipation policy. These made favorable note of his little address in which he predicted that the war would end in the removal of slavery, and that "when that cause is removed, simply by the operation of abolishing it, as the origin and agent of the treason that is without justification and without parallel, we shall henceforth be united, be only one country, having only one hope, one ambition, and one destiny."

Speech-making finally came to an end, and such of the visitors as were blessed with friends or good luck sought the retirement of their rooms, where in spite of brass-bands and glee-clubs, and the restless tramping of the less fortunate along the sidewalks, they slept the slumber of mental, added to physical, weariness.

There is neither record, evidence, nor well-founded tradition that Mr. Lincoln did any writing, or made any notes, on the journey between Washington and Gettysburg. The train consisted of four passenger-coaches, and either composition or writing would have been extremely troublesome amid all the movement, the noise, the conversation, the greetings, and the questionings which ordinarily courtesy required him to undergo in these surroundings; but still worse would have been the rockings and joltings of the train, rendering writing virtually impossible. Mr. Lincoln carried in his pocket the autograph manuscript of so much of his address as he had written at Washington the day before. Precisely what that was the reader can now see by turning to the facsimile reproduction of the original draft, which is for the first time printed and made public in this article. It fills one page of the letter-paper at that time habitually used in the Executive Mansion, containing the plainly printed blank heading; both paper and print giving convincing testimony to the simple and economical business methods then prevailing in the White House.

Source: Nicolay, John. 1894 "Lincoln's Gettysburg Address." Reprinted from *The Century Magazine*, February, 4–5.

NOAH BROOKS, WASHINGTON IN LINCOLN'S TIME (1896)

Noah Brooks was a journalist and a friend of Abraham Lincoln. Brooks was the Washington correspondent for The Sacramento Union *during the Civil War. He was a loyal confidant of the president and often provided Lincoln with political intelligence. His unusual access to Lincoln and the White House provided Brooks with the opportunity to observe and record many interesting conversations with the president. In 1896, Brooks wrote about a conversation he had with Lincoln on November 8, 1863, about the president's upcoming speech in Gettysburg.*

One November day—it chanced to be the Sunday before the dedication of the national cemetery at Gettysburg—I had an appointment to go with the President to Gardner, the photographer, on Seventh Street, to fulfil a long-standing engagement. Mr. Lincoln carefully explained that he could not go on any other day without interfering with the public business and the photographer's business, to say nothing of his liability to be hindered by curiosity-seekers "and other seekers" on the way thither. Just as we were going down the stairs of the White House, the President suddenly remembered that he needed a paper, and, after hurrying back to his office, soon rejoined me with a long envelope in his hand. When we were fairly started, he said that in the envelope was an advance copy of Edward Everett's address to be delivered at the Gettysburg dedication on the following Tuesday. Drawing it out, I saw that it was a one-page supplement to a Boston paper, and that Mr. Everett's address nearly covered both sides of the sheet. The President expressed his admiration for the thoughtfulness of the Boston orator, who had sent this copy of his address in order that Mr. Lincoln might not traverse the same lines that the chosen speaker of the great occasion might have laid out for himself. When I exclaimed at its length, the President laughed and quoted the line, "Solid men of Boston, make no long orations," which he said he had met somewhere in a speech by Daniel Webster. He said that there was no danger that he should get upon the lines of Mr. Everett's oration, for what he had ready to say was very short, or, as he emphatically expressed it, "short, short, short." In reply to a question as to the speech having been already written, he said that it was written, "but not finished." He had brought the paper with him, he explained, hoping that a few minutes of leisure while waiting for the movements of the photographer and his processes would give him a chance to look over the speech. But we did not have to wait long between the sittings, and the President, having taken out the envelope and laid it on a little table at his elbow, became so engaged in talk that he failed to open it while we were at the studio. A disaster overtook the negative of that photograph, and after a very few prints had been made from it, no more were possible. In the picture which the President gave me, the envelope containing Mr. Everett's oration is seen on the table by the side of the sitter, recalling the incident and Lincoln's quotation of Boston's "long orations."

Source: Brooks, Noah. 1896. *Washington in Lincoln's Time.* New York: Century, 285–87.

ABRAHAM LINCOLN, SPEECH AT WILLS HOUSE (NOVEMBER 18, 1863)

John Nicolay stated that it was Lincoln's usual practice in writing speeches to take "great deliberation" in arranging his thoughts and "molding his phrases mentally" before committing them to written form. It was not in Lincoln's nature to wait until the last minute to craft a speech, and he did not like to adlib his remarks. Nicolay did not know exactly when Lincoln began work on the Gettysburg Address, but he was sure Lincoln worked on it weeks before he left the nation's capital for Gettysburg. He was also positive that Lincoln did not compose it on the train to Gettysburg.

Lincoln demonstrated his reluctance to speak without sufficient preparation on the night of November 18, 1863, in Gettysburg, Pennsylvania. A crowd of well-wishers went to the Wills House and serenaded Lincoln. They called for the president to make an impromptu speech. Lincoln finally appeared before the assemblage and informed them that he would not make a speech because he had not prepared one. Nicolay later wrote that "Mr. Lincoln showed himself only long enough to utter the few commonplace excuses politeness require." Below are Lincoln's remarks to the crowd gathered at Wills House on November 18.

I appear before you, fellow-citizens, merely to thank you for this compliment. The inference is a very fair one that you would hear me for a little while at least, were I to commence to make a speech. I do not appear before you for the purpose of doing so, and for several substantial reasons. The most substantial of these is that I have no speech to make. In my position it is somewhat important that I should not say any foolish things. [A voice: If you can help it.] It very often happens that the only way to help it is to say nothing at all. Believing that is my present condition this evening, I must beg of you to excuse me from addressing you further.

Source: Nicolay, John. 1894. "Lincoln's Gettysburg Address." Reprinted from *The Century Magazine*, February, 5.

Further Reading

Andrews, Mary Raymond Shipman. 1906. *The Perfect Tribute*. New York: Charles Scribner and Sons.

Arnold, Isaac N. 1866. *The History of Abraham Lincoln and the Overthrow of Slavery*. Chicago: Clark.

Barton, William E. 1950. *Lincoln at Gettysburg: What He Intended to Say; What He Said; What He Was Reported to Have Said; What He Wished He Had Said*. New York: Peter Smith.

Baster, Roy P., ed. 1953. *The Collected Works of Abraham Lincoln*. New Brunswick, NJ: Rutgers University Press.

Borih, Gabor. 2006. *The Gettysburg Gospel: The Lincoln Speech That Nobody Knows*. New York: Simon and Schuster.

Brooks, Noah. 1896. *Washington in Lincoln's Time*. New York: Century.

Burlingame, Michael. 2013. *A Day Long to Be Remembered: Lincoln in Gettysburg*. New York: Wild Perceptions.

Conant, Sean. 2015. *The Gettysburg Address: Perspectives on Lincoln's Greatest Speech*. New York: Oxford University Press.

Dixon, David T. 2015. *The Lost Gettysburg Address: Charles Anderson's Civil War Odyssey*. Santa Barbara, CA: B-List History.

Elmore, A. E. 2009. *Lincoln's Gettysburg Address: Echoes of the Bible and Book of Common Prayer*. Carbondale: Southern Illinois University Press.

Gramm, Kent. 2001. *November: Lincoln's Elegy at Gettysburg*. Bloomington: Indiana University Press.

Holzer, Harold. n.d. "Lincoln's 'Flat Failure.' The Gettysburg Myth Revisited." *Journal of the Gilder Lehrman Institute*. Accessed September 20, 2017. https://www.gilderlehrman.org/history-by-era/american-civil-war/essays/lincoln%e2%81.

Klement, Frank L. 1993. *The Gettysburg Soldiers Cemetery and Lincoln's Address: Aspects and Angles*. Shippensburg, PA: White Maine.

Knorowski, Carla, ed. 2015. *Gettysburg Replies: The World Responds to Abraham Lincoln's Gettysburg Address.* Guilford, CT: Rowan and Littlefield.

Kunhardt, Philip N. 1983. *A New Birth of Freedom: Lincoln at Gettysburg.* Boston: Little, Brown.

Lambert, Major William H. 1909. "The Gettysburg Address: When Written, How Received, Its True Form." *Pennsylvania Magazine of History and Biography.*

Nicolay, John G. 1894. "Lincoln's Gettysburg Address." *The Century Magazine,* 596–609.

Nicolay, John G., and John M. Hay. 1890. *Abraham Lincoln: A History.* 10 vols. New York: Century.

Olson, Steven P. 2005. *Lincoln's Gettysburg Address: A Primary Source Investigation.* New York: Rosen.

Peatman, Jared. 2013. *The Long Shadow of Lincoln's Gettysburg Address.* Carbondale: Southern Illinois University Press.

Poore, Benjamin Perley, and Allen Thorndike Rice, eds. 1886. *Reminiscences of Lincoln by Distinguished Men of His Times.* New York: North American Publishing.

Staff, National Constitution Center. 2016. "Myths and Mysteries about the Gettysburg Address." *Constitution Daily.* National Constitution Center, November 19. Accessed April 16, 2018. https//constitutioncenter.org /blog/myths-and-mysteries-about-the-gettysburg-address.

Warren, Louis A. 1964. *Lincoln's Gettysburg Declaration: "A New Birth of Freedom."* Fort Wayne, IN: Lincoln National Life Foundation.

White, Ronald C., Jr. 2005. *The Eloquent President: A Portrait of Lincoln through His Words.* New York: Random House.

Wieck, Carl F. 2002. *Lincoln's Quest for Equality: The Road to Gettysburg.* DeKalb: Northern Illinois University Press.

Wills, Gary. 1992. *Lincoln at Gettysburg: The Words That Remade America.* New York: Simon and Schuster.

Wilson, Douglas L. 2006. *Lincoln's Sword: The Presidency and the Power of Words.* New York: Knopf.

Zeitz, Joshua. 2014. *Lincoln's Boys: John Hay, John Nicolay, and the War for Lincoln's Image.* New York: Penguin.

7

Grant Was a Butcher

What People Think Happened

Next to Abraham Lincoln, Gen. Ulysses S. Grant did more than any other individual to preserve the Union. His military genius, flexibility, perseverance, and offensive acumen made him the most successful general in the Civil War. His victories at Fort Henry and Fort Donelson were among the first Union successes and raised morale in the North. They also opened the door to the capture of Nashville, Tennessee, the first Southern state capital to come under Union control. In 1863, Grant's capture of Vicksburg put the Mississippi River under Union control and split the Confederacy in half. At Chattanooga, in the fall of 1863, he rescued the Army of the Cumberland from the jaws of defeat and forced the Confederate Army of Tennessee under the command of Gen. Braxton Bragg to retreat into Georgia. In the spring of 1864, Grant launched his Overland Campaign that one year later led to the surrender of Robert E. Lee and the Army of Northern Virginia at Appomattox Court House. By the end of the war, Grant had received the surrender of three Confederate armies. This feat made Grant the most successful general in American history to that point in time.

Despite his unparalleled success, Grant's critics developed the myth that the general's victories were the result of his overwhelming manpower and resources rather than his military skill or ability. The myth claims that Grant had no regard for human life, that he used brute force to bludgeon Confederate foes into submission, that he was only able to defeat superior Southern commanders because his troops outnumbered the Confederate forces, and that he was willing to accept extremely high Union casualties as the "butcher's price" for victory. This myth began during the Civil War and has persisted into the 21st century.

The myth that Grant carelessly wasted the lives of his soldiers originated with the costly Union victory at Shiloh. On the morning of April 6, 1862, Confederate forces attacked Grant's army at Pittsburg Landing, Tennessee. Southern troops drove the stunned Union forces back about two miles but did not break the Northern line. The following morning, Grant, reinforced with 25,000 men, pushed the Confederates back and forced them to retreat to Corinth, Mississippi. The Battle of Shiloh was the bloodiest battle in American history to that point in time. The Union suffered 13,000 casualties, while the Confederate figure was 10,700.

Though Shiloh was a Union victory, military leaders and politicians blamed Grant for the heavy Union losses. They blamed the carnage on Grant's unpreparedness for battle and the false rumor that Grant was intoxicated at the time of the Confederate attack. After Shiloh, Gen. Henry W. Halleck, Union commander of the Western Theater, appointed Grant his deputy commander. This appointment effectively removed Grant from command of his army and left him with nothing to do during the Corinth Campaign of 1862.

Grant's career rebounded with victories at Vicksburg and Chattanooga. In 1864, Lincoln appointed Grant general in chief of all Union armies. Grant made his headquarters with Gen. George Gordon Meade's Army of the Potomac and in effect was its strategic field commander. In May 1864, Grant launched the Overland Campaign. His goals were to annihilate Lee's army and capture Richmond, the Confederate capital. For the next six weeks, Grant's and Lee's forces fought a series of horrific battles from the wilderness around Fredericksburg to the entrenchments of Petersburg, Virginia.

Casualties were extremely high on both sides. From the Battle of the Wilderness (May 5) to Petersburg (June 18), Union forces suffered 64,000 casualties, while the Confederate number was 37,000. Union casualty numbers were so high during this campaign that some Republican leaders feared the party would not renominate Lincoln as president.

Grant's critics claimed that his disregard for his soldiers' lives and his sole dependence on bludgeoning tactics led to unacceptably high casualty numbers for this campaign. They also argued that Grant's calculation (Lincoln called it the "terrible arithmetic")—that the Union could afford casualties while the South could not—increased the frightful figures.

Mary Todd Lincoln told her seamstress, Elizabeth Keckley, that Grant "is a butcher and is not fit to be a head of an army. He loses two men to the enemy's one." On June 4, 1864, the day after the Battle of Cold Harbor, secretary of the navy Gideon Welles confided in his diary: "Still there is a heavy loss, but we are becoming accustomed to sacrifice. Grant has not great regard for human life." The heavy casualties at Shiloh created the image of Grant as a butcher of his men. The devastating losses during the Overland Campaign confirmed it.

How the Story Became Popular

The myth that Grant was a butcher who needlessly spent the lives of his soldiers to achieve victory has persisted into the 21st century. The myth has remained resilient and alive for a variety of reasons, including Lee's General Orders No. 9, lost cause apologists, the writings of Grant and other Union officers, and the sympathetic treatment of Lee by Southern historians.

On April 10, 1865, one day after he surrendered his army to Grant, Lee issued General Orders No. 9. In his farewell statement to the Army of Northern Virginia, Lee informed his troops that they had served their country with "unsurpassed courage and fortitude." Lee said that he had "been compelled to yield to the overwhelming numbers and resources" of the Union. Lee's contention that Grant defeated his army simply because the North had the advantage in resources and manpower became the mantra of the defeated South. This conception not only provided the Confederates with a convenient rationale for defeat but also permanently tarnished Grant's reputation.

Lee's explanation of his defeat soon became ensconced in the tenets of the lost cause. Edward Pollard coined the term in 1866 in his work *The Lost Cause: A New Southern History of the War of the Confederates.* Pollard and other Southern apologists were determined that their version of history would shape the thought of future generations. They hoped to justify their actions and find something positive in the devastating defeat of the Confederacy. Lost cause advocates believed that Lee was the best and brightest general to fight in the Civil War. They saw Confederate forces as gallant and brave soldiers who only lost because of the overwhelming disadvantages they faced in the war. Lost cause advocates also thought Grant was a butcher and paled in comparison to Lee as a commander.

Lt. Gen. Jubal Early and other Confederate generals lambasted Grant and his strategies in their postwar writings. Early was the first to vilify

Grant and malign his leadership style, writing in his autobiography that Lee did all he could for "the success of the cause" but was overwhelmed by the resources of the North. The Union's boundless resources coupled with the lack of concern for his men allowed Grant to defeat a man of superior military intellect. Confederate general Evander Law wrote that during the Overland Campaign, captured Union prisoners complained about "the useless butchery" Grant subjected them to during the march toward Richmond. Walter Taylor, one of Lee's adjutants, wrote in 1906 that Grant "put a lower estimate upon the value of human life than any of his predecessors." Confederate officers enshrined Lee in the pantheon of great generals and demoted Grant to the rank of butcher.

The perpetuators of the myth used Grant's own words against him and the writings of his comrades. On July 22, 1865, General Grant filed a report with the War Department on the activities of the Armies of the United States from 1864 to 1865. In his report, Grant stated that in 1864, it was his firm conviction that peace could not be achieved until "the military power of the rebellion was entirely broken." Grant put forth two strategies to achieve his goal. First, he would "use the greatest number of troops practicable against the armed force of the enemy." Second, he planned "to hammer continuously against the armed forces of the enemy and his resources, until by mere attrition, if in no other way, there should be nothing left to him but an equal submission with the loyal section of our common country." Grant's own words suggest that he employed a war of attrition based on superior resources to defeat the undermanned and overwhelmed Confederates.

Mark Twain published Grant's memoirs shortly after the general's death in 1885. In his memoirs, Grant confessed that he "regretted that the last assault at Cold Harbor was ever made." The assault on June 3, 1864, against fixed Confederate defenses resulted in nearly 7,000 Union casualties. Grant wrote, "At Cold Harbor no advantage whatever was gained to compensate for the heavy loss we sustained." In the same passage, Grant said he also regretted the assault on Vicksburg on May 22, 1863. This attack also resulted in high casualties with no advantage gained against the fortifications of this key Southern city on the Mississippi River. Lost cause apologists and military historians have used Grant's candid criticism of himself to bolster their argument that Grant was a reckless leader who carelessly spent human life to purchase victory.

Gen. Joshua Chamberlain, the iconic Union hero of the second day at Gettysburg, wrote a stream-of-consciousness memoir about the Appomattox Campaign (April 1865). In his work, *The Passing of the Armies*,

Chamberlain provided the reader with a succinct description of the 1864 Overland Campaign. His description contained a veiled criticism of Grant's leadership. Chamberlain described "reckless front attacks" where there were "butcherings in slaughter pens." The "deepest loss" was the result of the "ever alert enemy" who overmatched Union leadership. Chamberlain claimed that after Cold Harbor, superiors no longer asked for casualty reports. When he asked them why, they answered "because the country would not stand it, if they knew." Chamberlain's book published in 1914 did little to restore the luster to Grant's reputation.

Historians in the 20th century continued to perpetuate the butcher myth about Lee. Douglas Southhall Freeman's *R. E. Lee: A Biography* and *Lee's Lieutenants: A Study in Command* elevated Lee to the stature of sainthood. Clifford Dowdy in his work *Lee* wrote that "Grant took no count of losses." Both authors depicted Grant as a general whose only strategy was to relentlessly hammer smaller forces until he won by attrition.

The myth of Grant the butcher continues into the 21st century. In 2003, Bruce Smith began his review of Gordon Rhea's book on Cold Harbor for the Associated Press with this statement: "Ask most school children and they will tell you that Robert E. Lee was a military genius while Ulysses S. Grant was a butcher." James R. Kennedy and Walter Donald Kennedy, in their 2008 work *The South Was Right!*, portray Union generals as evil and dim-witted leaders who only managed to defeat the South by extreme advantages in both manpower and resources. In his 2010 book *The American Civil War: A Military History*, the renowned British military historian John Keegan wrote that "most of Grant's battles were costly in casualties." As Gordon Rhea concludes in his work on Cold Harbor, "The ghost of 'Grant the butcher' still haunts Civil War lore."

PRIMARY SOURCE DOCUMENTS

ELIZABETH KECKLEY, *BEHIND THE SCENES: OR, THIRTY YEARS A SLAVE AND FOUR YEARS IN THE WHITE HOUSE* (1868)

Elizabeth Keckley was born a slave in 1818 in Dinwiddie, Virginia. She became a seamstress and eventually purchased freedom for herself and her son. In 1860, she arrived in Washington, D.C., and made dresses for wealthy clients. Margaret Mclean arranged a meeting between Keckley and Mary Todd Lincoln. Keckley became Mrs. Lincoln's dressmaker and confidant. She also became Mrs. Lincoln's personal dresser and helped the First Lady prepare for events in the White House. In 1868, she published her autobiography, Behind the Scenes: Or, Thirty Years a Slave and Four Years in the White House. *Her work is both a slave narrative and personal look at the Lincoln family.*

In this excerpt from her autobiography, Keckley recalls a conversation between Lincoln and his wife in which the First Lady described Grant as "a butcher."

Mrs. Lincoln could not tolerate General Grant. "He is a butcher," she would often say, "and is not fit to be at the head of an army."

"But he has been very successful in the field," argued the President.

"Yes, he generally manages to claim a victory, but such a victory! He loses two men to the enemy's one. He has no management, no regard for life. If the war should continue four years longer, and he should remain in power, he would depopulate the North. I could fight an army as well myself. According to his tactics, there is nothing under the heavens to do but to march a new line of men up in front of the rebel breastworks to be shot down as fast as they take their position, and keep marching until the enemy grows tired of the slaughter. Grant, I repeat, is an obstinate fool and a butcher."

"Well, mother, supposing that we give you command of the army. No doubt you would do much better than any general that has been tried." There was a twinkle in the eyes, and a ring of irony in the voice.

I have often heard Mrs. Lincoln say that if Grant should ever be elected President of the United States she would desire to leave the country, and remain absent during his term of office.

Source: Keckley, Elizabeth. 1868. *Behind the Scenes or Thirty Years a Slave and Four Years in the White House.* New York: G. W. Carleton, 132–34.

EDWARD POLLARD, *THE LOST CAUSE* (1866)

After the defeat of the Confederacy in 1865, Southerners initiated a movement to justify secession and explain why the South lost the war. Southern historian and journalist Edward A. Pollard called this movement the "lost cause." One of the major tenets of the lost cause is that the North prevailed in this sectional conflict because of their overwhelming manpower and resource advantage. Lost cause apologists also asserted that Grant was a poor general who had no respect for human life and that he was only able to defeat the noble Lee through a war of attrition.

In this excerpt from The Lost Cause: A New Southern History of the War of the Confederates, *Pollard provides his assessment of Grant in comparison to General Lee.*

On the Federal side a new and important actor was to appear on the scene. Gen. Ulysses S. Grant, who had had a long run of success in the West, had been appointed lieutenant-general and commander-in-chief of all the Federal forces, and was now to answer the expectation of his admirers by a campaign in Virginia and the repetition of the enterprise upon the Confederate capital. The Richmond journals complimented him as a "man of far more energy and ability than any that had yet commanded the Army of the Potomac," but" his performances would bear no comparison whatever to those of Gen. Lee."

The new Federal commander in Virginia was one of the most remarkable accidents of the war. That a man without any marked ability, certainly without genius, without fortune, without influence, should attain the position of leader of all the Federal armies, and stand the most conspicuous person on that side of the war, is a phenomenon which would be inexplicable among any other people than the sensational and coarse mobs of admiration in the North. Gen. Grant's name was coupled with success; and this circumstance alone, without regard to merit of personal agency, without reference to any display of mental quality in the event, was sufficient to fix him in the admiration of the Northern public. It mattered not that Grant had illustrated no genius; it mattered not that he had smothered Fort Donelson by numbers; it mattered not that he had succeeded at Vicksburg through the glaring incompetency of a Confederate commander, and by the weight of eighty thousand men against twenty odd thousand; the North was prepared to worship him, without distinguishing between accident and achievement, and to entitle him the hero of the war.

It is a curious commentary on the justice of popular judgment, that while Grant was thus elevated to power and fame, the man who rescued him at Perryville and again at Shiloh, and whose heroism and genius had saved there the consequences of his stupidity, should be languishing in obscurity. This man was Gen. Buell. It was he who had contributed most to Grant's success, and whose masterly manoeuvres had done more to reclaim the Mississippi Valley for the Federals than any other commander, and who now had been sacrificed to the spirit of political intrigue. At a time when popular passion clamored for the desolation of the South, Gen. Buell persisted, with a firmness rarer and more admirable even than he exhibited in the crisis of battle, in conducting the war on the principles of humanity; and by this noble moderation he incurred the displeasure of the faction that controlled the Government at Washington. The Radicals waged a war of extermination; but he proposed, with the sagacity of a statesman, to conciliate the good will of the South, while he overcame its resistance by an exertion of physical force. His system was too refined for the comprehension, and too liberal for the vindictive temper of the dominant party, and he was forced to relinquish the command of the superb army he had organized, and to resign a commission which he might have illustrated by splendid achievements.

It is some consolation to reflect that the verdict of history is neither the sensation of a mob nor the fiat of a political faction. Gen. Grant will have his proper place surely and exactly assigned in the ultimate records of merit in the war. "No one will deny this man credit for many good qualities of heart and great propriety of behaviour. He had that coarse, heavy obstinacy, which is as often observed in the Western backwoodsman as in a higher range of character. But he contained no spark of military genius; his idea of war was to the last degree rude—no strategy, the mere application of the vis inertice; he had none of that quick perception on the field of action which decides it by sudden strokes; he had no conception of battle beyond the momentum of numbers. Such was the man who marshalled all the material resources of the North to conquer the little army and overcome the consummate skill of Gen. Lee. He, who was declared the military genius of the North, had such a low idea of the contest, such little appreciation of the higher aims and intellectual exercises of war that he proposed to decide it by a mere competition in the sacrifice of human life. His plan of operations, as he himself described it, was "to hammer continuously against the armed force of the enemy and his resources, until by mere attrition, if in no other way, there should be nothing left to him but an equal submission with the loyal section of our common country to the Constitution and laws of the land."

Source: Pollard, Edward. 1866. *The Lost Cause: A New Southern History of the War of the Confederates.* New York: E. B Trust, 509–10.

ULYSSES S. GRANT, *PERSONAL MEMOIRS OF U. S. GRANT* (1883)

After Ulysses S. Grant left the White House in 1877, he became involved in an investment firm owned by his son, Ulysses S. Grant Jr., and Geoffrey Ward. When the firm of Grant and Ward failed in 1884, Grant became penniless.

At the same time, doctors diagnosed him with terminal throat cancer. Grant decided to write and publish his memoirs to support his family after his death. He finished the manuscript five days before he died. Mark Twain published the two-volume set after Grant's death. About 350,000 copies were sold, and Julia Grant received about $450,000 in royalties. Grant's memoirs were well written and provide a candid self-assessment of himself and his foes.

In this excerpt, Grant expresses his regret for ordering frontal attacks and the loss of life that ensued at Vicksburg and Cold Harbor.

I have always regretted that the last assault at Cold Harbor was ever made. I might say the same thing of the assault of the 22d of May, 1863, at Vicksburg. At Cold Harbor no advantage whatever was gained to compensate for the heavy loss we sustained. Indeed, the advantages other than those of relative losses, were on the Confederate side. Before that, the Army of Northern Virginia seemed to have acquired a wholesome regard for the courage, endurance, and soldierly qualities generally of the Army of the Potomac. They no longer wanted to fight them "one Confederate to five Yanks." Indeed, they seemed to have given up any idea of gaining any advantage of their antagonist in the open field. They had come to much prefer breastworks in their front to the Army of the Potomac. This charge seemed to revive their hopes temporarily; but it was of short duration. The effect upon the Army of the Potomac was the reverse. When we reached the James River, however, all effects of the battle of Cold Harbor seemed to have disappeared.

There was more justification for the assault at Vicksburg. We were in a Southern climate, at the beginning of the hot season. The Army of the Tennessee had won five successive victories over the garrison of Vicksburg in the three preceding weeks. They had driven a portion of that army from Port Gibson with considerable loss, after having flanked them out of their stronghold at Grand Gulf. They had attacked another portion of the same army at Raymond, more than fifty miles farther in the interior of the State, and driven them back into Jackson with great loss in killed, wounded, captured and missing, besides loss of large and small arms: they had captured the capital of the State of Mississippi, with a large amount of materials of war and manufactures. Only a few days before, they had beaten the enemy then penned up in the town first at Champion's Hill, next at Big Black River Bridge, inflicting upon him a loss of fifteen thousand or more men (including those cut off from returning) besides large losses in arms and ammunition. The Army of the Tennessee had come to believe that they could beat their antagonist under any circumstances. There was no telling how long a regular siege might last. As I have stated, it was the beginning of the hot season in a Southern climate. There was no telling what the casualties might be among Northern troops working and living in trenches, drinking surface water filtered through rich vegetation, under a tropical sun. If Vicksburg could have been carried in May, it would not only have saved the army the risk it ran of a greater danger than from the bullets of the enemy, but it would have given us a splendid army, well equipped and officered, to operate elsewhere with. These are reasons justifying the assault. The only benefit we gained—and it was a slight one for so great a sacrifice—was that the men worked cheerfully in the trenches after that, being satisfied with digging the enemy out. Had the assault not been made, I have no doubt that the majority of those engaged in the siege of Vicksburg would have believed that had we assaulted it would have proven successful, and would have saved life, health and comfort.

Source: Grant, Ulysses S. 1885. *Personal Memoirs of Ulysses S Grant.* Vol. 3. New York: Charles L. Webster, ch. 55.

JOSHUA CHAMBERLAIN, *THE PASSING OF THE ARMIES* (1915)

Joshua Lawrence Chamberlain is a Civil War icon. The college professor turned general was wounded six times in combat. He is best known as the commander of the 20th Maine. Chamberlain and his regiment gained notoriety for their heroic defense of the Little Round Top on the second day of the Battle of Gettysburg. Congress awarded Chamberlain the Medal of Honor for his "conspicuous gallantry" in defending the extreme left flank of the Union defensive lines.

After the war, Chamberlain served four terms as the governor of Maine and also later became president of Bowdoin College. In his later years, he wrote The Passing of the Armies, *a stream-of-consciousness memoir about the Appomattox Campaign in April 1865.*

In this excerpt from The Passing of the Armies, *Chamberlain describes the horrors of the Overland Campaign in the spring of 1864. He also claims that the military suppressed casualty reports so the public would not be alarmed by the increasing number of dead and wounded Union soldiers in this deadly series of battles in Virginia.*

Then the rushing, forced flank-movements, known and overmatched by the ever alert enemy; followed by reckless front attacks, where highest valor was deepest loss; buffetings on bloody angles; butcherings in slaughter pens,—all the way down to the fateful Chickahominy once more—a campaign under fire for twenty-seven days and nights together; morning reports at last not called for, and when we asked explanation our superiors answered,—confidentially, lest it seem disloyal: "Because the country would not stand it, if they knew."

What wonder that men who have passed through such things together,—no matter on which side arrayed,—should be wrought upon by that strange power of a common suffering which so divinely passes into the power of a common love.

Source: Chamberlain, Joshua. 1915. *The Passing of the Armies.* New York: G. P. Putman's Sons, ch. 1.

What Really Happened

In his defense of British soldiers at the Boston Massacre trial, John Adams stated that "facts are stubborn things." The facts show that Grant was not a butcher but instead was the Civil War's most successful general. He won four major campaigns and compelled the surrender of three different Confederate armies. His success was based on imagination, speed, flexibility, maneuver, and persistence as well as an aggressive command style. In his victories, he generally had a lower casualty rate than his Confederate foes. During the war, troops commanded by Grant suffered fewer casualties than the forces led by Robert E. Lee.

Grant's first success was along the Tennessee and the Cumberland Rivers. In January 1862, Grant seized Fort Henry on the Tennessee River. In February, Grant captured Fort Donelson on the Cumberland River and accepted the surrender of Gen. Simon Bolivar Buckner's army. When Buckner asked Grant for terms of surrender, Grant replied, "No terms except an unconditional and immediate surrender can be accepted." These words became famous and provided the general with the moniker "unconditional surrender Grant." The defense of Nashville became untenable with the fall of Fort Donelson, and Confederate forces evacuated the Tennessee capital on February 23. In these two victories, Grant suffered about 3,000 casualties to around 16,000 for the Confederates.

On April 6, 1862, Confederate forces attacked Grant's army at Pittsburg Landing, Tennessee. On the first day of the battle, Confederate troops drove the outnumbered Union soldiers back about two miles. Grant received reinforcements throughout the night. The next morning,

Grant counterattacked and regained the ground he had lost the previous day. By 3:30 p.m., the beaten Southern army retreated toward Corinth, Mississippi. The two-day battle known as Shiloh was the bloodiest battle to that point in American history. Grant's victorious forces suffered 13,000 casualties, while the defeated Confederates endured 10,700 casualties. While Grant's army suffered more casualties than the South at Shiloh, the Confederacy lost a higher percentage of troops (24 percent) than did Grant's army (20 percent).

Grant's Vicksburg Campaign (March 29 to July 4, 1863) was a masterpiece of military leadership. Vicksburg was one of the last Confederate strongholds on the Mississippi River. The Vicksburg fortifications prevented Union ships from sailing from the North to the port of New Orleans. Jefferson Davis called Vicksburg the Gibraltar of America because eight miles of trenches encircled the city. Vicksburg's fortifications were anchored by nine massive forts, some with walls 20 feet thick. Swampy ground to the north and the river to the west made Vicksburg virtually impregnable to attack.

In his 1863 campaign, Grant crossed the Mississippi River from the west bank to Bruinsburg. Living off the land, Grant fought five battles against Confederate forces that outnumbered him in the theater of operations. Grant won all five battles, captured Jackson (Mississippi's capital), and then laid siege to Vicksburg. On July 4, 1863, Lt. Gen. John C. Pemberton surrendered his army and Vicksburg to Grant. Grant's victory cut the Confederacy in half and opened the river to Union ships all the way to the Gulf of Mexico. Coupled with the Southern defeat at Gettysburg, Grant's victory at Vicksburg helped to seal the fate of the Confederacy. Over the three-month campaign, Grant inflicted 38,000 casualties on Confederate forces while suffering 10,100 himself.

In the fall of 1863, Confederate forces trapped the Union army of the Cumberland in Chattanooga, Tennessee. The Confederate Army of Tennessee under the command of Gen. Braxton Bragg held the high ground above the city and had choked off most of the supplies headed to Union troops. The loss of an entire Union army to the Confederacy would be devastating and undo all the Union successes gained in 1863.

Lincoln sent Grant to Chattanooga to extricate the Army of the Cumberland from its precarious situation. The president provided Grant with reinforcements from the Army of the Potomac and the Army of the Tennessee. The Battle of Chattanooga commenced on November 23. Grant's troops successfully dislodged Confederate forces from the high ground of Missionary Ridge and Lookout Mountain, a feat rarely accomplished in the Civil War. By the afternoon of November 25, Bragg's army was routed and retreated to Georgia. Grant had not only done the impossible, driving the enemy from fixed positions on the high ground, but he did it with fewer casualties (5,800) than the Confederates (6,700). Grant's victory rescued the Army of the Cumberland and set the stage for the Atlanta Campaign.

Lincoln appointed Grant general in chief of all the Union armies in March 1864. Grant made his headquarters with General Meade's Army of the Potomac. Grant instructed Meade that "Lee's army will be your objective point. Wherever Lee goes there you will go also." In what became known as the Overland Campaign, Grant hoped to maneuver the Army of the Potomac around Lee's right flank. This strategy would allow the Army of the Potomac to slip in between Lee's forces and Richmond. Lee would then be compelled to abandon his defensive strategy and attack the Army of the Potomac in order to save Richmond.

By the spring of 1864, Lee, Davis, and other Confederate leaders realized their best chance to win their independence was to keep Lincoln from being reelected president for four more years. The key to turning the Northern electorate against Lincoln was to make the war more costly in terms of human life. If the Confederacy could increase Union casualty rates, Northern voters might seek a negotiated end to the conflict by electing a peace Democrat instead of Lincoln. Lee now fought defensively in entrenched positions. Lee's strategy forced Grant to attack him, and this resulted in high casualties for both sides. When his attacks failed, Grant tried to maneuver Lee out of position, only to find Lee entrenched at another site.

Constant fighting occurred in this manner for six weeks as the two armies fought each other from the wilderness outside Fredericksburg, Virginia, until they reached the entrenchments of Petersburg. Grant's casualties for the campaign were approximately 64,000 men or 41 percent of his army. Grant inflicted 37,000 casualties on the Confederates, costing Lee about 46 percent of the Army of Northern Virginia. Grant imposed a higher percentage of casualties on Lee's army even though Grant had the disadvantage of having to attack the Confederates, who had the distinct advantage of fighting defensively from entrenched positions.

At the conclusion of the Overland Campaign, Lee had retreated to Petersburg, where Grant laid siege to the city and the remnants of the Army of Northern Virginia. Grant's siege of Petersburg eventually led to the capture of the Confederate capital at Richmond and the downfall of the Confederacy. Lee's forces abandoned their Petersburg fortifications in early April 1865 and headed toward the western part of the state. The Army of the Potomac pursued and surrounded them. With no hope of escape, Lee surrendered the Army of Northern Virginia to Grant at Appomattox Court House on April 9, 1865.

Throughout all his campaigns in the Civil War, Grant's forces suffered approximately 153,600 casualties. Grant lost about 15 percent of the men he took into combat. His greatest losses occurred during the Overland Campaign. In comparison, Lee suffered over 209,000 casualties or over 20 percent of the men he commanded. During the course of the war, Grant took about 55,400 fewer casualties than Lee.

In conclusion, Grant was not a butcher. He was a skilled general who outthought, outmaneuvered, and outfought his opponents. He generally took fewer casualties in terms of both numbers and percentages than his foes. He accomplished this feat while having the disadvantage of fighting on both the strategic and tactical offensive. Grant's forces endured substantially fewer casualties than the general favored by his lost cause critics, Robert E. Lee. Grant won all four major campaigns he fought in during the war and received the surrender of three Confederate armies. Despite "the stubborn facts," the lore of Grant the butcher still exists today.

PRIMARY SOURCE DOCUMENTS

ALEXANDER MCCLURE, LINCOLN ON GRANT AFTER THE BATTLE OF SHILOH (1892)

Alexander Kelly McClure was born in Sherman's Valley, Pennsylvania, in 1828. McClure was a journalist, editor, and historian. He was an ardent abolitionist and joined the Republican Party in 1855. Prior to the Civil War, he served in both houses of the Pennsylvania legislature. During the Civil War, McClure served as an assistant adjutant general and helped to provide 17 Pennsylvania regiments to the Union army. In 1864, Confederate troops under the command of Gen. Jubal Early occupied Chambersburg, Pennsylvania, and burned McClure's estate, Norland, to the ground.

After the war, McClure again served in the Pennsylvania senate. In 1875, he founded The (Philadelphia) Times *and remained its editor until 1901. In 1892, he published a biography of Lincoln entitled* Abraham Lincoln and Men of War-Times. *In this work, McClure described a meeting he had with Lincoln shortly after the costly Union victory at Shiloh. McClure suggested to Lincoln that the president should fire Grant because of the general's negligence during the battle. Lincoln's succinct retort to McClure that "I can't fire this man; he fights" spoke volumes about Lincoln's growing confidence in General Grant.*

The few of to-day who can recall the inflamed condition of public sentiment against Grant caused by the disastrous first day's battle at Shiloh will remember that he was denounced as incompetent for his command by the public journals of all parties in the North, and with almost entire unanimity by Senators and Congressmen without regard to political faith. Not only in Washington, but throughout the loyal States, public sentiment seemed to crystallize into an earnest demand for Grant's dismissal from the army. His victories of Forts Henry and Donelson, which had thrilled the country a short time before, seemed to have been forgotten, and on every side could be heard the emphatic denunciation of Grant because of his alleged reckless exposure of the army, while Buell was universally credited with having saved it. It is needless to say that owing to the excited condition of the public mind most extravagant reports gained ready credence, and it was not uncommon to hear Grant denounced on the streets and in all circles as unfitted by both habit and temperament for an important military command. The clamor for Grant's removal, and often for his summary dismissal, from the army surged against the President from every side, and he was harshly criticized for not promptly dismissing Grant, or at least relieving him from his command. I can recall but a single Republican member of Congress who boldly defended Grant at that time. Elihu B. Washburne, whose home was in Galena, where Grant had lived before he went into the army, stood nearly or quite alone among the members of the House in wholly justifying Grant at Shiloh, while a large majority of the Republicans of Congress were outspoken and earnest in condemning him.

I did not know Grant at that time; had neither partiality nor prejudice to influence my judgment, nor had I any favorite general who might be benefited by Grant's overthrow, but I shared the almost universal conviction of the President's friends that he could not sustain himself if he attempted to sustain Grant by continuing him in command. Looking solely to the interests of Lincoln, feeling that the tide of popular resentment was so overwhelming against Grant that Lincoln must yield to it, I had repeated conferences with some of his closest friends, including Swett and Lamon, all of whom agreed that Grant must be removed from his command, and complained of Lincoln for his manifest injustice to himself by his failure to act promptly in Grant's removal. So much was I impressed with the importance of prompt action on the part of the President after spending a day and evening in Washington that I called on Lincoln at eleven o'clock at night and sat with him alone until after one o'clock in the morning. He was, as usual, worn out with the day's exacting duties, but he did not permit me to depart until the Grant matter had been gone over and many other things relating to the war that he wished to discuss. I pressed upon him with all the earnestness I could command the immediate removal of Grant as an imperious necessity to sustain himself. As was his custom, he said but little, only enough to make me continue the discussion until it was exhausted. He sat before the open fire in the old Cabinet room, most of the time with his feet up on the high marble mantel, and exhibited un- usual distress at the complicated condition of military affairs. Nearly every day brought some new and perplexing military complication. He had gone through a long winter of terrible strain with McClellan and the Army of the Potomac; and from the day that Grant started on his Southern expedition until the battle of Shiloh he had had little else than jarring and confusion among his generals in the West. He knew that I had no ends to serve in urging Grant's removal, beyond the single desire to make him be just to himself, and he listened patiently.

I appealed to Lincoln for his own sake to remove Grant at once, and in giving my reasons for it I simply voiced the admittedly overwhelming protest from the loyal people of the land against Grant's continuance in command. I could form no judgment during the conversation as to what effect my arguments had upon him beyond the fact that he was greatly distressed at this new complication. When I had said everything that could be said from my standpoint, we lapsed into silence. Lincoln remained silent for what seemed a very long time. He then gathered himself up in his chair and said in a tone of earnestness that I shall never forget: "I can't spare this man; he fights." That was all he said, but I knew that it was enough, and that Grant was safe in Lincoln's hands against his countless hosts of enemies. The only man in all the nation who had the power to save Grant was Lincoln, and he had decided to do it. He was not influenced by any personal partiality for Grant, for they had never met, but he believed just what he said—"I can't spare this man; he fights." I knew enough of Lincoln to know that his decision was final, and I knew enough of him also to know that he reasoned better on the subject than I did, and that it would be unwise to attempt to unsettle his determination. I did not forget that Lincoln was the one man who never allowed himself to appear as wantonly defying public sentiment. It seemed to me impossible for him to save Grant without taking a crushing load of condemnation upon himself; but Lincoln was wiser than all those around him, and he not only saved Grant, but he saved him by such well-concerted effort that he soon won popular applause from those who were most violent in demanding Grant's dismissal.

The method that Lincoln adopted to rescue Grant from the odium into which he had, to a very large degree, unjustly fallen was one of the bravest and most sagacious acts of his administration. Halleck was commander of the military division consisting of Missouri, Kentucky, Tennessee, and possibly other States, but he remained at his headquarters in St. Louis until after the battle of Shiloh. Lincoln's first move was to bring Halleck to the field, where he at once superseded Grant as commander of the army. This relieved public apprehension and soon calmed the inflamed public sentiment that was clamoring for Grant's dismissal. Lincoln knew that it would require time for the violent prejudice against Grant to perish, and he calmly waited until it was safe for him to give some indication to the country of his abiding faith in Grant as a military commander. Halleck reached the army at Pittsburg Landing on the 11th of April, four days after the battle had been fought, and of course his presence on the field at once made him the commanding officer. On the 30th of April, when the public mind was reasonably well prepared to do justice to Grant, an order was issued assigning him "as second in command under the major-general commanding the department."

Source: McClure, Alexander. 1892. *Abraham Lincoln and Men of War-Times*. Philadelphia: Times, 178–80.

JAMES RUSHLING, *MEN AND THINGS I SAW IN CIVIL WAR DAYS* (1899)

Lt. Col. James Rushling was on Maj. Gen. George Sickles's staff. General Sickles commanded Third Corps in the Army of the Potomac. On the second day of the Battle of Gettysburg, Sickles's right leg was badly wounded. Surgeons amputated his leg and sent him to Washington, D.C., to recuperate. On July 5, 1863, Rushling and President Lincoln visited Sickles at a private residence on F Street. The men discussed Gettysburg, and then the conversation turned to Grant and Vicksburg.

In this excerpt from Rushling's Men and Things I Saw in Civil War Days, *Lincoln expresses his confidence in Grant and his willingness to tie his fate to the general's.*

The first to speak was General Sickles, who, between the puffs of his cigar, presently resumed, as follows: "Well, Mr. President, what are you thinking about Vicksburg, nowadays? How are things getting along down there?"

"O," answered Mr. Lincoln, very gravely, "I don't quite know. Grant is still pegging away down there. As we used to say out in Illinois, I think he 'will make a spoon or spoil a horn' before he gets through. Some of our folks think him slow and want me to remove him. But, to tell the truth, I kind of like U. S. Grant. He doesn't worry and bother me. He isn't shrieking for reinforcements all the time. He takes what troops we can safely give him, considering our big job all around—and we have a pretty big job in this war—and does the best he can with what he has got, and doesn't grumble and scold all the while. Yes, I confess. I like General Grant—U. S. Grant—'Uncle Sam Grant!' [dwelling humorously on this last name.] There is a great deal to him, first and last. And, Heaven helping me, unless something happens more than I see now, I mean to stand by Grant a good while yet."

"So, then, you have no fears about Vicksburg either, Mr. President?" added General Sickles.

"Well, no: I can't say that I have," replied Mr. Lincoln, very soberly; "the fact is—but don't say anything about this either just now—I have been praying to almighty God for Vicksburg also. I have wrestled with him and told him how much we need the Mississippi, and how it ought to flow unvexed to the sea, and how that great valley ought to be forever free, and I reckon He understands the whole business down there, 'from A to Izzard.' I have done the very best I could to help General Grant along, and all the rest of our generals, though some of them don't think so, and now it is kind of borne in on me that somehow or other we are going to win at Vicksburg too. I can't tell how soon. But I believe we will. For this will save the Mississippi and bisect the Confederacy; and be in line with God's laws besides. And if Grant only does this thing down there—I don't care much how, so he does it right—why, Grant is my man and I am his the rest of this war!"

Of course, Mr. Lincoln did not then know that Vicksburg had already fallen, on July 4, and that a United States gunboat was then speeding its way up the Mississippi to Cairo with the glorious news that was soon to thrill the country and the civilized world through and through. Gettysburg and Vicksburg! Our great twin Union victories! What were they not to us in that fateful summer of 1863? And what would have happened to the American Republic had both gone the other way? Of course, I do not pretend to say that Abraham Lincoln's faith and prayers saved Gettysburg and Vicksburg. But they certainly did not do the Union any harm. And to him his serene confidence in victory there, because of these, was a comfort and a joy most beautiful to behold, on that memorable July 5, 1863.

Source: Rushling, James F. 1899. *Men and Things I Saw in Civil War Days*. New York: Curtis and Jennings, 16–17.

LETTER TO GENERAL GRANT FROM LINCOLN
(APRIL 30, 1864)

In March 1864, Grant became general in chief of all Union armies. Grant had won Lincoln's confidence with his victories at Vicksburg and Chattanooga, and his grand strategy was to have all Union armies simultaneously attack their Confederate counterparts. This military strategy was known as concentration in time. If Union armies could successfully execute this strategy, the Confederates would be unable to reinforce any of their armies, and the Union could use its manpower advantage to its fullest potential. Grant, himself, would direct the Army of the Potomac's campaign against Lee.

In his letter dated April 30, 1864, Lincoln again expressed confidence in Grant's leadership and gave him free rein in his assault on Lee. The president did, however, warn Grant to avoid "any great disaster." Lincoln feared that "any great disaster" could cost him renomination by the Republican Party or reelection in November. Southern independence would be all but assured with Lincoln no longer president of the United States.

APRIL 30, 1864

    EXECUTIVE MANSION, WASHINGTON, APRIL 30, 1864

    LIEUTENANT GENERAL GRANT.

    Not expecting to see you again before the Spring campaign opens, I wish to express in this way, my entire satisfaction with what you have done up to this time, so far as I understand it. The particulars of your plans I neither know or seek to know. You are vigilant and self-reliant; and, pleased with this, I wish not to obtrude any constraints or restraints upon you. While I am very anxious that any great disaster, or the capture of our men in great numbers, shall be avoided, I know these points are less likely to escape your attention than they would be mine—If there is anything wanting which is within my power to give, do not fail to let me know it.

    And now with a brave army, and a just cause, may God sustain you.

    Yours very truly,

    A. Lincoln

Source: Grant, U. S. 1886. "Preparing for the Wilderness Campaign." *The Century Magazine* 16, no. 4 (February): 581.

Further Reading

Badeau, Adam. 1868. *Military History of Ulysses S. Grant, from April, 1861 to April, 1865.* New York: D. Appleton.

Bonekemper, Edward H., III. 2010. *Ulysses S. Grant: A Victor, Not a Butcher: The Military Genius of the Man Who Won the Civil War.* Washington, D.C.: Regnery.

Bonekemper, Edward H., III. 2012. *Grant and Lee.* Washington, D.C.: Regnery History.

Brands, H. W. 2012. *The Man Who Saved the Union: Ulysses S. Grant in War and Peace.* New York: Doubleday.

Catton, Bruce. 1954. *U.S. Grant and the American Military Tradition.* Boston, MA: Little, Brown.

Catton, Bruce. 1960. *Grant Moves South.* Boston, MA: Little, Brown.

Catton, Bruce. 1968. *Grant Takes Command.* Boston, MA: Little, Brown.

Chernow, Ron. 2017. *Grant.* London: Penguin.

Farina, William. 2007. *Ulysses S. Grant, 1861–1864: His Rise from Obscurity to Military Greatness.* Jefferson, NC: McFarland.

Flood, Charles Bracelen. 2005. *Grant and Sherman: The Friendship that Won the Civil War.* New York: Harper Perennial.

Fulter, Major Gen J. F. C. 1957. *Grant and Lee, a Study in Personality and Leadership.* Bloomington: Indiana University Press.

Grant, Ulysses S. 1990. *Ulysses S. Grant: Memoirs and Selected Letters: Personal Memoirs of U. S. Grant/Selected Letters, 1939–1865.* Edited by Mary D. McFeeley and William S. McFeeley. New York: Library of America.

Larke, Julian K. 2010. *General Grant and His Campaigns.* Manoa, HI: Biographical Cruder Research.

Lloyd, Lewis. 1950. *Captain Sam Grant.* Boston, MA: Little, Brown.

Longacre, Edward G. 2006. *General Ulysses S. Grant: The Soldier and the Man.* Cambridge, MA: First Da Capo.

Macartney, Clarence Edward. 1953. *Grant and His Generals.* Freeport, NY: Books for Libraries Press.

McFeeley, William S. 1981. *Grant: A Biography.* New York: W. W. Norton.

McWhiney, Grady. 1995. *Battle in the Wilderness: Grant Meets Lee.* Fort Worth, TX: Ryan Place.

Mosier, John. 2015. *Grant: A Biography.* New York: St. Martin's.

Perret, Geoffrey. 2009. *Ulysses S. Grant: Soldier and President.* New York: Modern Library.

Porter, Horace. 1897. *Campaigning with Grant.* New York: Putnam.

Rhea, Gordon C. 2000. *To the North Anna River: Grant and Lee, May 13–25, 1864.* Baton Rouge: Louisiana State University Press.

Sherman, Don. 2017. *Ulysses S. Grant Biography: The Complete Biography of the Commanding General of the Union and 18th President of the*

United States; Based on the Life and Personal Memoirs of Ulysses Grant. Charleston, SC: CreateSpace.

Simpson, Brooks D. 2014. *Ulysses S. Grant: Triumph over Adversity, 1822–1865.* Boston: Houghton Mifflin.

Smith, Jean Edward. 2001. *Grant.* New York: Simon and Schuster.

Thayer, William M. 1885. *From Tannery to the White House: The Life of Ulysses S. Grant: His Boyhood, Youth, Manhood, Public and Private Life and Services.* Boston: James H. Earle.

Waugh, Joan. 2009. *U. S. Grant: American Hero, American Myth.* Chapel Hill: University of North Carolina Press.

White, Ronald C. 2017. *American Ulysses: A Life of Ulysses S. Grant.* New York: Random House.

8

Civil War Medicine Was Barbaric

What People Think Happened

By its very nature, war is grotesque, gruesome, and barbaric. The object is to kill and maim enemy soldiers so your country can achieve its goals. The American Civil War was no different from other wars. The official estimate is that 620,000 soldiers died in the Civil War, 360,000 in the Union army and 260,000 Confederates. More recent estimates based on comparative census data from 1860 and 1870 place the figure at closer to 750,000. Disease killed two-thirds of the soldiers who died in the four-year struggle. The Civil War remains the deadliest war in American history.

The misconception developed that this catastrophic loss of life in such a short period was partially the result of the primitive and barbaric nature of American medicine. Many Americans believed surgeons performed unnecessary amputations because they lacked the skill to save the limb by other means. They also believed that surgeons amputated limbs without the use of anesthesia, causing the wounded solider unspeakable pain and suffering. The final element of the misconception is that American medical care was not up to the standards of the era.

The misconception that American medical care was barbaric and not state of the art originally derived from two sources. First, both sides in the Civil War were woefully unprepared for the medical issues associated with large armies and battles. Second, eyewitness reports from soldiers, medical personnel, and reporters provided readers with horrific views of hospitals and medical care.

There were fewer than 100 doctors in the U.S. Army when the Civil War began in 1861. Fort Leavenworth in Kansas had the largest military hospital, with 40 beds. There was only one hospital in Washington, D.C. The army had virtually no ambulance corps or triage system. Surgeons had little training and experience in their craft. As the war progressed, the medical establishment gained the knowledge and experience to redress these issues. The difficulty in converting the military medical establishment from a time of peace to a war footing created the misconception that American medicine was not state of the art for the time.

Reports from soldiers and medical personnel about doctors and hospitals also originated the misconception of primitive and barbaric medical treatment. Prior to joining the army, soldiers had not seen death, disease, and destruction on the scale that existed during the Civil War. No experience prepared them for the horrific sights and smells they would experience in combat and its aftermath. Grotesque wounds, pools of blood, and amputated arms and legs stacked like cordwood became all too common sights for soldiers, who shared their experiences with readers on the home front.

Lt. Col. W. W. Blackford of the First Virginia Cavalry, who witnessed an amputation, wrote home, "Tables about breast high had been erected upon which screaming victims were having legs and arms cut off. The surgeons and their assistants, stripped to the waist and bespattered with blood, stood around, some holding the poor fellows while others, armed with long, bloody knives and saws, cut and sawed away with frightful rapidity, throwing the mangled limbs on a pile nearby as soon as removed." A Union soldier described a field hospital established in a barn in this manner: "About the building you could see the hogs belonging to the farm eating [amputated] arms and other portions of the body." The images provided by these two soldiers, as well as the testimony of others, have convinced generations of Americans that Civil War medicine was primitive and barbaric.

Medical personnel on both sides described the difficult if not deplorable conditions they witnessed during the war. Kate Cumming was a nurse in a Confederate hospital in Corinth, Mississippi. In her diary, she wrote about the conditions she witnessed in April 1862, shortly after the Battle of Shiloh. She wrote, "The foul air from this mass of human beings at first made me giddy and sick, but I soon got over it. We have to walk, and when we give the men anything kneel, in blood and water: but we think nothing of it." In *Specimen Days and Collect*, poet Walt Whitman described a brick mansion in Falmouth, Virginia, used as a hospital shortly after the Battle of Fredericksburg. Whitman wrote, "Out doors, at the foot of a tree within ten yards of the front of the house, I notice a heap of amputated feet, legs, arms, hands and a full load for a one-horse cart." The unprepared Confederate and Union military establishments coupled with the gruesome eyewitness testimony of soldiers and medical personnel led to the misconception that American Civil War medicine was primitive and barbaric.

How the Story Became Popular

A number of factors perpetuated the myth that Civil War medicine was primitive and barbaric. At the time of the Civil War, the practice of medicine was in transition. It was moving to care based more on research and evidence than tradition. At the time of the Civil War, the humoral theory of disease dominated the practice of medicine. This theory postulated that miasma, or toxins in the air, caused diseases. There were no antibiotics at the time because doctors did not yet understand the connection of germs to disease. Doctors treated diseases such as typhoid, cholera, diarrhea, and dysentery with special diets, mercury pills, and purging.

The research of Louis Pasteur and Robert Koch helped to establish germ theory in the 1880s as the predominant cause of disease. This theory states that microscopic organisms such as bacteria and viruses are the main cause of many illnesses. Germ theory revolutionized the treatment of diseases and reduced the number of deaths caused by them. When compared to germ theory and its treatments, medicine based on humoral theory appears primitive and barbaric even though it was state-of-the-art medicine at the time of the Civil War.

The medical community did not fully understand the relationship between cleanliness and infectious disease at the time of the Civil War. Doctors did not sterilize surgical equipment between operations. They rarely washed their hands and did not change their surgical garments. Almost 39 percent of the soldiers who died from wounds received in battle succumbed to infection that set in after treatment. Joseph Lister, a British surgeon, is hailed as the founder of antiseptic medicine. He introduced new principles of cleanliness that transformed surgical practice in the late 1880s. His use of carbolic acid as an antiseptic greatly reduced the risk of postoperative infection. Sterile operating procedure and antiseptic medicine are such common practices today that people can't believe Civil War doctors did not know about or practice them.

At the start of the war, neither side had a well-organized ambulance corps. There were few ambulances, and civilian teamsters were pressed into service to drive them. Both armies assigned regimental musicians, cooks, and other noncombatants as stretcher-bearers. The individuals had little training and often fled in terror once the battle commenced. Wounded soldiers were often left on the battlefield for days, where they suffered and died from their wounds. William W. Averell, a Union cavalry officer, described the impact of this disorganized ambulance corps in an article published in *Battles and Leaders* after the war. He wrote that on July 2, 1862, the morning after the Battle of Malvern Hill, "over five thousand dead and wounded were on the ground, enough were alive and moving to give the field a singular crawling effect." Descriptions like Averell's seem to confirm that the military medical establishment was insensitive to the needs of its soldiers.

The amputation of a limb is a frightful thought for any human being. Three out of every four surgical procedures doctors performed during the Civil War were amputations. Surgeons amputated more limbs in the Civil War than in any other war in American history. Union surgeons performed 29,980 amputations, while 28,000 Confederate soldiers lost limbs as a result of their wounds. The mortality rate for patients who underwent amputation was about 26.3 percent. The sheer number of amputations, the gruesome nature of the procedure, and the sight of maimed veterans led people to conclude that Civil War doctors were "butchers" and "quacks" who solved most medical problems by sawing something off.

Most Americans believe that surgeons amputated limbs without the use of anesthesia. In a survey conducted by the Mutter Museum of the College of Physicians of Philadelphia, 89 percent of the respondents thought that amputations performed during the Civil War were done without the aid of anesthesia. In fact, surgeons did not use anesthesia in only 5 percent of the amputation procedures. It is the ghastly and gruesome nature of the small number of amputations performed without the use of anesthesia that captured the imagination of the American public and fostered the misconception that anesthesia was not uniformly used during the Civil War. Hollywood and historical fiction have reinforced this misconception. They have provided viewers and readers with vivid scenes from field hospitals where blood-spattered surgeons saw off the limbs of fully conscious patients.

At the start of the Civil War, the U.S. Army had only one military hospital, located at Fort Leavenworth in Kansas. There was no effective system of treating wounded soldiers on the battlefield and providing them with aftercare. No one foresaw the immense number of casualties that would be produced by the war. Military authorities turned barns, houses, and warehouses into makeshift hospitals. The fetid, unsanitary, and overcrowded conditions of hospitals led soldiers to conceal wounds or diseases to avoid treatment. In December 1862, the poet Walt Whitman described the division hospitals at Falmouth, Virginia, as "merely tents, and sometimes very poor ones, the wounded lying on the ground, lucky if their blankets are spread on layers of pine or hemlock twigs or small leaves." During the war, both sides made massive improvements to their hospital systems and the medical care delivered at these facilities. Despite these improvements, it is the vision of early Civil War hospitals that remains lodged in American popular memory.

There were fewer than 100 doctors in the U.S. Army at the start of the Civil War. They were overwhelmed by the high numbers of casualties. They were also inexperienced. At that time, doctors only went to medical school for two years, each comprised of two four-month semesters. Professors taught students through the lecture method, and medical students did not receive any clinical experience until they entered their own practice. At the onset of the war, most doctors did not have experience with the wounds or diseases they would soon encounter during the war. Though the number of doctors and their competence level increased during the war, soldiers and generations of Americans embrace the stereotype of the "bad doctor." This stereotype is based on the large number of amputations doctors carried out and their inability to cure diseases. The low esteem for doctors was also based on the personal misbehavior of some physicians. During the war, the Union alone initiated military justice proceedings against 622 surgeons. The charges included drunkenness, embezzlement, rape, desertion, and stealing food.

The misconception that American Civil War medicine was not state of the art and was barbaric started with the letters and the testimony of soldiers and medical personnel. The lack of preparedness, high numbers of amputations, comparison with modern medicine, and the low repute afforded Civil War doctors has perpetuated the misconception into the 21st century.

PRIMARY SOURCE DOCUMENTS

WALT WHITMAN, *SPECIMEN DAYS AND COLLECT*, "DOWN AT THE FRONT" (DECEMBER 21, 1862)

Walt Whitman was an American poet, essayist, and journalist. He founded a weekly newspaper, Long-Islander, *and was an editor for papers in New York and New Orleans. In 1855, he published his first edition of* Leaves of Grass.

Throughout his lifetime, Whitman continued to add to the work and pub-lished several additional editions. At the beginning of the Civil War, Whitman worked as a freelance journalist. He visited the wounded in New York City hospitals, and, in December 1862, he traveled to Washington, D.C., to care for his wounded brother. Whitman was moved by his experience in the hospi-tal and decided to become a volunteer nurse.

In 1882, Whitman published Specimen Days and Collect. *In this work, Whitman provides the reader with intimate observations and reflections about his experiences during the Civil War and afterward. The excerpt below is Whitman's description of a Union hospital in Falmouth, Virginia, used to treat the wounded after the battle of Fredericksburg in December 1862.*

FALMOUTH, VA., opposite Fredericksburg, December 21, 1862.— Begin my visits among the camp hospitals in the army of the Potomac. Spend a good part of the day in a large brick mansion on the banks of the Rappahannock, used as a hospital since the battle—seems to have receiv'd only the worst cases. Out doors, at the foot of a tree, within ten yards of the front of the house, I notice a heap of amputated feet, legs, arms, hands and a full load for a one-horse cart. Several dead bodies lie near, each cover'd with its brown woolen blanket. In the door-yard, towards the river, are fresh graves, mostly of officers, their names on pieces of barrel-staves or broken boards, stuck in the dirt. (Most of these bodies were subsequently taken up and transported north to their friends.) The large mansion is quite crowded upstairs and down, everything impromptu, no system, all bad enough, but I have no doubt the best that can be done; all the wounds pretty bad, some frightful, the men in their old clothes, unclean and bloody. Some of the wounded are rebel soldiers and officers, prisoners. One, a Mississippian, a captain, hit badly in leg, I talk'd with some time: he ask'd me for papers, which I gave him. (I saw him three months afterward in Washington, with his leg amputated, doing well.) I went through the rooms, downstairs and up. Some of the men were dying. I had nothing to give at that visit, but wrote a few letters to folks home, mothers, Also talk'd to three or four, who seem'd most susceptible to it, and needing it.

Source: Whitman, Walt. 1882–83. *Specimen Days and Collect.* Philadelphia: Rees Welsh, 26.

THE REMINISCENCES OF CARL SCHURZ (JULY 1863)

Carl Schurz was born in Liblar, Germany, in 1829 and took part in the German revolutionary movement of 1848. He fled Germany after the revolutionary movement failed and eventually settled in the United States. He became a lawyer and practiced law in Milwaukee. During the Civil War, Schurz was a major general and commanded a division in the mostly German XI Corps of the Army of the Potomac. After the war, Schurz served in the U.S. Senate and was secretary of the interior. He also became a vocal advocate for civil service reform.

His memoirs, The Reminiscences of Carl Schurz, *was published in 1907, after his death. In this excerpt from his memoirs, Schurz describes the hospital conditions at Gettysburg in July 1863.*

There were more harrowing experiences in store for me that day. To look after the wounded of my command, I visited the places where the surgeons were at work. At Bull Run, I had seen only on a very small scale what I was now to behold. At Gettysburg the wounded—many thousands of them—were carried to the farmsteads behind our lines. The houses, the barns, the sheds, and the open barnyards were crowded with moaning and wailing human beings, and still an unceasing procession of stretchers and ambulances was coming in from all sides to augment the number of the sufferers. A heavy rain set in during the day—the usual rain after a battle— and large numbers had to remain unprotected in the open, there being no room left under roof. I saw long rows of men lying under the eaves of the buildings, the water pouring down upon their bodies in streams. Most of the operating tables were placed in the open where the light was best, some of them partially protected against the rain by tarpaulins or blankets stretched upon poles. There stood the surgeons, their sleeves rolled up to the elbows, their bare arms as well as their linen aprons smeared with blood, their knives not seldom held between their teeth, while they were helping a patient on or off the table, or had their hands otherwise occupied; around them pools of blood and amputated arms or legs in heaps, sometimes more than man-high. Antiseptic methods were still unknown at that time. As a wounded man was lifted on the table, often shrieking with pain as the attendants handled him, the surgeon quickly examined the wound and resolved upon cutting off the injured limb. Some ether was administered and the body put in position in a moment. The surgeon snatched his knife from between his teeth, where it had been while his hands were busy, wiped it rapidly once or twice across his blood-stained apron, and the cutting began. The operation accomplished, the surgeon would look around with a deep sigh, and then—"Next!"

And so it went on, hour after hour, while the number of expectant patients seemed hardly to diminish. Now and then one of the wounded men would call attention to the fact that his neighbor lying on the ground had given up the ghost while waiting for his turn, and the dead body was then quietly removed. Or a surgeon, having been long at work, would put down his knife, exclaiming that his hand had grown unsteady, and that this was too much for human endurance—not seldom hysterical tears streaming down his face. Many of the wounded men suffered with silent fortitude, fierce determination in the knitting of their brows and the steady gaze of their bloodshot eyes. Some would even force themselves to a grim jest about their situation or about the "skedaddling of the rebels." But there were, too, heart-rending groans and shrill cries of pain piercing the air, and despairing exclamations, "Oh, Lord! Oh, Lord!" or "Let me die!" or softer murmurings in which the words "mother" or "father" or "home" were often heard.

I saw many of my command among the sufferers, whose faces I well remembered, and who greeted me with a look or even a painful smile of recognition, and usually with the question what I thought of their chances of life, or whether I could do anything for them, sometimes, also, whether I thought the enemy were well beaten. I was sadly conscious that many of the words of cheer and encouragement I gave them were mere hollow sound, but they might be at least some solace for the moment.

Source: Bancroft, Frederick, and William Dunning, eds. 1907. *The Reminiscences of Carl Schulz.* Vol. 3. New York: McClure, 39–40.

What Really Happened

Civil War medical care was state of the art by the standards of the time. The high use of amputation coupled with the revolutionary medical changes that followed the war gave generations of Americans the image that Civil War medical care was both primitive and barbaric. The truth is that Civil War medical care adjusted to the needs and demands of large-scale modern warfare with innovations that saved lives. Some of these innovations became the basis of modern medical care.

In the Civil War, disease caused twice as many deaths as combat. This number seems exceedingly high by modern standards. For the 1860s, it was remarkably low and demonstrated a marked improvement in health care compared to previous wars. In the Napoleonic wars, eight soldiers died of disease to every soldier killed on the battlefield. In the Mexican War, the ratio was seven to one.

Union surgeon general William Hammond and the U.S. Sanitary Commission were two reasons for the reduced death rate due to disease.

Hammond was the author of *A Treatise on Hygiene: With Special Reference to the Military Service*. The U.S. government widely distributed Hammond's book to its doctors and hospital staff. Hammond's work stressed that diet, sanitation, and hygienic practices played a large role in the soldiers' overall health.

Hammond also increased the number and quality of military hospitals. There was one small military hospital at the start of the war. By 1865, there were 350 Union hospitals in operation. Most of the hospitals were built in pavilion style. This style hospital featured a cluster of small, well-ventilated buildings that housed 40 to 60 patients. The design prevented communicable diseases from spreading from one unit to another. The mortality rate in this style of hospital was an incredibly low 8 percent, lower than in any previous war in American history.

Union civilians formed the U.S. Sanitary Commission in 1861. The Sanitary Commission advocated for cleanliness in camps and medical facilities as well as improved living conditions for soldiers. The commission sent inspectors to camps to instruct soldiers on proper drainage, cooking, latrine building, and safe water supply. It sent medicines, bandages, and even its own doctors and nurses to field hospitals. The commission also encouraged doctors to keep detailed records that could be used as the foundation for future medical research. The advocacy and watchdog work of the Sanitary Commission was essential to reducing mortality rates during the Civil War.

The disorganized and unprofessional medical corps left wounded soldiers to die unattended on the battlefields. In 1862, William Hammond appointed Dr. Jonathan Letterman the surgeon general of the Army of the Potomac. Letterman's first task was to create an ambulance corps for the Army of the Potomac. Under Letterman's system, ambulances were removed from the control of the quartermaster and could only be used for medical purposes. Medical officers chose and specially trained the drivers and stretcher-bearers. Only ambulance corps personnel could remove the wounded from the battlefield. Each regiment was assigned three ambulances that were posted near the front so they could be within a short distance of the wounded once the battle commenced. The ratio of ambulances to soldiers was 1 to 150. The first real test for Letterman's system was the Battle of Antietam. During the battle, Letterman's ambulance corps removed all of the 10,000 wounded Union soldiers to field hospitals in 24 hours. Both sides in the conflict adapted Letterman's system, and it saved countless lives.

Letterman also developed a more effective three-layered system for treating wounded soldiers. The first stop for a wounded soldier was the primary station. This was a tent just out of rifle range where doctors assessed wounds and provided the first treatment. The more seriously wounded soldiers were sent to field hospitals located in buildings one and a half to two miles away from the front. Surgeons performed surgery and other serious procedures here. After treatment, soldiers were sent to general hospitals in larger cities to recuperate from their wounds. Armies still employ the basics of this system in the 21st century.

Confederate and Union surgeons performed approximately 55,000 amputations during the war. The high number of amputations resulted from both sides' use of the minie ball. French officer Claude-Etienne Minie invented the .58 caliber bullet named for him. The minie ball flattens on impact with a body, and the wound grows larger as the bullet travels through the tissue. It shatters bone below and above impact, bringing bits of cloth, skin, and bacteria into the wound. The usual treatment for an extremity hit by a minie ball was amputation. In many instances, this was the only way to save a soldier's life.

Three out of every four surgical procedures performed during the Civil War were amputations. Both sides allowed only the most skilled surgeons to perform this procedure. It took a surgeon about 2 to 10 minutes to amputate a limb. The survival rate was about 73.7 percent. The farther the amputation was from the torso, the greater the chance the patient would survive the procedure. Contrary to popular belief, anesthesia was used in 95 percent of all amputations. Surgeons used both ether and chloroform to put patients into a temporary sleep during operations. The use of anesthesia was both effective and safe, and there were only 43 anesthesia-related deaths during the war.

The conception that doctors were butchers and quacks was more myth than reality. The mortality rates for disease, amputations, and hospital patients were lower than for any previous war for which there are statistics. Surgeons amputated limbs because of the devastating impact of the minie ball, not because they were butchers. They managed to save the lives of almost 75 percent of the soldiers they operated on during the war. The Union military prosecuted about 5 percent of the doctors who served in the army. Almost all these were charged with criminal activity and not malpractice. The other 95 percent were competent physicians of solid character.

The Civil War produced a number of medical advances. The pavilion-style hospital became the standard design for both civilian and military hospitals. Letterman's ambulance corps, hospital system, and triage procedure became standard medical operations for militaries throughout the world. Hammond's insistence on cleanliness and sanitation cut mortality rates in camps and hospitals even before the introduction of germ theory and antiseptic medicine. Confederate physician Dr. Julian J. Chisolm developed a 2.5-inch inhaler that used only one-eighth the amount of chloroform used by Union doctors to sedate patients. Civil War surgeons pioneered plastic surgery. Dr. Gordon Buck and others reconstructed eyelids, noses, cheeks, and lips. Doctors also abandoned heroic medical techniques, such as bloodletting and blistering.

In conclusion, Civil War doctors practiced state-of-the-art medicine for their era. Mortality rates for disease, amputations, and hospital stays were lower in the Civil War than in any previous war. The devastating impact of the minie ball forced surgeons to amputate limbs to save lives. The almost universal use of anesthesia during amputation provided patients with some measure of relief during surgical procedures. The high death toll in the war, nearly 2 percent of the entire American population, hides the fact that military and civilian medical care made important advances during the Civil War.

PRIMARY SOURCE DOCUMENTS

GEN. GEORGE MCCLELLAN, SPECIAL ORDERS NO. 147 (AUGUST 2, 1862)

At the start of the Civil War, the Union army did not have an organized, professional ambulance corps. The quartermaster controlled the ambulances. Civilian teamsters drove the ambulances, and untrained noncombatants served as stretcher-bearers. Quartermasters often employed ambulances to move supplies rather than the wounded, and teamsters and stretcher-bearers fled when combat commenced. As a consequence, wounded soldiers languished and died on the battlefield without treatment.

When Dr. Jonathan Letterman became the surgeon general of the Army of the Potomac in 1862, he developed an ambulance corps to effectively move wounded soldiers from the battlefield to primary care units and field hospitals. Medical officers now controlled the ambulances, and enlisted men were trained as drivers and stretcher-bearers. The first test of Letterman's system was the Battle of Antietam, where the ambulance corps moved all 10,000 wounded Union soldiers from the battlefield to treatment facilities in 24 hours.

On August 2, 1862, Major General McClellan issued Special Orders No. 147. McClellan's order established Letterman's ambulance system for the Army of the Potomac. Special Orders No. 147 appears below.

"The following regulations for the organization of the ambulance corps and the management of ambulance trains, are published for the information and government of all concerned. Commanders of Army Corps will see that they are carried into effect without delay.

"1. The ambulance corps will be organized on the basis of a captain to each Army Corps, as the commandant of the ambulance corps; a first lieutenant for a division, second lieutenant for a brigade, and a sergeant for each regiment.

"2. The allowance of ambulances and transport carts will be: one transport cart, one four-horse and two two-horse ambulances for a regiment; one two-horse ambulance for each battery of artillery; and two two-horse ambulances for the headquarters of each Army Corps. Each ambulance will be provided with two stretchers.

"3. The privates of the ambulance corps will consist of two men and a driver to each ambulance, and one driver to each transport cart.

"4. The captain is the commander of all the ambulances and transport carts in the Army Corps, under the direction of the Medical Director. He will pay special attention to the condition of the ambulances, horses, harness, etc., requiring daily inspections to be made by the commanders of the division ambulances, and reports thereof to be made to him by these officers. He will make a personal inspection once a week of all the ambulances, transport carts, horses, harness, etc., whether they have been used for any other purpose than the transportation of the sick and wounded and medical supplies, reports of which will be transmitted, through the Medical Director of the Army Corps, to the Medical Director of the Army every Sunday morning. He will institute a drill in his corps, instructing his men in the most easy and expeditious method of putting men in and taking them out of the ambulances, taking men from the ground, and placing and carrying them on stretchers, observing that the front man steps off with the left foot and the rear man with the right, etc. He will be especially careful that the ambulances and transport carts are at all times in order, provided with attendants, drivers, horses, etc., and the kegs rinsed and filled daily with fresh water, that he may be able to move at any moment. Previous to, and in time of action, he will receive from the Medical Director of the Army Corps his orders for the distribution of the ambulances and the points to which he will carry the wounded, using the light two-horse ambulances for bringing men from the field, and the four-horse ones for carrying those already attended to further to the rear, if the Medical Director considers it necessary. He will give his personal attention to the removal of the sick and wounded from the field and to and from the hospitals, going from point to point to ascertain what may be wanted, and to see that his subordinates (for whose conduct he will be responsible) attend to their duties in taking care of the wounded, treating them with gentleness and care, and removing them as quickly as possible to the places pointed out, and that the ambulances reach their destination. He will make a full and detailed report, after every action and march, of the operations of the ambulance corps.

"5. The first lieutenant assigned to the ambulance corps of a division will have complete control, under the commander of the whole corps and the Medical Director, of all the ambulances, transport carts, ambulance horses, etc., in the division. He will be the acting assistant quartermaster for the division ambulance corps, and will receipt and be responsible for the property belonging to it, and be held responsible for any deficiency in ambulances, transport carts, horses, harness, etc., pertaining to the ambulance corps of the division. He will have a travelling cavalry forge, a blacksmith, and a saddle; who will be under his orders to enable him to keep his train in order. He will receive a daily inspection report of all the ambulances, horses, etc., under his charge from the officer in charge of brigade ambulance corps; will see that the subordinates attend strictly to their duties at all times, and will inspect the corps under his charge once a week, a report of which inspection he will transmit to the commander of the ambulance corps.

"6. The second lieutenant in command of the ambulances of a brigade will be under the immediate orders of the commander of the ambulance corps for the division, and have superintendence of the ambulance corps for the brigade.

"7. The sergeant in charge of the ambulance corps for a regiment will conduct the drills, inspections, etc., under the orders of the commander of the brigade ambulance corps, and will be particular in enforcing rigidly all orders he may receive from his superior officers. The officers and non-commissioned officers of this corps will be mounted.

"8. The detail for this corps will be made with care by Commanders of Army Corps, and no officer or man will be detailed for this duty except those known to be active and efficient, and no man will be relieved except by orders from these headquarters. Should any officer or man detailed for this duty be found not fitted for it, representation of the fact will be made by the Medical Director of the Army Corps to the Medical Director of this Army.

"9. Two medical officers from the reserve corps of Surgeons of each division and an hospital steward, who will be with the medicine wagon, will be detailed by the Medical Director of the Army Corps to accompany the ambulance train when on the march, the train of each division being kept together, and will see that the sick and wounded are properly attended to. A medicine wagon will accompany each train.

"10. The officers connected with the corps must be with the trains on a march, observing that no one rides in the ambulances without the authority of the Medical officers, except in urgent cases; but men must not be allowed to suffer when the Medical officers cannot be found. Use a sound discretion in this matter, and be especially careful that the men and drivers are in their proper places. The place for the ambulances is in front of all wagon trains.

"11. When in camp the ambulances, transport carts, and ambulance corps will be parked with the brigade, under the supervision of the commander of the corps for the brigade. They will be used on the requisition of the regimental Medical officers, transmitted to the commander of the brigade ambulance corps, for transporting the sick to various points and procuring medical supplies, and for nothing else. The non-commissioned officer in charge will always accompany the ambulances or transport carts when on this or any other duty, and he will be held responsible they are used for none other than their legitimate purposes. Should any officer infringe upon this order regarding the uses of ambulances, etc., he will be reported by the officer in charge to the commander of the train, all the particulars being given.

"12. The officer in charge of a train will at once remove every thing not legitimate, and if there be not room for it in the baggage wagons of the regiment, will leave it on the road. Any attempt by a superior officer to prevent him from doing his duty in this or any other instance, he will promptly report to the Medical Director of the Army Corps, who will lay the matter before the Commander of the Corps. The latter will, at the earliest possible moment, place the officer offending in arrest for trial for disobedience of orders.

"13. Good serviceable horses will be used for the ambulances and transport carts, and will not be taken for any other purpose, except by orders from these headquarters.

"14. The uniform of this corps is—for privates, a green band, two inches broad, around the cap, a green half-chevron, two inches broad, on each arm above the elbow, and to be armed with revolvers; non-commissioned officers to wear the same band around the cap as the privates, chevrons two inches broad, and green, with the point toward the shoulder, on each arm above the elbow.

"15. No person will be allowed to carry from the field any wounded or sick except this corps.

"16. The commanders of the ambulance corps, on being detailed, will report without delay to the Medical Director at these headquarters for instructions. All division, brigade, or regimental Quartermasters having any ambulances, transport carts, ambulance horses, or harness, etc., in their possession, will turn them in at once to the commander of the division ambulance corps.

"By command of Maj.-Gen. MCCLELLAN.

"(Signed) S. WILLIAMS,

Assistant Adjutant-General."

Source: Letterman, Jonathan. 1866. *Medical Recollections of the Army of the Potomac.* New York: D. Appleton, 24–30.

JOSEPH BARNES, *MEDICAL AND SURGICAL HISTORY OF THE WAR OF THE REBELLION, 1861–1865* (1883)

In 1870, the surgeon general of the U.S. Army, Joseph K. Barnes, prepared and edited the first volume of Medical and Surgical History of the War of the Rebellion, 1861–1865. *Barnes and others completed this six-volume work in 1888. The work included statistical summaries related to wounds, diseases, and deaths in both the Union and Confederate armies. Its 3,000 pages also contain charts and tables as well as photographs and lithographs of specimens and wounded veterans. It is the basic primary source of information on medical care in the Civil War. Below is an excerpt that discusses the use of anesthetics during the Civil War.*

It was impracticable to determine the total number of cases in which anesthetics were employed during the war, but as near as can be ascertained they were used in no less than eighty thousand (80,000) instances. Time and clerical assistance did not allow of the examination of this enormous number of cases in detail, and in treating of this subject we must confine our remarks to the number of major operations in which the agents used were definitely ascertained. Of eight thousand nine hundred cases chloroform was used in six thousand seven hundred and eighty-four, or 76.2 per cent, ether in one thousand three and five, or 14.7 per cent., a mixture of chloroform and ether in eight hundred and eleven, or 9.1 per cent. These percentages differ somewhat from the percentages given in the preliminary report, where it was stated that chloroform was used in 60 per cent., ether in 30 per cent., and ether and chloroform in 10 per cent.: but at that time the percentage of the different agents had been principally derived from the reports of general hospitals, and in which ether was frequently used. When, afterwards, the operations performed in the field hospitals were examined, where chloroform was almost uniformly used, the percentage of the cases in which the latter agent was employed increased to 76.2 per cent, as above indicated, while the number of cases in which ether or the mixture of ether and chloroform was used was proportionally decreased.

The inestimable value of the use of anesthesia in military surgery will hardly be denied at this date, although it has been claimed that the effect of anesthetics in the treatment of shot injuries are deleterious, inasmuch as they add to the depression caused by the shock, and retard union by first intention, and predispose to hemorrhages and pyaemia. It is possible that in two hundred and fifty-four cases in which it was asserted that no anesthetic was given the surgeons were actuated by such objections, as no reasons have been assigned why anesthetics were not administered. How far the use of anesthetics has contributed to the saving of life during the late war it is impossible to say, as we have no statistics to make this comparison. It may be stated, however, that their use has undoubtedly influenced the favorable percentages of mortality after major operations pointed out in different sections of this and the proceeding volumes.

From the rapidity of its effects, and from the small quantity required—qualities which can only be appreciated at their proper values by the field surgeon when surrounded by hundreds of wounded anxiously awaiting speedy relief—chloroform was preferred by nearly all the field surgeons, and their testimony as to its value and efficacy is almost unanimous, although all recommend the greatest care in its administration. It is, perhaps, best to allow the different medical officers to speak for themselves on this subject: Surgeon C. J. Walton, 21st Kentucky, administered "chloroform in every painful operation, but did not keep the patients under its influence longer than was absolutely necessary, withdrawing it as soon as the cutting was completed. While I could not dispense with chloroform, I must protest against the extravagant and indiscreet use of it. It is a most potent agent and should be used with the utmost caution. *In no case were we displeased with it effect.*" Surgeon B. B. Breed, U.S. V.: "Chloroform was almost universally employed as an anesthetic, and without bad effect in any case. Whenever practicable, I employed ether in preference to chloroform, preferring, both from personal experience and observation, the delay and discomfort in its administration to the possible danger from the use of the latter. On the field of battle, however, chloroform is the safe and preferable agent." Assistant Surgeon C. Bacon, Jr.: "The anesthetic I have seen used has invariably been chloroform. Among the great number of cases in which I have witnessed its administration I have seen but one death resulting from its use. I have, however, frequently seen cases in which its use required extreme care, and, at times, have been obliged to desist in its administration in cases of great exhaustion consequent upon long-established injuries. I have frequently seen the use of chloroform attended with bad results when improperly administered. As an anesthetic I think chloroform should be given in prompt and efficient dose. The desired effect being attained, its administration should be discontinued; in this manner less chloroform is required, thereby avoiding to a great extent its toxical effect." Surgeon D. P. Smith U.S.V.: "I have in every instance but one, in the army, employed chloroform, and in but one case have had reason to believe its use disastrous. In this instance it was given too profusely by an entirely incompetent person (since then dismissed from the medical corps) while I was amputating at the knee joint. The patient never reacted from the shock, but died about twelve hours subsequently."

Source: Barnes, Joseph. 1883. *The Medical and Surgical History of the War of the Rebellion (1861–1865)*. Part 3, Vol. 2. Washington, D.C.: Government Printing Office, 887–88.

DR. HUNTER HOLMES MCGUIRE, ADDRESS TO THE SOUTHERN SURGICAL AND GYNECOLOGICAL ASSOCIATION MEETING IN NASHVILLE, TENNESSEE (NOVEMBER 13, 1889)

Dr. Hunter Holmes McGuire was one of the 3,296 medical officers in the Confederate army. He served as the medical director of II Corps of the Army of Northern Virginia. He was also Lt. Gen. Thomas Jackson's personal surgeon. McGuire amputated Jackson's left arm on May 3, 1863, and attended to Jackson until the general died on May 10, 1863, at Guinea Station, Virginia.

After the war, Dr. McGuire became the president of the Southern Surgical and Gynecological Association. On November 13, 1889, McGuire gave a speech to this group at their meeting in Nashville, Tennessee. In his talk, Dr. McGuire praised the courage and virtues of Confederate surgeons. He specifically mentioned the use of chloroform during surgery. Below is an excerpt of Dr. McGuire's November 13, 1889, speech in Nashville.

And now of the Confederate surgeon let me say a word. How can I express, in adequate terms, my admiration for him! He possessed virtues peculiarly his own. Coming from civil life, it was wonderful to see how rapidly he adapted himself to the discipline of the army and conformed to the requirements of military life. The hardships he endured and the privations to which he was subjected soon transformed him from a novice to a veteran, and I can say, with truth, that before the war ended some of the best military surgeons in the world could be found in the Confederate army.

His scanty supply of medicines and hospital stores made him fertile in expedients of every kind. I have seen him search field and forest for plants and flowers, whose medicinal virtues he understood and could use. The pliant bark of a tree made for him a good tourniquet; the juice of the green persimmon, a styptic; a knitting needle, with its point sharply bent, a tenaculum, and a pen-knife in his hand, a scalpel and bistoury. I have seen him break off one prong of a common table-fork, bend the point of the other prong, and with it elevate the bone in depressed fracture of the skull and save life. Long before he knew the use of the porcelain-tipped probe for finding bullets, I have seen him use a piece of soft pine wood and bring it out of the wound marked by the leaden ball. Years before we were formally told of N'laton's method of inverting the body in chloroform narcosis, I have seen it practiced by the Confederate Surgeon. Many a time I have seen the foot of the operating-table raised to let the blood go, by gravitation, to the patient's head, when death from chloroform was imminent, and I will add that, in the corps to which I was attached (2d Corp ANV), chloroform was given over 28,000 times, and no death was ever ascribed to its use.

Many of the medical officers of this corps were wounded or killed on the field. One, I saw fall at Strasburg, amid the cheers of soldiers at the evidence he gave of devotion to duty. Another, at Sharpsburg, facing an assault before which even veterans quailed and fled, and a third I found upon the bloody field of Cold Harbor dying with a shell-wound through his side. As I knelt down beside him and told him his wound was mortal, he answered, "I am no more afraid to die than I was afraid to do my duty."

They were splendid specimens of a noble race—a race whose achievements astonished the world and wrung from the foe himself a full measure of praise. During the terrible six days which followed the retreat of our army from Richmond, the medical men, by their unswerving devotion to duty and cheerful support, contributed no little to inspire the heroism which turned our defeat into honor, and made Appomattox one of the proudest memories of the war.

Source: McGuire, Hunter Holmes. 1890. *Address of the President before the Southern Surgical and Gynecological Association.* Nashville, Tennessee. November 13, 1889. Richmond: Wm Ellis Jones, 8–9.

Further Reading

Adams, George W. 1961. *Doctors in Blue: The Medical History of the Union Army in the Civil War.* New York: Collier Books.

Alcott, Louisa May. 2006. *Civil War Hospital Sketches.* Mineola, NY: Dover Publications.

Barnes, Joseph H., ed. 1870–1888. *The Medical and Surgical History of the War of the Rebellion, 1861–1865.* 6 vols. Washington, D.C.: U.S. Government Printing Office.

Bollet, Alfred Jay. 2002. *Civil War Medicine: Challenges and Triumph.* Austerlitz, NY: Gallen Press.

Butts, Heather. 2014. *African American Medicine in Washington, DC: Healing the Capital during the Civil War Era.* Stroud, U.K.: History Press.

Cunningham, H. H. 1993. *Doctors in Gray: The Confederate Medical Service.* Baton Rouge: Louisiana State University Press.

Damman, Gordon, and Alfred Jay Bollet. 2007. *Images of Civil War Medicine: A Photographic History.* New York: Springer.

Denney, Robert E. 1995. *Civil War Medicine: Care and Comfort of the Wounded.* New York: Sterling Publishing.

Dewine, Shauna. 2017. *Learning from the Wounded: The Civil War and the Rise of American Medical Science.* Chapel Hill: University of North Carolina Press.

Dorwart, Bonnie Brice. 2009. *Death Is in the Breeze: Disease during the American Civil War.* Frederick, MD: National Museum of Civil War Medicine Press.

Dyer, J. Franklin, and Michael B. Chesson, eds. 2003. *The Journal of a Civil War Surgeon.* Lincoln: University of Nebraska Press.

Freemon, Frank R. 2001. *Gangrene and Glory: Medical Care during the American Civil War.* Champaign: University of Illinois Press.

Harwell, Richard B., ed. 1959. *Kate: The Journal of a Confederate Nurse.* Baton Rouge: Louisiana State University Press.

Letterman, Jonathan. 1866. *Medical Reflections of the Army of the Potomac.* New York: D. Appleton & Company.

Lowry, Thomas P., and Terry Reimer. 2010. *Bad Doctors: Military Justice Proceedings against 622 Civil War Surgeons.* Frederick, MD: National Museum of Civil War Medicine Press.

Maxwell, George. 2016. *Agent of Mercy: The Untold Story of Dr. Archibald S. Maxwell Civil War Surgeon and Iowa State Sanitary Agent.* Bellevue, WA: Amazon Digital Services.

Maxwell, William Q. 1956. *Lincoln's Fifth Wheel: The Political History of the United States Sanitary Commission.* New York: Longmans, Green & Company.

McGaugh, Scott. 2015. *Surgeon in Blue: Jonathan Letterman, the Civil War Doctor Who Pioneered Battlefield Care.* New York: Arcade.

Miller, Brian C. 2015. *Empty Sleeves: Amputation in the Civil War South.* Athens: University of Georgia Press.

Rutkow, Ira. 2015. *Bleeding Blue and Gray: Civil War Surgery and the Evolution of American Medicine.* Mechanicsburg, PA: Stackpole Books.

Schaadt, Mark J. 1998. *Civil War Medicine: An Illustrated History.* Nashville, TN: Cedarwood Publishing.

Schroeder-Lein, Glenna R. 1996. *Confederate Hospital on the Move: Samuel H. Stout and the Army of Tennessee.* Columbia: University of South Carolina Press.

Schroeder-Lein, Glenna R. 2008. *The Encyclopedia of Civil War Medicine.* New York: Routledge.

Slawson, Robert G. 2006. *Prologue to Change: African Americans in Medicine in the Civil War Era.* Frederick, MD: National Museum of Civil War Medicine Press.

Waite, Robert W. 1964. *Confederate Military Hospitals in Richmond.* Richmond, VA: Richmond Civil War Centennial Committee.

Wilbur, C. Keith. 1998. *Civil War Medicine.* Lanham, MD: Rowman & Littlefield.

9

Freed Slaves Were Promised 40 Acres and a Mule

What People Think Happened

Christmas Day, 1865, passed without the U.S. government providing the freedmen with 40 acres and a mule. So did New Year's Day, 1866, the third anniversary of the Emancipation Proclamation. Since the beginning of 1865, the persistent rumor that the government would redistribute confiscated Confederate land to formerly enslaved families spread like wildfire through the Southern black community. The freedmen saw the redistribution of land as a just and fair reparation for their years of uncompensated toil in the institution of slavery. Formerly enslaved persons commonly believed that the American government would provide them with "40 acres of land and a mule" as part of a land distribution policy.

For over 150 years, the misconception has persisted that the U.S. government promised formerly enslaved persons 40 acres and a mule in compensation for their years in slavery. "Forty acres and a mule" became a euphemism for the belief that the U.S. government was going to redistribute confiscated Confederate land to the freedmen. The origin of this misconception was Maj. Gen. William Tecumseh Sherman's Special Field Orders No. 15.

General Sherman took possession of Atlanta on September 3, 1864. He then decided to march through Georgia to Savannah. On November 15, Sherman's army left Atlanta for the Atlantic coast. On his famous "march to the sea," Sherman's troops lived off the land without a fixed base of supply. They also destroyed anything of military value to the Confederacy on their 285-mile trek to Savannah. As they moved through the Georgia countryside, Sherman's troops were joined by thousands of liberated former slaves. Sherman tried unsuccessfully to limit the number of free people to only able-bodied black males. The thousands of freed men, women, and children severely limited the mobility of Sherman's forces. On December 9, Union general Jefferson C. Davis ordered a pontoon bridge across Ebenezer Creek disassembled before the freed people following Sherman's army could cross it. This resulted in disaster. Hundreds of freed people drowned trying to swim the creek while Confederate troops captured hundreds of the stranded refugees.

When Sherman took control of Savannah on December 21, about 7,000 freed blacks arrived with his army. On January 9, 1865, Secretary of War Edwin Stanton arrived in Savannah to investigate the Ebenezer Creek incident. Stanton asked Sherman to arrange a meeting with the leaders of Savannah's black community. The meeting was held on January 12, on the second floor of Charles Green's mansion on Macon Street. Twenty black ministers were in attendance. They chose Garrison Frazier, a former slave and now Baptist minister, as their leader and spokesperson. Stanton asked Frazier how the freed people could take care of themselves. Frazier responded that the best way was "to have land, and turn it and till it by our own hand."

In response to Frazier's plea for land, Sherman issued Special Field Orders No. 15 five days after the meeting with the ministers. Sherman's order had three relevant parts. First, it set aside "the islands from Charleston, south, the abandoned rice fields along the rivers for thirty miles back from the sea, and the country bordering the St. John's River, Florida" for settlement by the freed people. Second, the communities established in this area could only be settled and governed by blacks. Finally, each family was to receive a "plot of not more than forty acres of tillable ground." The free people would have possessory title to the land. This granted them the right to use the land but not own it. Ownership was subject to presidential or congressional approval. Separate from Special Field Orders No. 15, Sherman loaned the freed people mules no longer fit for military duty to work the land. Sherman's orders and actions in January 1865 led to the enduring misconception that the freed people would receive 40 acres and a mule from the American government in reparation for their years in bondage.

How the Story Became Popular

The misconception that the freed people were going to receive 40 acres and a mule originated with Sherman's Special Field Orders No. 15. It was perpetuated by a series of events that commenced with the distribution of land in the area covered by Sherman's order. Sherman placed Gen. Rufus Saxton in charge of executing his orders. Saxton was a West Point graduate and an ardent abolitionist. By June 1865, about 40,000 black families had settled on 400,000 acres in the area designated in Sherman's order. The black settlement quickly became known as Sherman's Reservation. Saxton furnished the settlers with a possessory title that granted them the right to use but not own the land. The approval of the president or congress was necessary for legal land ownership. Black settlers, however, became convinced that they owned the land Saxton distributed to them through Sherman's order.

The next mention of distributing 40 acres of land to the freed people came on March 3, 1865, when Congress established the Bureau of Refugees, Freedmen and Abandoned Lands. This act authorized the bureau to lease "not more than forty acres" of abandoned or confiscated land to formerly enslaved persons. Blacks who leased the land would have the option to purchase the title from the U.S. government. The act did not give away free land but provided freed blacks with the eventual opportunity to become landowners.

On June 21, 1866, Congress passed the Southern Homestead Act. This legislation opened 46 million acres of public lands in Alabama, Arkansas, Florida, Louisiana, and Mississippi to settlement by the freed people. The law divided the land into 50-acre plots, not 40. The purchase price was five dollars. Settlers had to occupy and improve the land for five years before they could acquire full ownership title to the plot. Again, the government did not provide free land to formerly enslaved persons, only the opportunity of land ownership. Few blacks availed themselves of this land offer. When Congress repealed the Southern Homestead Act in 1876, blacks occupied only a few thousand acres of land available under this legislation.

Thaddeus Stevens was a radical Republican member of the House of Representatives from Pennsylvania. He was an outspoken abolitionist and believed that the freed people should receive reparations for their centuries of uncompensated toil. In a speech in Lancaster, Pennsylvania, during the summer of 1865, Stevens told his constituents that every black family "ought to receive 40 acres of land." Stevens said that this could be done by confiscating Confederate estates and the public lands of the rebellious states. Stevens believed that such action would break the power of the planter class while providing reparations for formerly enslaved persons. Such a plan would also ensure future black political support for the Republican Party.

In March 1867, Stevens sponsored H. R. 29 in the first session of the 40th Congress. Section 4 of the Reparations Bill provided formerly enslaved persons with land confiscated from Confederates during the war. The bill gave "each male who is the head of a family, forty acres; to each male adult, whether the head of a family or not, forty acres." Widows who were heads of families were also allotted 40 acres under the plan. The bill passed both houses of Congress but failed to become law when President Andrew Johnson vetoed it. The proposed bill helped to perpetuate the idea that the government was going to provide free land to black families, usually in the amount of 40 acres.

Word of free land spread quickly through the black communities of the South. Freedmen's Bureau agents, missionaries, teachers, and politicians used speeches, pamphlets, and newspapers to proliferate and encourage the belief that the freed people were going to receive 40 acres and a mule. For example, the commissioner of the Freedmen's Bureau, Maj. Gen. Oliver O. Howard, issued Circular No. 13 on July 28, 1865. In this circular, Howard instructed bureau agents that land distribution was the official policy of the Freedmen's Bureau. In 1865, abolitionists and civil rights advocates wrote in the *National Anti-Slavery Standard* that the American government should give freed black families "40 acres and a furnished cottage."

In the election of 1868, Republicans campaigned in the eight reconstructed Southern states on the promise to provide the freed people with 40 acres and a mule if elected to office. Elected officials never fulfilled their campaign promise, but black voters provided the Republicans with the margin of victory in six of the eight former Confederate states that participated in the 1868 presidential election. Republican candidates in the South made similar promises in the midterm elections of 1870 and the presidential election of 1872.

In the 1870s, swindlers and con men preyed on the hopes of Southern blacks that the U.S. government was going to award them 40 acres. The con men posed as government agents and sold four stripped pegs to the unsuspecting freedmen. The swindlers told the blacks to take the pegs and mark off 40 acres of land on their former master's estate. The con men provided a falsified deed for each set of stakes. The swindlers charged a dollar a stake and claimed this was a nominal fee to cover their expenses. Political promises coupled with the belief that they should receive reparations for their years of unpaid labor made Southern blacks easy victims for these unscrupulous swindlers.

The misconception lingered into the 20th and 21st centuries that the U.S. government promised the freed people 40 acres and a mule. It symbolizes the failure of the post–Civil War United States to provide reparations for slave labor and economic assistance to the freed people. The famous movie producer and director Spike Lee named his production company 40 Acres and a Mule Filmswork. Lee used the name of his company to remind Americans of their failure to compensate formerly enslaved persons and their ancestors for their centuries of uncompensated work. In 1989, Democrat John Conyers Jr. from Michigan led a campaign in the U.S. House of Representatives to study the provision of reparations to the ancestors of enslaved persons. House leadership numbered Conyers's proposed legislation HR 40. The bill's number is a symbolic reference to 40 acres and a mule.

In 2015, the *World News Daily Report* published a false report that the U.S. Supreme Court had awarded an ancestor of an enslaved man 40 acres of land and a mule. The *World News Daily Report* is a satirical "fake-news" website known more for its faux-journalism and audacity than for the truth. The website falsely claimed that the U.S. Supreme Court, in a narrow 5–4 decision, ruled that the federal government had to keep its promise and provide 40 acres and farm animals to the descendants of enslaved persons. The court's decision was based on Sherman's Special Orders No. 15, which the justices asserted had the legal status of law. The website claimed that the National Association for the Advancement of Colored People field director called the ruling a "historical step towards justice." This satirical story demonstrates how persistent the 40 acres and a mule misconception is and how deeply it has penetrated our historical consciousness.

PRIMARY SOURCE DOCUMENTS

GEN. WILLIAM T. SHERMAN, SPECIAL FIELD ORDERS NO. 15 (JANUARY 16, 1865)

Maj. Gen. William Tecumseh Sherman's march to the sea wreaked havoc on the Georgia countryside from Atlanta to Savannah (November 15 to December 21).

Sherman destroyed almost anything of use to the Confederacy in a path almost 285 miles long. Thousands of liberated slaves followed Sherman's army, creating logistical and mobility problems for the general.

Four days after meeting with black leaders in Savannah, Sherman issued Special Field Orders No. 15. The general intended the order to address the immediate problem of what to do with the large number of blacks following his army. The order set aside land on the coast of South Carolina, Georgia, and Florida for settlement by the displaced blacks. Each family would be eligible for a plot of 40 acres of land. The black homesteaders would only have possessory title to the land subject to the approval of the president or Congress. In a separate action, Sherman allowed the settlers to use army mules not fit for service. Sherman would later claim that the order was a temporary measure and did not provide the homesteaders with permanent ownership of the land. This order originated the misconception that the government was going to provide formerly enslaved persons with reparations in the form of free land and farm animals.

Special Field Orders No. 15.

Headquarters Military Division of the Mississippi,
In the Field, Savannah, Ga., January 16, 1865.

I. The islands from Charleston south, the abandoned rice-fields along the rivers for thirty miles back from the sea, and the country bordering the Saint Johns River, Fla., are reserved and set apart for the settlement of the BLACKS now made free by the acts of war and the proclamation of the President of the United States.

II. At Beaufort, Hilton Head, Savannah, Fernandina, Saint Augustine, and Jacksonville the blacks may remain in their chosen or accustomed vocations; but on the islands, and in the settlements hereafter to be established, no white person whatever, unless military officers and soldiers detailed for duty, will be permitted to reside; and the sole and exclusive management of affairs will be left to the freed people themselves, subject only to the United States military authority and the acts of Congress. By the laws of war and orders of the President of the United States the negro is free, and must be dealt with as such. He cannot be subjected to conscription or forced military service, save by the written orders of the highest military authority of the Department, under such regulations as the President or Congress may prescribe; domestic servants, blacksmiths, carpenters, and other mechanics will be free to select their own work and residence, but the young and able-bodied negroes must be encouraged to enlist as soldiers in the service of the United States, to contribute their share toward maintaining their own freedom and securing their rights as citizens of the United States. Negroes so enlisted will be organized into companies, battalions, and regiments, under the orders of the United States military authorities, and will be paid, fed, and clothed according to law. The bounties paid on enlistment may, with the consent of the recruit, go to assist his family and settlement in procuring agricultural implements, seed, tools, boats, clothing, and other articles necessary for their livelihood.

III. Whenever three respectable negroes, heads of families, shall desire to settle on land, and shall have selected for that purpose an island, or a locality clearly defined within the limits above designated, the inspector of settlements and plantations will himself, or by such sub-ordinate officer as he may appoint, give them a license to settle such island or district, and afford them such assistance as he can to enable them to establish a peaceable agricultural settlement. The three parties named will subdivide the land, under the supervision of the inspector, among themselves and such others as may choose to settle near them, so that each family shall have a plot of not more than forty acres of tillable ground, and when it borders on some water channel with not more than 800 feet water front, in the possession of which land the military authorities will afford them protection until such time as they can protect themselves or until Congress shall regulate their title. The quartermaster may, on the requisition of the inspector of settlements and plantations, place at the disposal of the inspector one or more of the captured steamers to ply between the settlements and one or more of the commercial points, heretofore named in orders, to afford the settlers the opportunity to supply their necessary wants and to sell the products of their land and labor.

IV. Whenever a negro has enlisted in the military service of the United States he may locate his family in any one of the settlements at pleasure and acquire a homestead and all other rights and privileges of a settler as though present in person. In like manner negroes may settle their families and engage on board the gunboats, or in fishing, or in the navigation of the inland waters, without losing any claim to land or other advantages derived from this system. But no one, unless an actual settler as above defined, or unless absent on Government service, will be entitled to claim any right to land or property in any settlement by virtue of these orders.

V. In order to carry out this system of settlement a general officer will be detailed as inspector of settlements and plantations, whose duty it shall be to visit the settlements, to regulate their police and general management, and who will furnish personally to each head of a family, subject to the approval of the President of the United States, a possessory title in writing, giving as near as possible the description of boundaries, and who shall adjust all claims or conflicts that may arise under the same, subject to the like approval, treating such titles altogether as possessory. The same general officer will also be charged with the enlistment and organization of the negro recruits and protecting their interests while absent from their settlements, and will be governed by the rules and regulations prescribed by the War Department for such purpose.

VI. Brig. Gen. R. Saxton is hereby appointed inspector of settlements and plantations and will at once enter on the performance of his duties. No change is intended or desired in the settlement now on Beaufort Island, nor will any rights to property heretofore acquired be affected thereby.

By order of Maj. Gen. W. T. Sherman:

L. N. DAYTON, Assistant Adjutant-General.

—William T. Sherman, Military Division of the Mississippi; 1865 series—Special Field Order 15, January 16, 1865.

Source: *The War of the Rebellion: A Compilation of the Official Records of the Union and Confederate Armies.* Vol. 47, Part 2. 1880–1901. Washington, D.C.: Government Printing Office, 60–62.

LAW CREATING THE FREEDMEN'S BUREAU, U.S. CONGRESS (MARCH 3, 1865)

On March 3, 1865, the U.S. Congress created the Bureau of Refugees, Freedmen and Abandoned Lands. The public soon referred to it as the Freedmen's Bureau. Congress charged this agency with providing the freed people with temporary relief and education as they made the transition from slavery to freedom. Section 4 of the act allowed the freed people to lease confiscated or abandoned land in the South from the U.S. government. The plots of land were not to exceed 40 acres. At the end of three years or any time in between, the homesteaders could purchase the land at its assessed value. Though the act had no provision for free land, it continued to perpetuate the misconception that freed blacks would receive 40 acres of land in reparation for their years in slavery.

CHAP. XC.–An Act to establish a Bureau for the Relief of Freedmen and Refugees.

Be it enacted by the Senate and House of Representatives of the United States of America in Congress assembled, That there is hereby established in the War Department, to continue during the present war of rebellion, and for one year thereafter, a bureau of refugees, freedmen, and abandoned lands, to which shall be committed, as hereinafter provided, the supervision and management of all abandoned lands, and the control of all subjects relating to refugees and freedmen from rebel states, or from any district of country within the territory embraced in the operations of the army, under such rules and regulations as may be prescribed by the head of the bureau and approved by the President. The said bureau shall be under the management and control of a commissioner to be appointed by the President, by and with the advice and consent of the Senate, whose compensation shall be three thousand dollars per annum, and such number of clerks as may be assigned to him by the Secretary of War, not exceeding one chief clerk, two of the fourth class, two of the third class, and five of the first class. And the commissioner and all persons appointed under this act, shall, before entering upon their duties, take the oath of office prescribed in an act entitled "An act to prescribe an oath of office, and for other purposes," approved July second, eighteen hundred and sixty-two, and the commissioner and the chief clerk shall, before entering upon their duties, give bonds to the treasurer of the United States, the former in the sum of fifty thousand dollars, and the latter in the sum of ten thousand dollars, conditioned for the faithful discharge of their duties respectively, with securities to be approved as sufficient by the Attorney-General, which bonds shall be filed in the office of the first comptroller of the treasury, to be by him put in suit for the benefit of any injured party upon any breach of the conditions thereof.

SEC. 2. And be it further enacted, That the Secretary of War may direct such issues of provisions, clothing, and fuel, as he may deem needful for the immediate and temporary shelter and supply of destitute and suffering refugees and freedmen and their wives and children, under such rules and regulations as he may direct.

SEC. 3. And be it further enacted, That the President may, by and with the advice and consent of the Senate, appoint an assistant commissioner for each of the states declared to be in insurrection, not exceeding ten in number, who shall, under the direction of the commissioner, aid in the execution of the provisions of this act; and he shall give a bond to the Treasurer of the United States, in the sum of twenty thousand dollars, in the form and manner prescribed in the first section of this act. Each of said commissioners shall receive an annual salary of two thousand five hundred dollars in full compensation for all his services. And any military officer may be detailed and assigned to duty under this act without increase of pay or allowances. The commissioner shall, before the commencement of each regular session of congress, make full report of his proceedings with exhibits of the state of his accounts to the President, who shall communicate the same to congress, and shall also make special reports whenever required to do so by the President or either house of congress; and the assistant commissioners shall make quarterly reports of their proceedings to the commissioner, and also such other special reports as from time to time may be required.

SEC. 4. And be it further enacted, That the commissioner, under the direction of the President, shall have authority to set apart, for the use of loyal refugees and freedmen, such tracts of land within the insurrectionary states as shall have been abandoned, or to which the United States shall have acquired title by confiscation or sale, or otherwise, and to every male citizen, whether refugee or freedman, as aforesaid, there shall be assigned not more than forty acres of such land, and the person to whom it was so assigned shall be protected in the use and enjoyment of the land for the term of three years at an annual rent not exceeding six per centum upon the value of such land, as it was appraised by the state authorities in the year eighteen hundred and sixty, for the purpose of taxation, and in case no such appraisal can be found, then the rental shall be based upon the estimated value of the land in said year, to be ascertained in such manner as the commissioner may by regulation prescribe. At the end of said term, or at any time during said term, the occupants of any parcels so assigned may purchase the land and receive such title thereto as the United States can convey, upon paying therefor the value of the land, as ascertained and fixed for the purpose of determining the annual rent aforesaid.

SEC. 5. And be it further enacted, That all acts and parts of acts inconsistent with the provisions of this act, are hereby repealed.

APPROVED, March 3, 1865.

Source: *U.S. Statutes at Large, Treaties and Proclamations of the United States of America.* Vol. B. 1866. Boston: Little, Brown, 507–09.

REPARATIONS BILL FOR THE AFRICAN SLAVES IN THE UNITED STATES (1867)

Thaddeus Stevens was a radical Republican from Pennsylvania. On March 11, 1867, he proposed H. R. 29 in the House of Representatives. Section 4 of the bill would provide formerly enslaved persons with 40 acres of land. The act would redistribute the land Union forces confiscated from rebels during the Civil War. The settlers would own the land and not simply have possessory title to it. The bill passed Congress but was vetoed by Andrew Johnson. Congress never provided reparations to formerly enslaved persons, but they continued to hope for free land as compensation for their years in slavery.

Whereas it is due to justice, as an example to future times, that some future punishment should be inflicted on the people who constituted the "confederate States of America" both because they, declaring on unjust war against the United States for the purpose of destroying republican liberty and permanently establishing slavery, as well as, for the cruel and barbarous manner in which they conducted said war, in violation of all the laws of civilized warfare, and also to compel them to make some compensation for the damages and expenditures caused by the said war:

Therefore, Be it enacted by the Senate and House of Representatives of the United States of America in Congress assembled. That all the public lands belonging to the ten States that formed the government of the so-called Confederate States of America shall be forfeited by said States and become forthwith vested in the United States.

SEC. 2. And be it further enacted. That the President shall forthwith proceed to cause the seizure of such of the property belonging to the belligerent enemy as is deemed forfeited by the act of July 17, A. D. 1862, and hold and appropriate the same as enemy's property, and to proceed to condemnation with that already seized.

SEC. 3. And be it further enacted, That in lieu of the proceeding to condemn the property thus seized enemy's property. as is provided by the act of July A. D. 1862, two commissions or more, as by him may be deemed necessary, shall be appointed by the President for each of the said "Confederate States," to consist of three persons each, one of whom shall be an officer of the late or present Army, and two shall be civilians, neither of whom shall be citizens of the State for which he shall be appointed; that the said commissions shall proceed adjudicate and Condemn the property foresaid, under such forms and proceedings is shall be prescribed by the Attorney General of the United States, whereupon the title to said property shall become vested in the United States.

SEC. 4. And be it further enacted. That out of the lands thus seized and confiscated the slaves who have been liberated by the operations of the war and the amendment to the constitution or otherwise, who resided in said "confederate States" on the 4th day of March, A. D. 1861, or since, shall have distributed to them as follows, namely: to each male person who is the head of a family, forty acres; to each adult male, whether the head of a family or not, forty acres, to each widow who is the head of a family, forty acres—to be held by them in fee-simple, but to be inalienable for the next ten years after they become seized thereof.

For the purpose of distributing and allotting said land the Secretary of War shall appoint as many commissions in each State as he shall deem necessary, to consist of three members each, two of whom at least shall not be citizens of the State for which he is appointed. Each of said commissioners shall receive a salary of $3,000 annually and all his necessary expenses. Each commission shall be allowed one clerk, whose salary shall be $2,000 per annum.

The title to the homestead aforesaid shall be vested in trustees for the use of the liberated persons aforesaid. Trustees shall be appointed by the Secretary of War, and shall receive such salary as he shall direct, not exceeding $3,000 per annum. At the end of ten years the, absolute title to said homesteads shall be conveyed to said owners or to the heirs of such as are then dead.

SEC. 5. And be it further enacted, That out of the balance of the property thus seized and confiscated there shall be raised, in the manner hereinafter provided, a sum equal to fifty dollars, for each homestead, to be applied by the trustees hereinafter mentioned toward the erection of buildings on the said homesteads for the use of said slaves; and the further sum of $500,000,000, which shall be appropriated as follows, to wit: $200,000,000 shall be invested in United States six per cent, securities; and the interest thereof shall be semi-annually added to the pensions allowed by law to pensioners who have become so by reason of the late war; $300,000,000, or so much thereof as may Be need, shall be appropriated to pay damages done to loyal citizens by the civil or military Operations of the government lately called the "confederate States of America."

Source: HR 29. 40th Congress, 1st Session, 1867.

What Really Happened

The persistent misconception that the U.S. government was going to provide formerly enslaved persons with reparations in the form of 40 acres and a mule originated with Sherman's Special Field Orders No. 15. The misconception became entrenched in the Southern black community. The reality was that neither Congress nor the president approved measures to provide free land or any other form of reparation to the freed people.

Major General Sherman issued Special Field Orders No. 15 as a military necessity. He needed to free his army from the encumbrance of thousands of freed blacks who followed his forces and restricted his mobility. Sherman's orders gave the black settlers possessory not fee-simple title to the land. Under possessory title, blacks could farm and use the land but would not own it. Outright ownership of the land would require a fee-simple title. As a military commander, Sherman did not have the power to grant such a title. This would require the approval of the president through an executive order or congressional legislation. Sherman wrote in his memoirs that his order did not give the settlers a fee-simple title to the land. He wrote "all that was designated by these special field orders was to make temporary provisions for the freedmen and their families during the rest of the war, or until Congress should take action."

The president and Congress never took the necessary action to secure black ownership of the land on "Sherman's Reservation." Andrew Johnson became president on April 15, 1865, after the assassination of Abraham Lincoln. Johnson launched a lenient pardon policy that restored most rights to former Confederates who swore an oath of allegiance to the United States of America. The restoration of rights included the return of confiscated property to their former owners. Many of the former owners of land that comprised Sherman's Reservation wanted their property returned to them.

General Howard, commissioner of the Freedmen's Bureau, responded to Johnson's pardon policy by issuing Circular #13. This circular informed bureau agents that land redistribution was the official policy of the agency. Johnson countermanded Howard's circular and told the general that the pardoned Confederates could reclaim their land. The president instructed Howard to negotiate an acceptable agreement between the black settlers and former landowners. Howard tried to encourage blacks to surrender their land in return for being hired as laborers by their former owners. The plan met with great resistance from blacks on Edisto Island, South Carolina, and other areas of Sherman's Reservation.

Despite resistance, the U.S. government returned about 350,000 of the original 400,000 acres of confiscated land to its former owners. In July 1866, the reauthorization of the Freedmen's Bureau included a section that returned all the land that Sherman granted to black homesteaders in 1865 to the former owners. The government provided the freed people who continued to occupy these lands with two options: work as wage laborers or leave. The army evicted those who chose to stay but could not produce a deed for the land.

Radical Republicans in Congress sought to provide the freed people with land but not for free. Land ownership was a sign of status in the mid-19th century. Property rights were sacred, and most Americans in this era did not favor massive land redistribution, especially from white owners to freed blacks. The 1865 congressional act that created the Freemen's Bureau reflected this opinion. The act authorized the bureau to lease not more than 40 acres of confiscated or abandoned land to the freed people. The act allowed black settlers to use the land for a term of three years. Rent for the land would be based on a percentage of the assessed value of the property in 1860. At the end of the term, or during it, the occupants had the option of purchasing the land from the U.S. government at the assessed value.

Under the Freedmen's Bureau Act, the government leased land to blacks. If the occupants wanted clear title to the land, they had to purchase it. There was also no mention of the use or provision of farm animals to work the homestead. President Johnson's land ownership restoration policy thwarted the act's intention to provide land to the freed people. By 1867, former white owners had reclaimed most of the land the government earmarked for use and ownership by black settlers.

Congress passed the Southern Homestead Act in June 1866. This legislation opened for settlement 46 million acres of public land in five former Confederate states. The act divided the land into parcels of 80 acres. This amount was extended to 160 acres in June 1865. For the first six months of the act, only free blacks and loyal whites were allowed access to the land. The law required the homesteaders to occupy and improve the land before they could acquire full ownership. The price of a plot was five dollars. The act did not allow former Confederates to purchase homesteads until January 1, 1867.

The Southern Homestead Act did not accomplish its purpose of providing land ownership to the free people for a variety of reasons. The land was generally of inferior condition, and free blacks lacked the money to buy farm animals and implements to cultivate the land. Southern bureaucrats often did not comply with the law and failed to inform blacks of their right to use and own the land. Southern whites also used violence to drive black settlers off their homesteads. When Congress finally repealed the law in June 1876, free blacks had entered fewer than 4,500 claims for land over the 10-year period. In 1876, the government issued fewer than 1,000 property certificates to blacks. Forty acres and a mule remained an unfulfilled dream for Southern blacks.

On March 11, 1867, Speaker of the House Thaddeus Stevens proposed H.R. 29. Section 4 of this bill called for the land confiscated in the former

Confederate States of America to be redistributed to the freed people in plots of 40 acres. At the end of 10 years of occupation and use, the U.S. government would grant absolute title to the homesteads to the settlers or their heirs. Stevens saw this provision as a punishment for rebellion and a way to ensure the economic independence of the free people. The bill made it through the House and Senate but was vetoed by Johnson, who favored returning confiscated property to its former owners. The rejection of H.R. 29 doomed the idea of land redistribution and reparations for the remainder of the 19th century.

The question of land redistribution, reparations for slavery, and even pensions for formerly enslaved persons continued to appear on the congressional docket for over a century without resolution. In 1989, 122 years after Stevens introduced H.R. 29, Representative John Conyers Jr. (D, MI) introduced H.R. 40. This bill would establish a commission to study reparation proposals for African Americans and "to examine slavery and discrimination in the colonies and the United States from 1619 to the present and recommend appropriate remedies." Conyers has introduced the bill in the every session of the House since 1989. He introduced the latest version into the 114th Congress on January 6, 2015. Like its previous iterations, this bill died in Congress and, for the time being, so have the hopes of the ancestors of formerly enslaved persons of receiving 40 acres and a mule.

In conclusion, the misconception that the government would provide the freed people with 40 acres and a mule originated with Sherman's Special Field Orders No. 15. The homesteaders on "Sherman's Reservation" only received possessory title to the land, which President Johnson revoked with his pardon and land restoration policy. Congress reinforced Johnson's actions when it provided a provision for returning the land to its former owners in the Freedmen's Bureau Act of 1866. No U.S. law ever promised or offered the freed people free land or farm animals. Also, Congress has never provided reparations to formerly enslaved persons or their ancestors.

PRESIDENT ANDREW JOHNSON, AMNESTY PROCLAMATION, RESTORATION OF RIGHTS OF PROPERTY EXCEPTION IN SLAVES (MAY 29, 1865)

Andrew Johnson issued an amnesty proclamation on May 29, 1865. In this proclamation, the president granted amnesty to all persons who directly or indirectly participated in the rebellion unless excluded by special circumstances. Individuals covered under the special circumstances provision would have to file a different application that the president would review on a case-by-case basis. Amnesty was contingent on taking an oath of allegiance to the United States and to defend its constitution. Once an individual received amnesty, the government would restore his or her confiscated property, except for enslaved persons. The president's proclamation negated Sherman's Special Field Orders No. 15 and rendered any land redistribution scheme based on confiscated property impossible to enact. After Johnson issued his amnesty proclamation, 40 acres and a mule became an aspiration but never a reality.

WASHINGTON, May 29.

By the President of the United States of America:

A PROCLAMATION.

Whereas, The President of the United States, on the 8th day of December, A.D. eighteen hundred and sixty-three, and on the 26th day of March, A.D. eighteen hundred and sixty-four, did, with the object to suppress the existing rebellion, to induce all persons to return to their loyalty, and to restore the authority of the United States, issue proclamations offering amnesty and pardon to certain persons, who had directly or by implication participated in the said rebellion; and

Whereas, Many persons, who had so engaged in said rebellion, have, since the issuance of said proclamations, failed or neglected to take the benefits offered thereby; and

Whereas, Many persons, who have been justly deprived of all claim to amnesty or pardon thereunder, by reason of their participation, directly or by implication, in said rebellion, and continued hostility to the Government of the United States since the date of said proclamations, now desire to apply for and obtain amnesty and pardon;

To the end, therefore, that the authority of the Government of the United States may be restored, and that peace, order and freedom may be established, I, ANDREW JOHNSON, President of the United States, do proclaim and declare that I hereby grant to all persons who have directly or indirectly participated in the existing rebellion, except as hereinafter excepted, amnesty and pardon, with restoration of all rights of property, except as to slaves, and except in cases where legal proceedings under the laws of the United States providing for the confiscation of property of persons engaged in rebellion have been instituted; but on the condition, nevertheless, that every such person shall take and subscribe the following oath or affirmation, and thenceforward keep and maintain said oath inviolate, and which oath shall be registered for permanent preservation, and shall be of the tenor and effect following, to wit:

"I, _____, do solemnly swear or affirm, in presence of Almighty God, that I will henceforth faithfully support and defend the Constitution of the United States and the Union of the States thereunder. And that I will, in like manner, abide by and faithfully support all laws and proclamations which have been made during the existing rebellion with reference to the emancipation of slaves, so help me God."

The following classes of persons are excepted from the benefits of this proclamation:

First—All who are or shall have been pretended civil or diplomatic officers, or otherwise domestic or foreign agents of the pretended Confederate Government.

Second—All who left judicial stations under the United States to aid the rebellion.

Third—All who shall have been military or naval officers of said pretended Confederate Government above the rank of Colonel in the army or Lieutenant in the navy.

Fourth—All who left seats in the Congress of the United States to aid the rebellion.

Fifth—All who resigned or tendered resignations of their commissions in the army or navy of the United States, to evade duty in resisting the rebellion.

Sixth—All who have engaged in any way in treating otherwise than lawfully as prisoners of war persons found in the United States service, as officers, soldiers, seamen, or in other capacities.

Seventh—All persons who have been or are absentees from the United States for the purpose of aiding the rebellion.

Eighth—All military and naval officers in the rebel service who were educated by the government in the Military Academy at West Point, or the United States Naval Academy.

Ninth—All persons who held the pretended offices of Governors of States in insurrection against the United States.

Tenth—All persons who left their homes within the jurisdiction and protection of the United States and passed beyond the Federal military lines into the so-called Confederate States, for the purpose of aiding the rebellion.

Eleventh—All parties who have been engaged in the destruction of the commerce of the United States upon the high seas, and all persons who have made raids into the United States from Canada, or been engaged in destroying the commerce of the United States upon the lakes and rivers that separate the British Provinces from the United States.

Twelfth—All persons who at the time when they seek to obtain the benefits hereof by taking the oath herein prescribed, are in military naval, or civil confinement, or custody, or under bonds of the civil, military or naval authorities or agents of the United States, as prisoners of war, or persons detained for offences of any kind either before or after conviction.

Thirteenth—All persons who have voluntarily participated in said rebellion, and the estimated value of whoso taxable property is over twenty thousand dollars.

Fourteenth—All persons who have taken the oath of amnesty as prescribed in the President's Proclamation of December 8, A.D., 1863, or an oath of allegiance to the Government of the United States since the dates of said proclamation, and who have not thenceforward kept and maintained the same inviolate—provided that special application may be made to the President for pardon by any person belonging to the excepted classes, and such clemency will be liberally extended as may be consistent with the facts of the case and the peace and dignity of the United States.

The Secretary of State will establish rules and regulations for administering and recording the said amnesty oath so as to insure its benefit to the people and guard the government against fraud.

[L.S.] In testimony whereof I have hereunto set my hand and caused the seal of the United States to be affixed. Done at the City of Washington the Twenty-ninth day of May, in the year of Our Lord, one thousand eight hundred and sixty-five, and of the Independence of the United States the eighty-ninth.

By the President: ANDREW JOHNSON. WM. H. SEWARD, Secretary of State.

Source: Richardson, James D., ed. 1920. *A Compilation of the Messages and Papers of the Presidents 1789–1897.* Vol. 6. Washington, D.C.: Government Printing Office, 310–12.

LETTERS FROM THE COMMITTEE OF FREEDMEN ON EDISTO ISLAND TO THE FREEDMEN'S BUREAU COMMISSIONER (OCTOBER 20, 1865)

One of the most successful settlements on "Sherman's Reservation" was on Edisto Island, South Carolina. By the fall of 1865, many former owners of the land that comprised Sherman's Reservation wanted their property back after accepting the terms of Johnson's amnesty policy. Johnson ordered the commissioner of the Freedmen's Bureau, Oliver O. Howard, to negotiate an agreement where the freed people would return the land to the former owners.

Howard met with the black residents of Edisto Island and asked them to surrender their land in return for a guarantee that the former owners would hire them as laborers. The black homesteaders refused to leave the land and put their reasons in a letter to Howard and a petition to President Johnson. The 1866 Freedmen's Bureau Act included a provision to return the property on Sherman's Reservation to its former owners. By 1867, almost 80 percent of the land on Sherman's Reservation had been restored to the white owners. Below is a letter to General Howard and a petition to President Johnson from a committee of black residents on Edisto Island defending their right and claim to their lands on Sherman's Reservation.

[Edisto Island, S.C., October 20 or 21, 1865]

General It Is with painfull Hearts that we the committe address you, we Have thorougholy considered the order which you wished us to Sighn, we wish we could do so but cannot feel our rights Safe If we do so,

General we want Homestead's; we were promised Homestead's by the government, If It does not carry out the promises Its agents made to us, If the government Haveing concluded to befriend Its late enemies and to neglect to observe the principles of common faith between Its self and us Its allies In the war you said was over, now takes away from them all right to the soil they stand upon save such as they can get by again working for your late and thier all time ememies.—If the government does so we are left In a more unpleasant condition than our former we are at the mercy of those who are combined to prevent us from getting land enough to lay our Fathers bones upon. We Have property In Horses, cattle, carriages, & articles of furniture, but we are landless and Homeless, from the Homes we Have lived In In the past we can only do one of three things Step Into the public road or the sea or remain on them working as In former time and subject to thire will as then. We can not resist It In any way without being driven out Homeless upon the road.

You will see this Is not the condition of really freemen

You ask us to forgive the land owners of our Island, You only lost your right arm. In war and might forgive them. The man who tied me to a tree & gave me 39 lashes & who stripped and flogged my mother & my sister & who will not let me stay In His empty Hut except I will do His planting & be Satisfied with His price & who combines with others to keep away land from me well knowing I would not Have any thing to do with Him If I Had land of my own.—that man, I cannot well forgive. Does It look as If He Has forgiven me, seeing How He tries to keep me In a condition of Helplessness

General, we cannot remain Here In such condition and If the government permits them to come back we ask It to Help us to reach land where we shall not be slaves nor compelled to work for those who would treat us as such we Have not been treacherous, we Have not for selfish motives allied to us those who suffered like us from a common enemy & then Haveing gained our purpose left our allies In thier Hands There Is no rights secured to us there Is no law likely to be made which our Hands can reach. The state will make laws that we shall not be able to Hold land even If we pay for It Landless, Homeless. Voteless. we can only pray to god & Hope for His Help, your Infuence & assistance With consideration of esteem your Obt Servts

   In behalf of the people
           Henry Bram
   Committe   Ishmael Moultrie
           yates Sampson

Source: Committee of Freedmen on Edisto Island, letter to South Carolina to the Freedmen's Bureau Commissioner. 1865. Vol. 64, Letters sent, Series 2. Washington Headquarters, Bureau of Refugees, Freedmen and Abandoned Lands: Abandoned Lands Record Group 105 National Archives.

ANDREW JOHNSON, VETO OF THE FREEDMEN'S BUREAU BILL (1866)

President Johnson's amnesty policy returned confiscated lands to former Confederate landowners who swore an oath of allegiance to the United States and its constitution. Johnson's policy negated any attempt to redistribute confiscated lands to blacks as reparations for slavery.

On February 19, 1866, Johnson sent a message to the U.S. Senate outlining the reasons he vetoed the Second Freedmen's Bureau Bill. In his veto missive, Johnson stated his objections to the sections of the bill that would allow the freed people to rent or purchase land confiscated during the Civil War. Below is an excerpt from Johnson's veto message explaining why he was against the redistribution of land to free blacks.

The third section of the bill authorizes a general and unlimited grant of support to the destitute and suffering refugees and freedmen, and their wives and children. Succeeding sections make provision for the rent or purchase of landed estates for freedmen, and for the erection, for their benefit, of suitable asylums and schools, the expenses to be defrayed from the treasury of the whole people. The Congress of the United States has never, heretofore, thought itself competent to establish asylums beyond the limits of the District of Columbia, except for the benefit of our disabled soldiers and sailors. It has never founded schools for any class of our own people, not even for the orphans of those who have fallen in the defence of the Union, but has left the care of their education to the much more competent and efficient control of the States, of communities, of private associations, and of individuals. It has never deemed itself authorized to expend the public money for the rent or purchase of homes for the thousands, not to say millions, of the white race who are honestly toiling from day to day for their subsistence. A system for the support of indigent persons in the United States was never contemplated by the authors of the Constitution. Nor can any good reason be advanced why, as a permanent establishment, it should be founded for one class or color of our people more than for another. Pending the war, many refugees and freedmen received support from the Government, but it was never intended that they should henceforth be fed, clothed, educated, and sheltered by the United States. The idea on which the slaves were assisted to freedom was, that on becoming free they would be a self-sustaining population. Any legislation that shall imply that they are not expected to attain a self-sustaining condition must have a tendency injurious alike to their character and their prosperity. The appointment of an agent for every county and parish will create an immense patronage, and the expense of the numerous officers and their clerks to be appointed by the President will be great in the beginning, with a tendency steadily to increase. The appropriations asked by the Freedmen's Bureau, as now established, for the year 1866, amount to $11,745,000. It may be safely estimated that the cost to be incurred under the pending bill will require double that amount, more than the entire sum expended in any one year under the administration of the second Adams. If the presence of agents in every parish and county is to be considered as a war measure, opposition or even resistance might be provoked, so that to give effect to their jurisdiction troops would have to be stationed within reach of every one of them, and thus a standing army be rendered necessary. Large appropriations would therefore be required to sustain and enforce military jurisdiction in every county or parish from the Potomac to the Rio Grande. The condition of our fiscal affairs is encouraging; but, in order to sustain the present measure of public confidence, it is necessary that we practice not merely customary economy, but, as far as possible, severe retrenchment.

In addition to the objections already stated, the fifth section of the bill proposes to take away land from its former owners, without any legal proceedings being first had, contrary to that provision of the Constitution which declares that no persons shall be deprived of life, liberty, or property without due process of law. It does not appear that a part of the lands which this section refers to may not be owned by minors or persons of unsound mind, or by those who have been faithful to all their obligations as citizens of the United States. If any portion of the land is held by such persons, it is not competent for any other authority to deprive them of it. If, on the other hand, it be found that the property is liable to confiscation, even then it cannot be appropriated to public purposes until, by due process of law, it shall have been declared forfeited to the Government.

There are still further objections to the bill, on grounds seriously affecting the class of persons to whom it is designed to bring relief. It will tend to keep the mind of the freedman in a state of uncertain expectation and restlessness, while to those among whom he lives it will be a source of constant and vague apprehension. Undoubtedly the freedman should be protected by the civil authorities, especially by the exercise of all the constitutional powers of the courts of the United States and of the States. His condition is not so exposed as may at first be imagined. He is in a portion of the country where his labor cannot well be spared. Competition for his services from planters, from those who are constructing or repairing railroads, or from capitalists in his vicinage, or from other States, will enable him to command almost his own terms. He also possesses a perfect right to change his place of abode, and if, therefore, he does not find in one community or State a mode of life suited to his desires, or proper remuneration for his labor, he can move to another where labor is more esteemed and better rewarded. In truth, however, each State, induced by its own wants and interests, will do what is necessary and proper to retain within its borders all the labor that is needed for the development of its resources. The laws that regulate supply and demand will maintain their force, and the wages of the laborer will be regulated thereby. There is no danger that the great demand for labor will not operate in favor of the laborer. Neither is sufficient consideration given to the ability of the freedmen to protect and take care of themselves. It is no more than justice to them to believe that, as they have received their freedom with moderation and forbearance, so they will distinguish themselves by their industry and thrift, and soon show the world that in a condition of freedom they are self-sustaining and capable of selecting their own employment and their own places of abode; of insisting for themselves on a proper remuneration, and of establishing and maintaining their own asylums and schools. It is earnestly hoped that instead of wasting away, they will, by their own efforts, establish for themselves a condition of respectability and prosperity. It is certain that they can attain to that condition only through their own merits and exertions. In this connection the query presents itself, whether the system proposed by the bill will not, when put into complete operation, practically transfer the entire care, support, and control of four millions of emancipated slaves to agents, overseers, or taskmasters, who, appointed at Washington, are to be located in every county and parish throughout the United States containing freedmen and refugees. Such a system would inevitably tend to such a concentration of power in the Executive as would enable him, if so disposed, to control the action of a numerous class, and to use them for the attainment of his own political ends.

Source: Foster, Lillian. 1866. *Andrew Johnson, His Life and Speeches*. New York: Richardson.

Further Reading

Beard, Richard. 2017. "A Promise Betrayed." *Civil War Times* 56, no. 8: 44–51.

Bolz, Herman A. 1976. *A New Birth of Freedom: The Republican Party and Freedman's Rights, 1861–1866*. Westport, CT: Greenwood Press.

Bonekemper, Edward H., III. 1970. "Negro Ownership of Real Property in Hampton and Elizabeth City County, Virginia, 1860–1870." *Journal of Negro History* 55, no. 3: 165–81.

Carpenter, John A. 1999. *Sword and Olive Branch: Oliver Otis Howard*. Bronx, NY: Fordham University Press.

Cimbala, Paul A., and Hans L. Trefousse, eds. 2005. *The Freedmen's Bureau: Reconstructing the American South after the Civil War*. Malabar, FL: Krieger.

Cimbala, Paul B. 2010. *The Great Task Remaining Before Us: Reconstruction as America's Continuing Civil War*. New York: Fordham University Press.

Cox, John, and Lawanda Cox. 1955. "General O. O. Howard and the 'Misrepresented Bureau.'" *Journal of Southern History* 19, no. 3: 427–56.

Davis, Burke. 1988. *Sherman's March: The First Full-Length Narrative of General William T. Sherman's Devastating March through Georgia and the Carolinas*. Visalia, CA: Vintage.

Engs, Robert Francis. 1978. *Freedom's First Generation: Black Hampton, Virginia, 1861–1890*. Philadelphia: University of Pennsylvania Press.

Fleming, Walter L. 1906. "Forty Acres and a Mule." *North American Review* 182, no. 594.

Foner, Eric. 2011. *Reconstruction: America's Unfinished Revolution, 1863–1877.* New York: HarperCollins.

Gates, Henry Louis, Jr. 2013. "The Truth Behind '40 Acres and a Mule.'" *The Root*, January 7. Accessed April 17, 2018. http://www.theroot .com/the-truth-behind-40-acres-and-a-mule-1790894780.

Gates, Paul Wallace. 1940. "Federal Land Policy in the South, 1866–1888." *Journal of Southern History* 6, no. 3: 303–30.

Levine, Bruce. 2014. *The Fall of the House of Dixie: The Civil War and the Social Revolution that Transformed the South.* New York: Random House.

McFeely, Robert Tracey. 1968. *Yankee Stepfather: General O. O. Howard and Freedmen.* New Haven, CT: Yale University Press.

Osborne, Linda Barrett. 2009. *Traveling the Freedom Road: From Slavery and the Civil War through Reconstruction.* New York: Harry N. Abrams.

Oubre, Charles F. 1978. *Forty Acres and a Mule: The Freedmen's Bureau and Black Land Ownership.* Baton Rouge: Louisiana State University Press.

Reid, Debra, and Evan P. Bennett, eds. 2012. *Beyond Forty Acres and a Mule: African American Landowning Families Since Reconstruction.* Gainesville: University Press of Florida.

Rose, Willie Lee. 1976. *Rehearsal for Reconstruction: The Port Royal Experiment.* New York: Oxford University Press.

Saville, Julie. 1994. *The Work of Reconstruction: From Slave to Wage Laborer in South Carolina 1860–1870.* New York: Cambridge University Press.

Sherman, William Tecumseh, and Charles Royster, eds. 2017. *Memoirs of Gen. William F. Sherman.* New York: Library of America.

Trudeau, Noah Andre. 2009. *Southern Storm: Sherman's March to the Sea.* New York: Harper Perennial.

Voegeli, Jacque V. 2003. "A Rejected Alternative: Union Policy and the Relocation of Southern 'Contrabands' at the Dawn of Emancipation." *Journal of Southern History* 69, no. 4: 765–90.

Williamson, Joel. 1965. *After Slavery: The Negro in South Carolina during Reconstruction 1861–1867.* Chapel Hill: University of North Carolina Press.

10

Lincoln's Assassination Was the Result of a Conspiracy

What People Think Happened

After the fall of Richmond and the surrender of Robert E. Lee's Army of Northern Virginia, stage actor and Southern sympathizer John Wilkes Booth assembled a cabal of drifters, spies, and Confederate deserters. Their mission was to assassinate the top leadership of the United States, causing chaos and confusion that might allow the Confederate government and military the opportunity to regroup and continue the rebellion. The targets of this dynastic assassination included President Lincoln, Vice President Johnson, Secretary of State William Seward, and General of the Armies Ulysses S. Grant.

On the night of April 14, 1865, the assassins struck. Booth, the leader and mastermind of the conspiracy, shot President Lincoln in the head while the president watched the comedy *Our American Cousin* at Ford's Theatre. Lincoln died the next morning at 7:22 a.m. in the Petersen house across the street from the theater. Lewis Powell attacked William Seward at home in his bed but failed to kill him. George Atzerodt never launched his attack on Vice President Johnson, who remained unscathed by the night's bloody events. Booth did not target Grant because the general was away from Washington visiting his children in Long Branch, New Jersey. Booth escaped capture on April 14 and remained on the run until April 26, when Union soldiers found him and an accomplice, David Herold, in a barn on Garrett's farm in Virginia. Herold surrendered, but Booth was shot and killed by Sgt. Boston Corbett as he moved about inside the burning barn. A military tribunal tried eight of the coconspirators and executed four of them, including Powell, Atzerodt, and Herold.

Immediately after Lincoln's death, two theories arose about the conspiracy to assassinate him. The simple conspiracy theory contended that John Wilkes Booth alone masterminded the entire plot to kill Lincoln without outside direction or aid. The grand conspiracy theories argued that Booth was a mere pawn in a larger conspiracy hatched by more powerful players. These theories held that players such as Jefferson Davis, Vice President Johnson, Edwin Stanton, and even the Catholic church directed Booth and the other coconspirators to assassinate Lincoln to benefit their interests. The grand conspiracy theories all rest on a framework of misconceptions, circumstantial evidence, and untruths.

The first and most persistent grand conspiracy theory arose immediately after Lincoln's assassination. The new president of the United States, Andrew Johnson, and Secretary of War Edwin Stanton both blamed Jefferson Davis and the Confederate government for the conspiracy. On May 2, 1865, President Johnson issued Proclamation 131, in which he contended that Jefferson Davis and other Confederate agents "incited, concerted, and procured" the "atrocious murder" of President Lincoln and the "attempted assassination" of William Seward. Johnson offered a $100,000 reward for the arrest of Jefferson Davis. It is clear from the proclamation that the president and the War Department did not consider Booth to be the mastermind of the assassination plot.

Why did Johnson, Stanton, and others allege that Davis and the Confederate government were the masterminds of the Lincoln assassination? In February of 1864, the Confederate Congress appropriated $5 million to support a clandestine operation against the North. Davis appointed Jacob Thompson and Clement Clay to head the Confederate Secret Service operating out of Canada. The group proposed and attempted acts of terrorism that ranged from infecting Union troops and government personnel with contagious diseases to poisoning the New York City water supply and burning down prominent hotels there. The Confederate Secret Service seemed to be willing to take any step to turn the tide of the war.

In April 1865, the U.S. military foiled an attempted attack by the Torpedo Bureau, a part of the Confederate War Department's Secret Service. On April 1, the bureau ordered Thomas Harney, an explosives expert, to infiltrate the defenses of Washington, D.C. Armed with detonators and fuses, Harney arrived in the nation's capital to build and explode a bomb.

Historians are not sure of Harney's specific target but speculate that the intended purpose of the torpedo may have been to decapitate Union leadership who were meeting at the White House. Union troops captured Harney on April 10 and foiled the intended attack in the nation's capital. Union officials believed that an attack of this nature would have required the permission of the Confederate president. This intuitive leap led to the later assumption by Johnson and Stanton that Davis must have also ordered Booth to carry out his attack on Lincoln and other Union leaders.

How the Story Became Popular

At the time of the assassination, President Johnson, the War Department, and the general public believed that Jefferson Davis and elements of the Confederate government conspired to kill Lincoln. The prosecution at the trial of Booth's coconspirators helped to perpetuate the grand conspiracy theory. The War Department, with the approval of President Johnson, employed a military tribunal to try the eight persons accused in the assassination plot. Maj. Gen. David Hunter presided over the other eight generals who decided the fate of the accused conspirators. U.S. Army judge advocate Gen. Joseph Holt led the prosecution team. Congressman John A. Bingham and Maj. Henry Burnett assisted Holt.

Prosecutors saw the military tribunal as a chance to prosecute not only the eight individuals on trial but also Jefferson Davis and members of the Confederate Secret Service. Witnesses at the trial described various acts of terrorism that Confederate Secret Service plotted against Northern targets. Several witnesses testified that by the fall of 1864, there was a Confederate plot to abduct or assassinate prominent Union leaders. Richmond Montgomery, a Union double agent operating in Canada, claimed that he heard Jacob Thompson of the Confederate Secret Service say it would be a "blessing to rid the world of Lincoln, Johnson, and Grant." In his summation of the prosecution's case, special judge advocate John Bingham provided the tribunal with a long, detailed list of circumstantial evidence and witness testimony that attempted to link Jefferson Davis and the Confederate Secret Service to the assassination of Lincoln.

Evidence and testimony provided to the military tribunal as well as Bingham's accusatory summation form the major arguments used by proponents of Confederate conspiracy theories. Proponents also point to the coded letters investigators found in Booth's trunk at the National Hotel in Washington as a link between the assassination plot and the Confederate government. In 1977, Joan L. Chaconas discovered a lost statement that one of the Lincoln assassination conspirators, George Atzerodt, gave to Baltimore provost marshal James McPhail on May 1, 1865. In his statement, Atzerodt told McPhail that Booth had knowledge of the Confederate plot to blow up the White House in the early spring of 1865.

The discovery of Atzerodt's lost statement rekindled interest in the Confederate grand conspiracy theory. Works such as William Tidwell's *April '65: Confederate Covert Action in the American Civil War*, Larry Stankey's *Wilkes Booth Came to Washington*, and John Fazio's *Decapitating the Union: Jefferson Davis, Judah Benjamin and the Plot to Assassinate Lincoln* all implicated Confederate leadership in the conspiracy to assassinate Lincoln. Historian William Hanchett's research also suggests Confederate influence in the death of Lincoln. One hundred and fifty years after the assassination of Lincoln, the idea still persists that Davis and the Confederate Secret Service masterminded the murder of Lincoln, and Booth was merely a pawn in this violent chess match.

The death of the assassin before authorities can interrogate him or her always spawns a wide variety of grand conspiracy theories. The death of John Wilkes Booth before he could be brought to trial was no exception. A Confederate plot to assassinate Lincoln was only one of many theories about the conspiracy to kill the president. The misconception that Vice President Johnson was involved in the plot to murder Lincoln gained traction in American public opinion immediately after the assassination.

The association of Johnson to the conspiracy to assassinate Lincoln is based on Booth's mysterious visit to Johnson's Washington residence. Approximately seven hours before Lincoln's assassination, Booth went to Kirkwood House to see Johnson. When a desk clerk told Booth that Johnson was not there, Booth left a cryptic note that stated, "Don't wish to disturb you. Are you at home?" Mary Todd Lincoln added her support to the Johnson conspiracy theory in a letter she wrote to her friend Sally Orne on March 15, 1866. Referring to the assassination in her letter, Mrs. Lincoln wrote Orne that "as sure, as you & I live, Johnson had some hand in all this." The fact that Johnson's would-be assassin, George Atzerodt, did not carry out the attack on the vice president added more grist to the rumor mill.

In 1866, Congress established a committee to investigate the assassination of Lincoln. The committee examined the allegation that Johnson was involved in the plot but found no evidence to substantiate the claim. Despite this finding, Congress reopened the matter during Johnson's impeachment hearing in 1867. Some members of the House of Representatives, like James Mitchell Ashley of Ohio, testified that they believed Johnson was involved in the plot to kill Lincoln. When pressed to produce actionable evidence to corroborate their testimony, the accusers were unable to do so. Again, Congress did not link Johnson to the assassination plot.

One of the key elements needed to link Johnson to Lincoln's assassination was to establish that Booth and Johnson knew each other prior to April 1865. In his 1907 work *Civil War Echoes*, author Hamilton Howard claimed that during Johnson's tenure as the military governor of Tennessee, observers often saw Booth and Johnson in each other's company. According to Howard, Booth and Johnson kept a pair of sisters as mistresses, and this was how their relationship with each other began. In the 1997 publication *"Right or Wrong, God Judge Me": The Writings of John Wilkes Booth*, John Rhodehamel and Louise Taper wrote that Booth and Johnson met at Wood's Theater in Nashville in February 1864. These works have helped to perpetuate the idea that Johnson and Booth conspired to kill Lincoln.

Another grand conspiracy theory is that Secretary of War Edwin Stanton was the architect behind the Lincoln assassination. Otto Eisenschiml, an Austrian-born chemist and oil executive, put forward this theory in his 1937 work *Why Was Lincoln Murdered*. In 1928, Eisenschiml began to research Lincoln's assassination and became convinced that Booth was not the mastermind of the plot. Instead, he placed the blame on Lincoln's secretary of war, Edwin Stanton. According to Eisenschiml, Stanton opposed Lincoln's soft stance on reconstruction and wanted the president out of the way so radical Republicans could impose a harsher, more punitive reconstruction policy on the conquered South.

Eisenschiml attempted to prove his faulty hypothesis with circumstantial evidence and perjured testimony from the military tribunal trial of the coconspirators. Eisenschiml alleged that Stanton did not provide Lincoln with adequate protection at Ford's Theatre and allowed Booth to escape into Maryland across the Navy Yard Bridge, the only exit from Washington, D.C., not sealed by Stanton after the assassination. Eisenschiml then claimed that Stanton had the military kill Booth to cover the secretary of war's role in the plot. He also alleged that Stanton suppressed evidence by removing incriminating material from Booth's diary and hooding the imprisoned coconspirators so they could not communicate with interviewers.

Eisenschiml's book had a wide audience, and many graduate schools required their students to read the work. Several other works supported and provided new insights on Eisenschiml's hypothesis. Theodore Roscoe's *The Web of Conspiracy* and David Balsiger and Charles Sellier's *The Lincoln*

Conspiracy introduced Eisenschiml's allegation to a new generation of grand conspiracy advocates. Sunn Classic Pictures turned the latter work into a movie of the same title in 1977.

The list of grand conspiracy theories does not stop with the Confederate government, Andrew Johnson, and Edwin Stanton. Other prominent theories have Lincoln being assassinated by a powerful group of international bankers, the Catholic church, Northerners who had invested in Southern cotton, and Northerner elites upset with Lincoln's reconstruction policy. Since Lincoln's assassination, the American public has been unwilling to accept John Wilkes Booth as the leader of the conspiracy to kill the president. Instead, they seem enthralled with the idea that more sinister and more prominent forces conspired to assassinate Lincoln.

PRIMARY SOURCE DOCUMENTS

ANDREW JOHNSON, PROCLAMATION 131: REWARDS FOR THE ARREST OF JEFFERSON DAVIS AND OTHERS (MAY 2, 1865)

Immediately after Abraham Lincoln was assassinated, President Johnson, Secretary of War Edwin Stanton, and a substantial portion of Americans believed that Confederate officials were involved in the plot. They based their suspicions on acts of terrorism planned and executed by Confederate agents located in Canada. They were also aware of a plot by the Confederate Torpedo Bureau to explode a bomb in Washington, perhaps at the White House. On May 2, 1865, President Johnson issued a proclamation for the apprehension and arrest of Jefferson Davis and several other Confederate officials believed involved in the assassination plot. The government offered a $100,000 reward for Jefferson and $10,000 to $25,000 for the remaining suspects. Johnson's proclamation was a key element in the conception that the Confederate government was involved in a grand conspiracy to kill Lincoln.

Whereas it appears from evidence in the Bureau of Military Justice that the atrocious murder of the late President, Abraham Lincoln, and the attempted assassination of the Hon. William H. Seward, Secretary of State, were incited, concerted, and procured by and between Jefferson Davis, late of Richmond, Va., and Jacob Thompson, Clement C. Clay, Beverley

Tucker, George N. Sanders, William C. Cleary, and other rebels and traitors against the Government of the United States harbored in Canada:

Now, therefore, to the end that justice may be done, I, Andrew Johnson, President of the United States, do offer and promise for the arrest of said persons, or either of them, within the limits of the United States, so that they can be brought to trial, the following rewards:

One hundred thousand dollars for the arrest of Jefferson Davis.

Twenty-five thousand dollars for the arrest of Clement C. Clay.

Twenty-five thousand dollars for the arrest of Jacob Thompson, late of Mississippi.

Twenty-five thousand dollars for the arrest of George N. Sanders.

Twenty-five thousand dollars for the arrest of Beverley Tucker.

Ten thousand dollars for the arrest of William C. Cleary, late clerk of Clement C. Clay.

The Provost-Marshal-General of the United States is directed to cause a description of said persons, with notice of the above rewards, to be published.

In testimony whereof I have hereunto set my hand and caused the seal of the United States to be affixed.

Done at the city of Washington, this 2d day of May, A. D. 1865, and of the Independence of the United States of America the eighty-ninth.

ANDREW JOHNSON.

By the President:

W. HUNTER,

Acting Secretary of State.

Source: Richardson, James D. 1900. *A Compilation of the Messages and Papers of the Presidents: Andrew Johnson.* Vol. 6, Part 2. Washington, D.C.: U.S. Congress, 307–08.

JOHN BINGHAM, PROSECUTION'S SUMMATION AT THE LINCOLN ASSASSINATION TRIAL (1865)

On May 1, President Johnson ordered that a special military commission try the eight conspirators linked to the Lincoln assassination. The nine officers on the commission held the fate of the accused conspirators in their hands. The commission convened on May 9 and began hearing testimony from 366 witnesses on May 12. As the proceedings drew to a conclusion in late June, Hon. John Bingham, special judge advocate, offered the government's reply to the defense and a summation of the prosecution's arguments. Bingham used this occasion to have a de facto trial of Davis and other Confederate officials in absentia. In his summation, Bingham provided the commission a detailed description of Confederate acts of terrorism during the war. Using circumstantial evidence and perjured testimony, he argued that Davis and other Confederates conspired with Booth to kill Lincoln. Bingham's summation, excerpted below, became a cornerstone for the Confederate grand conspiracy theory.

By all the testimony in the case, it is, in my judgment, made as clear as any transaction can be shown by human testimony, that John Wilkes Booth and John H. Surratt, and the several accused, David E. Herold, George A. Atzerodt, Lewis Payne, Michael O'Laughlen, Edward Spangler, Samuel Arnold, Mary E. Surratt and Samuel A. Mudd, did, with intent to aid the existing rebellion, and to subvert the Constitution and laws of the United States, in the month of October last, and thereafter, combine, confederate and conspire with Jefferson Davis, George N. Sanders, Beverley Tucker, Jacob Thompson, William C. Cleary, Clement C. Clay, George Harper, George Young, and others unknown, to kill and murder, within the military department of Washington, and within the intrenched fortification and military lines thereof, Abraham Lincoln, then President of the United States, and Commander-in-Chief of the army and navy thereof; Andrew Johnson, Vice-President of the United States; William H. Seward, Secretary of State, and Ulysses S. Grant, Lieutenant-General, in command of the armies of the United States; and that Jefferson Davis, the chief of this rebellion, was the instigator and procurer, through his accredited agents in Canada, of this treasonable conspiracy.

It is also submitted to the Court, that it is clearly established by the testimony that John Wilkes Booth, in pursuance of this conspiracy, so entered into by him and the accused, did, on the night of the 14th of April, 1865, within the military department of Washington, and the intrenched fortifications and military lines thereof, and with the intent laid, inflict a mortal wound upon Abraham Lincoln, then President and Commander-in-chief of the army and navy of the United States, whereof he died; that, in pursuance of the same conspiracy, and within the said department and intrenched lines, Lewis Payne assaulted, with intent to kill and murder, William H. Seward, then Secretary of State of the United States; that George A. Atzerodt, in pursuance of the same conspiracy, and within the said department, laid in wait, with intent to kill and murder Andrew Johnson, then Vice-President of the United States; that Michael O'Laughlen, within said department, and in pursuance of said conspiracy, laid in wait to kill and murder Ulysses S. Grant, then in command of the armies of the United States; and that Mary E. Surratt, David E. Herold, Samuel Arnold, Samuel A. Mudd and Edward Spangler did encourage, aid and abet the commission of said several sets in the prosecution of said conspiracy.

Source: United States Army Military Commission. 1865. *Trial of the Assassins and Conspirators of the Murder of Abraham Lincoln.* Philadelphia: Barclay, 119–20.

IMPEACHMENT INVESTIGATION TESTIMONY OF HON. JAMES M. ASHLEY TAKEN BEFORE THE JUDICIARY COMMITTEE (NOVEMBER 23, 1867)

Mary Todd Lincoln and others believed that Andrew Johnson may have conspired with Booth to assassinate Lincoln. Johnson conspiracy theorists believed that ascension to the highest office of the land served as the vice president's primary motive. They point to Booth's coming to Johnson's hotel on the day of the assassination as the key link to Johnson's involvement in Lincoln's murder. However, the congressional committee that investigated the Lincoln assassination found no evidence to implicate Johnson in the plot.

The Judiciary Committee of the House of Representatives reopened the allegations against Johnson during the president's impeachment investigation. Representative James Mitchell Ashley of Ohio testified that he believed Johnson was part of the plot to kill Lincoln. He stated that there was evidence to substantiate his claim but not enough to actually charge Johnson. The House of Representatives eventually passed 11 articles of impeachment. Most centered on Johnson's violation of the Tenure of Office Act (1867). There were no articles that implicated Johnson in Lincoln's death.

Below is an excerpt from James Ashley's testimony (A) before the House of Representatives Judiciary Committee on November 23, 1867.

A. I wrote a note of that import, I presume.

Q. Have you that statement?

A. I have not. I sent it to Matchett, but I think I can get it.

Q. Did that relate to a charge against the President of having had to do with the assassination of President Lincoln?

A. I think there is a declaration in that statement that he (Dunham) is cognizant of the existence of a letter which would implicate the President in a guilty knowledge of the assassination. He made that statement in his letter to me. But the greater part of the paper referred to knowledge which he professed to have of other matters.

There was nothing in the paper which was of any value to me, and I did not bring it to the notice, I think, of a single member of the committee.

Q. Did you not bring it to the notice of General Butler, and did not he and you have consideration of it?

A. No sir; I think I never showed it to him. I did not think there was enough in it to induce me to do so. The statements were so exaggerated that I did not spend much time over it after I got it. I finally said to Dunham: "If you get me the letters, then whatever aid I can give you I will."

Q. Did that statement refer to letters?

A. Yes, sir; I think so.

Q. Are you certain of it?

A. I think I can get the paper itself. I will not be positive about its contents. I sent the paper to Matchett after some publications came out in this city, and he told me the other day that he never got it until some days ago. I sent it by express. He said it was misdirected.

Q. In whose handwriting was that statement?

A. In Dunham's, as I have every reason to believe.

Q. You say that the statement was so exaggerated that you did not believe its contents?

A. I thought from numerous other statements which had been made to me that there might be such letters in existence; but the statement was so indefinite and so vague that I never sent a man to look into it, or "to work the ease up," as detectives call it. I believe I never showed the statement to any one.

Q. Did you ever show it to Mr. Butler?

A. I think not. I don't believe I ever showed it to a single man.

Q. Did you not make a statement of it to this committee?

A. I think I have said that I had such a statement from this man, but I believe I never read it to a single member of the committee.

Q. Did that paper relate to evidence which it was supposed would implicate Mr. Johnson in the assassination of Mr. Lincoln?

A. Yes, sir. There were paragraphs in the paper which related to Johnson's supposed guilty knowledge of the assassination.

Q. Was there a suggestion in that paper that certain proofs would be necessary in order to fasten that on Mr. Johnson?

A. No, sir; I think not.

Q. There was no such intimation in the paper?

A. I think not.

Q. Did this appear in the paper: "For the names of Dawson and Allen, used by them, leave blanks, or substitute the names of such persons as you know will take their place?"

A. No, sir. I am very clear that there was nothing like that in the statement.

Q. Why did you send that statement away after this talk about it in the papers?

A. I was at home in Toledo, and sent it here to Mr. Matchett because he wrote for any paper I might have from Dunham.

Q. Why did you not keep it for your own protection?

A. I did not need protection of that kind.

Q. Why did you not keep it for this committee?

A. I think I can get it for the committee now, if they want it.

Q. Did you think it of any use?

A. I did not think it of any use.

Q. Did you consider that, from its exaggerated or from its frivolous and unconnected statements, it was not truthful, so that you did not care anything about it on that account?

A. The statement was so indefinite that I did not think any detective would undertake to hunt up evidence upon it. It might have been true, for all I knew, but I certainly would not undertake to look it up.

Q. Have you not stated to members of the House of Representatives that you had evidence in your possession which would implicate Mr. Johnson in the assassination of Mr. Lincoln?

A. No; not evidence in my possession. I may have said that I had statements made, in writing and otherwise, by this man and that, which induced me to believe it. I may have said that.

Q. Have you ever brought that evidence on which you believe it before this committee?

A. No, sir.

Q. Why did you not?

A. I have spoken to members of this committee about it. I have had no evidence which I regarded as valid; it was only an isolated statement of parties here and there, and not sufficiently strong to warrant me in presenting it.

Q. Then do you say before this committee that you had no evidence against Mr. Johnson which you considered as valid?

A. Yes. I had no evidence which I regarded as sufficient for the conviction of a criminal before a jury, and hence I never presented it.

Q. You had no evidence in your possession which you considered of sufficient importance to be considered by this committee?

A. No; I had not. If I had I should have presented it.

Q. I repeat the question whether you have not told members of the House of Representatives that you had evidence in your possession which satisfied you that Mr. Johnson had taken part or was implicated in the assassination of Mr. Lincoln.

A. I have said that I believed, from all that I had been able to gather during this investigation, that Mr. Johnson had a guilty knowledge of the assassination.

Q. You have said that before. I repeat the question as I put it before, and I want an answer to it specifically.

Witness. Have I not answered it?

Mr. ELDRIDGE. No, sir; I think not. I repeat the question:

Q. Have you stated to members of the House of Representatives that you had evidence which satisfied you that Mr. Johnson was connected with or implicated in the assassination of Mr. Lincoln?

A. Yes, certainly I have.

Q. Then I ask you why did you not produce this evidence to the committee?

A. Because it was not of that legal character which would have justified me in presenting it. It satisfied me from my stand-point, and that is what I meant.

Q. Then what do you mean by saying that you had no evidence in your possession which you considered valid?

A. It was not that kind of evidence which would satisfy the great mass of men, especially the men who do not concur with me in my theory about this matter. I have had a theory about it. I have always believed that President Harrison and President Taylor and President Buchanan were poisoned, and poisoned for the express purpose of putting the Vice Presidents in the presidential office. In the first two instances it was successful. It was attempted with Mr. Buchanan, and failed. It succeeded with Mr. Taylor and Mr. Harrison. Then Mr. Lincoln was assassinated, and from my stand-point I could come to a conclusion which impartial men, holding different views, could not come. It would not amount to legal evidence.

Q. Do you mean to say you have formed an opinion and expressed it to members of Congress that there was evidence to implicate Mr. Johnson which was not legal evidence?

A. Yes sir; it satisfied me, just as a man will say that he is satisfied a person is guilty of murder even when he escapes in a trial before a jury.

Q. Then you stated to these men, when you did make this statement, a conclusion which was founded on evidence which you did not consider legal?

A. It was founded on isolated statements which standing alone, would have been of no legal value, and I think the majority of men would not have come to the conclusion I did on reading or hearing the statements made to me; hence I did not care to present it or come before the committee with it.

Source: *Impeachment Investigation Testimony Taken Before the Judiciary Committee of the House of Representatives in the Investigation of the Charges Against Andrew Johnson.* 1867. Second Session, 39th Congress and First Session, 40th Congress. Washington, D.C.: Government Printing Office.

What Really Happened

All the grand conspiracy theories reject the idea that a mere stage actor like John Wilkes Booth could be the mastermind and organizer of a complex plan of dynastic assassination. The grand conspiracy theorists support their hypotheses with innuendo, circumstantial evidence, perjured testimony, and half-truths. In the end, they all fail to connect the alleged mastermind to the assassination plot with direct, verifiable, irrefutable evidence.

Most historians accept the simple conspiracy theory that John Wilkes Booth organized and led the plot to assassinate Lincoln, Johnson, and Seward. The existing evidence supports the contention, and 150 years of research and investigation have not definitively proved otherwise.

The simple conspiracy theory contends that Booth, a Southern sympathizer, did not originally intend to assassinate Lincoln. He was a part of a Confederate Secret Service plan to kidnap Lincoln and bring him to Richmond. This would not only throw the Union government into chaos but also Lincoln could be used as a bargaining chip to gain the release of Southern soldiers from Union prisoner-of-war camps. Booth recruited associates to help him with the kidnapping venture, including George Atzerodt, David Herold, John Surratt, and Lewis Powell. He established contacts in southern Maryland, purchased weapons and provisions, and procured a boat.

Booth attempted to kidnap Lincoln on March 17, 1865. Booth received information that Lincoln would be attending a play, *Still Waters Run Deep*, at Campbell Military Hospital located several miles north of the White House. He assembled his band of men with the intent to capture Lincoln on his return trip to the White House. The kidnapping plot was foiled when Lincoln decided not to attend the play at the hospital. Instead, he attended an event at the National Hotel. Ironically, this was the same hotel where Booth was residing at the time.

The plot to kidnap the president quickly disintegrated with the fall of Richmond in the first week of April. The Confederate government was on the run. Lee's Army of Northern Virginia was on the verge of defeat. Union cavalry had closed escape routes south for the retreating Southerners. There was nowhere to take a kidnapped president and no one to take charge of him. Booth abandoned the plan to abduct the commander in chief.

On the evening of April 11, 1865, Booth went to the White House with Powell and Herold to hear a speech by Lincoln. In his speech, the president stated that he supported voting rights for literate black men and for blacks that served in the Union army. Booth, an avowed racist, said to Powell and Herold, "Now by God, I'll put him through. That is the last speech he will ever make." It was at this moment that Booth made his decision to kill Lincoln.

Booth's decision to kill Lincoln was not simply motivated by revenge. Booth believed that Lincoln posed a threat to white civilization. He thought Lincoln disregarded civil liberties protected by the Constitution and was positioning himself to be a dictator in the style of Julius Caesar. Booth also hoped the Confederacy could still be saved, as he wrote in his diary, by doing "something decisive & great." That decisive and great action would be the decapitation of Union leadership.

On Friday, April 14, Booth learned that Lincoln was going to attend a performance of *Our American Cousin* that evening at Ford's Theatre. Booth decided this venue would provide him with the perfect opportunity to kill the president. In the evening, Booth informed his fellow conspirators of his intent to assassinate Lincoln. He assigned Powell the task of killing Seward and ordered Atzerodt to murder Johnson. David Herold was to aid Booth in his escape to Maryland. All three attacks were to occur simultaneously at approximately 10:00 p.m.

Booth entered Ford's Theatre a short time after 10:00 p.m. He proceeded upstairs to the mezzanine. John Parker, the Washington Metropolitan policeman assigned to guard the passageway to the presidential box, had deserted his post. Parker left Charles Forbes, a White House footman, as Lincoln's only protection. Booth presented Forbes with his calling card, and the footman allowed the assassin through a lobby door that led to the presidential box. Booth opened the door of the box and barred it behind himself. He then moved quietly toward the president and shot Lincoln in the head with a .44 caliber Derringer at approximately at 10:13 p.m. When Maj. Henry Rathbone, a member of the presidential party, attempted to apprehend Booth, he sliced the major with a hunting knife. Booth then vaulted over the railing of the box onto the stage. Most historians believe that Booth broke his leg in the jump. When on the stage, he waved his knife and shouted "sic semper tyrannis" (thus always to tyrants; also the motto of the state of Virginia). Booth exited the rear door of the stage and left on horseback. Lincoln died the next morning at 7:22 a.m.

Around the same time on April 14, Lewis Powell gained entrance to the Seward house. He tried to kill the secretary of state but failed in his attempt. George Atzerodt made no attempt to kill Johnson and aimlessly wandered the streets of Washington for the rest of the night. Booth escaped on horseback to Maryland. The government organized a massive manhunt that tracked Booth and his accomplice Herold through Maryland and into Virginia. On April 26, soldiers from the 16th New York Cavalry found Booth and Herold hiding in a tobacco barn on the Garrett farm near Port Royal, Virginia. Herold surrendered to the authorities, but Sgt. Boston Corbett shot and mortally wounded Booth as he wandered around the inside of the burning barn.

By the end of April, the government had eight of Booth's coconspirators in custody. A special nine-member military tribunal tried the eight suspects. The trial lasted seven weeks, and 366 witnesses testified during the proceedings. On June 30, 1865, the tribunal found all eight conspirators guilty and sentenced four to death by hanging (Lewis Powell, George Atzerodt, David Herold, and Mary Surratt). The tribunal sentenced the other four (Samuel Mudd, Samuel Arnold, Michael O'Laughlen, and Edmund Spangler) to terms ranging from six years to life imprisonment. The government hung Powell, Surratt, Herold, and Atzerodt on July 7 in the Old Arsenal Penitentiary. The government charged a ninth conspirator, John Surratt, with Lincoln's murder in 1867. A hung jury forced the government to release Surratt. The government never retried him.

In conclusion, the simple conspiracy theory best fits the verifiable facts of the Lincoln assassination. The reality is that Booth was involved in a scheme to kidnap Lincoln. When events made this plan untenable, Booth, by himself, decided to assassinate Lincoln rather than kidnap him. He employed his cabal of kidnappers to execute his assassination plots. Though President Johnson, Edwin Stanton, and the tribunal prosecutors tried to link Jefferson Davis and the Confederate government to Booth's assassination plot, no solid evidence exists to support this claim. In fact, after two years in prison, the government released Davis on bail. Despite all the accusations made against Davis and the Confederate Secret Service, the government never changed any Confederate official in the assassination of Lincoln. After over 150 years of investigation by Congress, scholars, and experts, they have yet to find records or evidence that anyone in the Confederate government was directly involved in Booth's assassination plot. The same is true for the assertions that Vice President Johnson or Secretary of War Edwin Stanton masterminded or were involved in Lincoln's death. Even with the passage of time, it still seems unfathomable to many that an actor and a group of miscreant misfits could pull off the crime of the century without the aid of some more powerful ally.

PRIMARY SOURCE DOCUMENTS

GEORGE SHEA, LETTER TO THE EDITOR OF
THE NEW YORK TRIBUNE (JANUARY 24, 1876)

George Shea was the chief justice of the Marine Court of New York. He was also the principal agent in securing bail for Jefferson Davis and gaining his release from federal custody after two years of imprisonment. Prominent Northerners, such as Horace Greely and Gerrit Smith, actually posted bail for the former Confederate president. At the insistence of Greely, Shea went to Canada to inspect secret Confederate journals and papers to ensure there was no link between Davis and the mistreatment of Union prisoners of war as well as no involvement in the assassination of Lincoln. Shea's investigation found no evidence that Davis was involved in the plot to kill Lincoln or to willfully mistreat Union POWs. No Confederate official was charged or tried for the assassination of Lincoln.

In January 1876, Shea wrote a letter to the editor of The New York Tribune. In his letter, Shea explained and defended why he sought bail for the release of Jefferson Davis. In the excerpt below, Shea claims that most Republicans of the time did not believe Davis was part of the conspiracy to kill Lincoln.

There was a general agreement among the gentlemen of the Republican party whom I have mentioned that Mr. Davis did not, by thought or act, participate in a conspiracy against Mr. Lincoln; and none of those expressed that conviction more emphatically than Mr. Thaddeus Stevens. The single subject on which light was desired by them was concerning the treatment of our soldiers while in the hands of the enemy. The Tribune of May 17th, 1865, tells the real condition of feeling at that moment, and unequivocally shows that it was not favorable to Mr. Davis on this matter. At the instance of Mr. Greeley, Mr. Wilson and, as I was given to understand, of Mr. Stevens, I went to Canada the first week in January, 1866, taking Boston on my route, there to consult with Governor Andrew and others. While at Montreal, General John C. Breckinridge came from Toronto, at my request, for the purpose of giving me information. There I had placed in my possession the official archives of the Government of the Confederate States, which I read and considered—especially all those messages and other acts of the Executive with the Senate in its secret sessions concerning the care and exchange of prisoners. I found that the supposed inhuman and unwarlike treatment of their own captured soldiers by agents of our Government was a most prominent and frequent topic. That those reports current then—perhaps even to this hour—in the South were substantially incorrect is little to the practical purpose. From those documents—not made to meet the public eye, but used in secret session, and from inquiries by me of those thoroughly conversant with the state of Southern opinion at the time—it was manifest that the people of the South believed those reports to be trustworthy, and they individually, and through their representatives at Richmond, pressed upon Mr. Davis, as the Executive and as the Commander-in-Chief of the army and navy, instant recourse to active measures of retaliation, to the end that the supposed cruelties might be stayed. Mr. Davis's conduct under such urgency and, indeed, expostulation, was a circumstance all-important in determining the probability of this charge as to himself. It was equally and decisively manifest, by the same sources of information, that Mr. Davis steadily and unflinchingly set himself in opposition to the indulgence of such demands, and declined to resort to any measure of violent retaliation. It impaired his personal influence, and brought much censure upon him from many in the South, who sincerely believed the reports spread among the people to be really true. The desire that something should be attempted from which a better care of prisoners could be secured seems to have grown so strong and prevalent that, on July 2d, 1863, Mr. Davis accepted the proffered service of Mr. Alexander H. Stephens, the Vice-President, to proceed as a military commissioner to Washington. The sole purpose of Mr. Davis in allowing that commission appears, from the said documents, which I read, to have been to place the war on the footing of such as are waged by civilized people in modern times, and to divest it of a savage character, which, it was claimed, had been impressed on it in spite of all effort and protest; and alleged instances of such savage conduct were named and averred. This project was prevented, as Mr. Stephens was denied permission by our Administration to approach Washington, and intercourse with him prohibited. On his return, after this rejected effort to produce a mutual kindness in the treatment of prisoners, Southern feeling became more unquiet on the matter than ever; yet it clearly appears that Mr. Davis would not yield to the demand for retaliation.

The evidence tending to show this to be the true condition of the case as to Mr. Davis himself was brought by me and submitted to Mr. Greeley, and in part to Mr. Wilson. The result was, these gentlemen, and those others in sympathy with them, changed their former suspicion to a favorable opinion and a friendly disposition. They were from this time kept informed of each movement as made to liberate Mr. Davis, or to compel the Government to bring the prisoner to trial. All this took place before counsel, indeed before any one acting on his behalf, was allowed to communicate with or see him.

Source: Shea, George. 1876. "Letter to the Editor of the *New York Tribune*," January 24. As published in the *Southern Historical Society Papers* 1, no. 4: 319–24.

JOHN WILKES BOOTH, LETTER PUBLISHED IN *THE PHILADELPHIA INQUIRER* (APRIL 21, 1865)

In November of 1864, John Wilkes Booth deposited an envelope for safekeeping with his brother-in-law John S. Clarke. In January 1865, Booth returned to Clarke's residence and affixed his signature to the document in the envelope. After the assassination of Lincoln, Clarke turned the envelope over to William Millward, the U.S. marshal for the Eastern District of Pennsylvania. On April 21, 1865, The Philadelphia Inquirer *published Booth's letter. This document contains the best explanation of Booth's motives to first abduct Lincoln and later to assassinate him. The letter is written in the first person and does not support any conspiracy with Confederate officials.*

_____. _____. 1864

MY DEAR SIR,—You may use this as you thing most. But as some may wish to know when, who and why, and as I know not how to direct, I give it (in the words of your master)

"TO WHOM IT MAY CONCERN":

Right or wrong. God judge me, not man. For be my motive good or bad, of one thing I am sure, the lasting condemnation of the North.

I love peace more than life. Have loved the Union beyond expression. For four years have I waited, hoped and prayed for the dark clouds to break, and for a restoration of our former sunshine. To wait longer would be a crime. All hope for peace is dead. My prayers have proved as idle as my hopes. God's will be done. I go to see and share the bitter end.

I have ever held the South were right. The very nomination of ABRA-HAM LINCOLN, four years ago, spoke plainly, war—war upon Southern rights and institutions. His election proved it. "Await an overt act." Yes, till you are bound and plundered. What folly! The South was wise. Who thinks of argument or patience when the finger of his enemy presses on the trigger? In a foreign war I, too, could say, "country, right or wrong." But in a struggle such as ours, (where the brother tries to pierce the brother's heart,) for God's sake, choose the right. When a country like this spurns justice from her side she forfeits the allegiance of every honest freeman, and should leave him, untrameled by any fealty so ever, to act as his conscience may approve.

People of the North, to hate tyranny, to love liberty and justice, to strike at wrong and oppression, was the teaching of our fathers. The study of our early history will not let me forget it, and may it never.

This country was formed for the white, not for the black man. And looking upon African Slavery from the same stand-point held by the noble framers of our constitution. I for one, have ever considered if one of the greatest blessings (both for themselves and us,) that God has ever bestowed upon a favored nation. Witness heretofore our wealth and power; witness their elevation and enlightenment above their race elsewhere. I have lived among it most of my life, and have seen less harsh treatment from master to man than I have beheld in the North from father to son. Yet, Heaven knows, no one would be willing to do more for the negro race than I, could I but see a way to still better their condition.

But LINCOLN's policy is only preparing the way for their total annihilation. The South are not, nor have they been fighting for the continuance of slavery. The first battle of Bull Run did away with that idea. Their causes since for war have been as noble and greater far than those that urged our fathers on Even should we allow they were wrong at the beginning of this contest, cruelty and injustice have made the wrong become the right, and they stand now (before the wonder and admiration of the world) as a noble band of patriotic heroes. Hereafter, reading of their deeds, Thermopylae will be forgotten.

When I aided in the capture and execution of JOHN BROWN (who was a murderer on our Western border, and who was fairly tried and convicted, before an impartial judge and jury, of treason, and who, by the way, has since been made a god), I was proud of my little share in the transaction, for I deemed it my duty, and that I was helping our common country to perform an act of justice. But what was a crime in poor JOHN BROWN is now considered (by themselves) as the greatest and only virtue of the whole Republican party. Strange transmigration! Vice to become a virtue, simply because more indulge in it

I thought men, as now, that the Abolitionists were the only traitors in the land, and that the entire party deserved the same fate of poor old BROWN, not because they wish to abolish slavery but on account of the means they have ever endeavored to use to effect that abolition. If BROWN were living I doubt whether he himself would set slavery against the Union. Most or many in the North do, and openly curse the Union, if the South are to return and retain a single right guarantied to them by every tie which we once revered as sacred. The South can make no choice. It is either extermination or slavery for themselves (worse than death) to draw from. I know my choice.

I have also studied hard to discover upon what grounds the right of a State to secede has been denied, when our very name, United States, and the Declaration of Independence, both provide for secession. But there is no time for words. I write in haste. I know how foolish I shall be deemed for undertaking such a step as this, where, on the one side, I have many friends, and everything to make me happy, where my profession alone has gained me an income of more than twenty thousand dollars a year, and where my great personal ambition in my profession has such a great field for labor. On the other hand, the South have never bestowed upon me one kind word; a place now where I have no friends, except beneath the sod; a place where I must either become a private soldier or a beggar. To give up all of the former for the latter, besides my mother and sisters whom I love so dearly, (although they so widely differ with me in opinion,) seems insane; but God is my judge. I love justice more than I do a country that disowns it; more than fame and wealth; more (Heaven pardon me if wrong,) more than a happy home. I have never been upon a battle-field; but O, my countrymen, could you all but see the reality or effects of this horrid war, as I have seen them, (in every State save Virginia.) I know you would think like me, and would pray the Almighty to create in the Northern mind a sense of right and justice, (even should it possess no seasoning of mercy,) and that he would dry up this sea of blood between us, which is daily growing wider. Alas! poor country, is she to meet her threatened doom? Four years ago I would have given a thousand lives to see her remain (as I had always known her) powerful and unbroken. And even now, I would hold my life as naught to see her what she was. O, my friends, if the fearful scenes of the past four years had never been enacted, or if what has been had been but a frightful dream, from which we could now awake, with what overflowing hearts could we bless our

God and pray for his continued favor. How I have loved the old flag, can never now be known. A few years since and the entire world could boast of none so pure and spotless. But I have of late been seeing and hearing of the bloody deeds of which she has been made the emblem, and would shudder to think how changed she had grown. O, how I have longed to see her break from the mist of blood and death that circles round her folds, spoiling her beauty and tarnishing her honor. But no, day by day has she been dragged deeper and deeper into cruelty and oppression, till now (in my eyes) her once bright red stripes look like bloody gashes on the face of Heaven. I look now upon my early admiration of her glories as a dream. My love (as things stand to-day) is for the South alone. Nor do I deem it a dishonor in attempting to make for her a prisoner of this man, to whom she owes so much of misery. If success attends me, I go penniless to her side. They say she has found that "last ditch" which the North have so long derided, and been endeavoring to force her in, forgetting they are our brothers, and that it's impolitic to goad an enemy to madness. Should I reach her in safety and find it true, I will proudly beg permission to triumph or die in that same "ditch" by her side.

A Confederate doing duty upon his own responsibility. J. WILKES BOOTH.

Source: Booth, John Wilkes. 1865. Letter published in *The Philadelphia Inquirer*, April 21.

JOHN WILKES BOOTH'S DIARY (1865)

John Wilkes Booth recorded his thoughts about the assassination and his escape in a small, red 1864 appointment book. Booth probably made the entries sometime between April 17 and April 22, 1865. Col. Everton Conger took the diary from Booth's body and gave it to the chief of the War Department's National Detective Police, Lafayette Baker. Baker gave the diary to Edwin Stanton. The government never used the diary in the conspiracy trial. In 1867, the diary was discovered in a War Department file. There were several pages missing. Today, Booth's diary is on display in the museum at Ford's Theatre.

In his diary entries for April 13/14 and April 21, Booth again uses the first person. In the April 13/14 entry, Booth alludes to the failed abduction scheme and uses the pronoun "we" to designate a wider conspiracy to kidnap Lincoln. When he describes the assassination, he continuously uses the singular pronoun "I," suggesting that he acted alone. Booth also tried to justify the assassination in both diary entries. Conspiracy theorists dwell on Booth's statement that he left behind a little evidence to clear his name. Here Booth is not claiming to be a part of a wider conspiracy. Instead, he hoped that his rationalizations for assassinating Lincoln would vindicate his actions over time in the court of public opinion.

April 13, 14, Friday, the Ides.

Until today nothing was ever thought of sacrificing to our country's wrongs. For six months we had worked to capture, but our cause being almost lost, something decisive and great must be done. But its failure was owing to others, who did not strike for their country with a heart. I struck boldly, and not as the papers say. I walked with a firm step through a thousand of his friends, was stopped, but pushed on. A colonel was at his side. I shouted Sic semper before I fired. In jumping broke my leg. I passed all his pickets, rode sixty miles that night with the bone of my leg tearing the flesh at every jump. I can never repent it, though we hated to kill. Our country owed all her troubles to him, and God simply made me the instrument of his punishment. The country is not what it was. This forced Union is not what I have loved. I care not what becomes of me. I have no desire to outlive my country. The night before the deed I wrote a long article and left it for one of the editors of the National Intelligencer, in which I fully set forth our reasons for our proceedings. He or the govmt

Friday 21 –

After being hunted like a dog through swamps, woods, and last night being chased by gunboats till I was forced to return wet, cold, and starving, with every man's hand against me, I am here in despair. And why; For doing what Brutus was honored for, What made Tell a hero. And yet I, for striking down a greater tyrant than they ever knew am looked upon as a common cutthroat. My action was purer than either of theirs. One hoped to be great himself. The other had not only his countrys but his own, wrongs to avenge. I hoped for no gain. I knew no private wrong. I struck for my country and that alone. A country that groaned beneath this tyranny and prayed for this end. Yet now behold the cold hands they extend to me. God *cannot* pardon me if I have done wrong. Yet I cannot see any wrong except in serving a degenerate people. The little, the very little I left behind to clear my name, the Govmt will not allow to be printed. So ends all. For my country I have given up all that makes life sweet and Holy, brought misery upon my family, and am sure there is no pardon in the Heaven for me since man condemns me so. I have only *heard* of what has been done (except what I did myself) and it fills me with horror. God try and forgive me and bless my mother. To night I will once more try the river with the intent to cross, though I have a greater desire and almost a mind to return to Washington and in a measure clear my name which I feel I can do. I do not repent the blow I struck. I may before my God, but not to man.

I think I have done well, though I am abandoned, with the curse of Cain upon me. When if the world knew my heart, that one blow would have made me great, though I did desire no greatness. To night I try to escape these bloodhounds once more. Who, who can read his fate. God's will be done.

I have too great a soul to die like a criminal. Oh may he, may He spare me that and let me die bravely.

I bless the entire world. Have never hated or wronged anyone. This last was not a wrong, unless God deems it so. And it's with him, to damn or bless me. As for this brave boy with me, who often prays (yes, before and since) with a true and sincere heart, was it crime in him, if so, why can he pray the same. I do not wish to shed a drop of blood, but "I must fight the course." Tis all that's left to me.

Source: "Diary of John Wilkes Booth." 1867. *The New York Times*, May 22.

Further Reading

Bishop, James. 1955. *The Day Lincoln Was Shot.* New York: Harper.

Bryan, George S. 1940. *The Great American Myth.* New York: Carrick and Evans.

Chiniguy, Charles. 2014. *Fifty Years in the Church of Rome: The Conversion of a Priest.* North Charleston, SC: CreateSpace.

Dewitt, David M. 2008. *The Assassination of Abraham Lincoln and Its Expiation.* Whitefish, MT: Kessinger.

Eisenschiml, Otto. 1937. *Why Was Lincoln Murdered?* Boston: Little, Brown.

Fazio, John. 2015. *Decapitating the Union: Jefferson Davis, Judah Benjamin and the Plot to Assassinate Lincoln.* Jefferson, NC: McFarland.

Guttridge, Leonard F., and Ray A. Neff. 2003. *Dark Union: The Secret Web of Profiteers, Politicians, and Booth Conspirators.* Hoboken, NJ: John Wiley and Sons.

Hanchett, William. 1983. *The Lincoln Murder Conspiracies.* Urbana: University of Illinois Press.

Hanchett, William. 1991. "Lincoln's Murder: The Simple Conspiracy Theory." *Civil War Time Illustrated* 30, no. 5: 28–35, 70–71.

Hanchett, William. 1995. "The Happiest Days of His Life." *Civil War Times Illustrated* 34, no. 5: 76–88.

Harris, Thomas M., and Edward Hendrie. 2014. *Rome's Responsibility for the Assassination of Abraham Lincoln.* Great Mountain Publishing.

Hingham, Charles. 2004. *Murdering Mr. Lincoln: A New Detection of the 19th Century's Most Famous Crime.* Beverly Hills, CA: New Millennium Press.

Holzer, Harold, Craig L. Symonds, and Frank J. Williams, eds. 2010. *The Lincoln Assassination: Crime and Punishment, Myth and Memory.* New York: Fordham University Press.

Kauffman, Michael W. 2005. *American Brutus: John Wilkes Booth and the Lincoln Conspiracies.* New York: Random House.

Lauglin, Clara E. 2012. *The Death of Lincoln: The Story of Booth's Plot, His Deed, and the Penalty.* Charleston, SC: Nabu Press.

Madonna, Jerrod. 2011. *A Threat to the Republic: The Secret of the Lincoln Assassination that Preserved the Union.* North Charleston, SC: CreateSpace.

McLoughin, Emmett. 1963. *An Inquiry into the Assassination of Abraham Lincoln.* New York: L. Stuart.

Mills, Robert Lockwood. 1994. *It Didn't Happen the Way You Think. The Lincoln Assassination: What the Experts Missed.* Bowie, MD: Heritage Books.

Norton, Rojer J. n.d. *Lincoln Assassination Theories: A Simple Conspiracy or a Grand Conspiracy.* Accessed April 17, 2018. http://rojerjnorton.com/Lincoln74.html.

Pitman, Benn. 1865. *The Assassination of President Lincoln and the Trial of the Conspirators.* New York: Moore, Wilstach & Baldwin.

Starkey, Larry. 1976. *Wilkes Booth Came to Washington.* New York: Random House.

Steers, Edward, Jr. 2001. *Blood on the Moon: The Assassination of Abraham Lincoln.* Lexington: University Press of Kentucky.

Steers, Edward, Jr., and Harold Holzer, eds. 2009. *The Lincoln Assassination Conspirators: Their Confinement and Execution, as Recorded in the Letterbook of John Frederick Hartranft.* Baton Rouge: Louisiana State University Press.

Swanson, James. 2006. *Manhunt: The 12-Day Chase for Lincoln's Killer.* New York: HarperCollins.

Tidwell, William A., James O. Hall, and David Winfred Gaddy. 1997. *Come Retribution: The Confederate Secret Service and the Assassination of Lincoln.* New York: Barnes and Noble Books.

Turner, Thomas Reed. 1991. *Beware the People Weeping: Public Opinion and the Assassination of Abraham Lincoln.* Baton Rouge: Louisiana State University Press.

Bibliography

Abbot, Karen. 2014. *Liar, Temptress, Soldier, Spy. Four Women Undercover in the Civil War*. New York: Harper.

Attie, Jeanie. 1998. *Patriot Toil: Northern Women and the American Civil War*. Ithaca, NY: Cornell University Press.

Barney, William L. 1990. *Battleground for the Union: The Era of the Civil War and Reconstruction, 1848–1877*. Englewood Cliffs, NJ: Prentice Hall.

Blight, David W. 1989. *Frederick Douglass' Civil War: Keep the Faith with Jubilee*. Baton Rouge: Louisiana State University Press.

Blight, David W. 2002. *Race and Reunion: The Civil War in American Memory*. Cambridge, MA: Harvard University Press.

Boritt, Gabor S., ed. 1996. *Why the Civil War Came*. New York: Oxford University Press.

Brown, Thomas J. 2004. *The Public Art of Civil War Commemoration: A Brief History with Documents*. Boston: Bedford/St. Martins.

Bruce, Levine. 1992. *Half Slave and Half Free: The Roots of the Civil War*. New York: Hill and Wang.

Burton, David H. 1995. *Clara Barton: In the Service of Humanity*. Westport, CT: Greenwood.

Catton, Bruce. 1960. *The Civil War*. Boston: Houghton Mifflin.

Catton, Bruce. 1982. *Reflections on the Civil War*. New York: Beakley Books.

Chadwick, Bruce. 2001. *The Reel Civil War: Myth Making in American Film*. New York: Knopf.

Cimbala, Paul A., and Randall M. Miller, eds. 2002. *An Uncommon Time: The Civil War and the Northern Home Front*. New York: Fordham.

Cornish, Dudley T. 1956. *The Sable Arm: Negro Troops in the Union Army, 1861–1865*. New York: W. W. Norton.

Creighton, Margaret. 2005. *The Colors of Courage: Gettysburg's Forgotten History—Immigrants, Women, and African Americans in the Civil War's Defining Battle.* New York: Basic Books.

Donald, David Herbert. 1995. *Lincoln.* New York: Simon and Schuster.

Durden, Robert F. 1972. *The Gray and Black: The Confederate Debate on Emancipation.* Baton Rouge: Louisiana State University Press.

Dyer, Frederick H. 1908. *A Compendium of the War of the Rebellion.* Des Moines, IA: Dyer.

Egerton, Douglas R. 2017. *Thunder at the Gates: The Black Civil War Regiments that Redeemed America.* New York: Basic Books.

Fahs, Alice. 2001. *The Imagined Civil War: Popular Literature of the North and South, 1861–1865.* Chapel Hill: University of North Carolina Press.

Faust, Drew Gilpin. 1990. *Mothers of Invention: Women of the Slaveholding South in the American Civil War.* Chapel Hill: University of North Carolina Press.

Fellman, Michael, Leslie J. Gordon, and Daniel E. Sutherland. 2003. *The Civil War and Its Aftermath.* New York: Longman.

Fishel, Edwin C. 1996. *The Secret War for the Union: The Untold Story of Military Intelligence in the Civil War.* Boston: Houghton Mifflin.

Foote, Shelby. 1958–1978. *The Civil War: A Narrative.* 3 vols. New York: Random House.

Gallagher, Gary W. 1997. *The Confederate War.* Cambridge, MA: Harvard University Press.

Gerteis, Louis S. 1973. *From Contraband to Freedman: Federal Policy toward Southern Blacks, 1861–1865.* Westport, CT: Greenwood.

Giewapp, William E., ed. 2001. *The Civil War and Reconstruction: A Documentary Collection.* New York: W. W. Norton.

Goodwin, Doris Kearns. 2005. *Team of Rivals: The Political Genius of Abraham Lincoln.* New York: Simon and Schuster.

Grant, Susan-Mary, and Brian Holden Reid, eds. 2000. *The American Civil War.* New York: Longman.

Hagerman, Edward. 1988. *The American Civil War and the Origins of Modern Warfare.* Bloomington: Indiana University Press.

Harris, William C. 1999. *With Charity for All. Lincoln and the Restoration of the Union.* Lexington: University Press of Kentucky.

Hattaway, Herman. 1997. *Shades of Blue and Gray: An Introductory Military History of the Civil War.* Columbia: University of Missouri Press.

Hedtke, James R. 2006. *Civil War Professional Soldiers, Citizen Soldiers, and Native American Soldiers of Genesee County, New York: Ordinary Men of Valor.* Lewiston, NY: Edwin Mellen.

Hesseltine, William B. 1930. *Civil War Prisons: A Study in Psychology.* Columbus: Ohio University Press.

Hettle, Wallace, ed. 2017. *The Confederate Homefront: A History in Documents.* Baton Rouge: Louisiana State University Press.

Holzer, Harold. 2004. *Lincoln at Cooper Union: The Speech that Made Abraham Lincoln President.* New York: Simon and Schuster.

Horwitz, Tony. 1998. *Confederates in the Attic: Dispatches from the Unfinished Civil War.* New York: Pantheon.

Irvine, Dallas. 1966. *Military Operations of the Civil War: A Guide-Index to the Official Records of the Union and Confederate Armies, 1861–1865.* Washington, DC: Civil War Centennial Commission.

Johannsen, Robert W., and Wendy Hamand Venet, eds. 2003. *The Union in Crisis 1850–1877.* Acton, MA: Copley.

Keegan, John. 2009. *The American Civil War: A Military History.* New York: Alfred A. Knopf.

Mahin, Dean B. 1999. *One War at a Time: The International Dimensions of the American Civil War.* Washington, DC: Brassey's.

Manning, Chandra. 2007. *What This Civil War Was Over: Soldiers, Slavery, and the Civil War.* New York: Alfred A. Knopf.

McPherson, James M. 1969. *The Struggle for Equality: Abolitionists and the Negro in the Civil War and Reconstruction.* Princeton, NJ: Princeton University Press.

McPherson, James M. 1987. *Battle Cry for Freedom.* New York: Oxford University Press.

McPherson, James M. 1997. *For Cause and Comrades: Why Men Fought in the Civil War.* New York: Oxford University Press.

McPherson, James M. 2001. *Ordeal by Fire: The Civil War and Reconstruction.* 3rd ed. New York: McGraw Hill.

Moe, Richard. 2001. *The Last Full Measure: The Life and Death of the First Minnesota Volunteers.* St. Paul: Minnesota Historical Society.

Murdock, Eugene C. 1987. *The Civil War in the North: A Selective Annotated Bibliography.* New York: Garland.

Nelson, Scott, and Carol Sheriff. 2005. *A People at War: Civilians and Soldiers in America's Civil War, 1854–1877.* New York: Oxford University Press.

Nevins, Allan. 1960. *The War for the Union: War Becomes Revolution, 1862–1863.* New York: Scribner.

Nevins, Allan, James I. Robertson Jr., and Bell I. Wiley. 1967. *Civil War Books: A Critical Bibliography.* Vol. 2. Baton Rouge: Louisiana State University Press.

Oates, Stephen B. 1997. *The Approaching Fury: Voices of the Storm, 1820–1861.* New York: Harper Perennial.

Palwdan, Phillip S. 1988. *"A People's Contest": The Union and the Civil War, 1861–1865.* New York: Harper and Row.

Perman, Michael. 1993. *The Coming of the American Civil War.* 3rd ed. Lexington, MA: D. C. Heath.

Potter, David M. 1976. *The Impending Crisis, 1848–1861.* New York: Harper and Row.

Pressley, Thomas J. 1954. *Americans Interpret Their Civil War.* Princeton, NJ: Princeton University Press.

Pryor, Elizabeth Brown. 2007. *Reading the Man: A Portrait of Robert E. Lee through His Private Letters.* New York: Penguin.

Reagan, John H. 1906. *Memoirs with Special Reference to Secession and the Civil War.* New York: Neale.

Reid, Mitchell. 1993. *The Vacant Chair: The Northern Soldier Leaves Home.* New York: Oxford University Press.

Rhodes, James Ford. 2000. *History of the Civil War, 1861–1865.* New York: Bartleby.

Robertson, James, Jr. 1997. *Stonewall Jackson: The Man, the Soldier, the Legend.* New York: Macmillan.

Roland, Charles P. 1991. *An American Iliad: The Story of the Civil War.* New York: McGraw-Hill.

Rose, Willie Lee. 1964. *Rehearsal for Reconstruction: The Port Royal Experiment.* Indianapolis, IN: Bobbs-Merrill.

Sears, Stephen W. 2017. *Lincoln's Lieutenants: The High Command of the Army of the Potomac.* Boston: Houghton Mifflin Harcourt.

Smith, John David. 2002. *Black Soldiers in Blue: African American Troops in the Civil War.* Chapel Hill: University of North Carolina Press.

Stampp, Kenneth M. 1950. *And the War Came: The North and the Secession Crisis.* Baton Rouge: Louisiana State University Press.

Stephens, Joseph E. 1999. *1863: The Birth of the Nation.* New York: Bantam Books.

Stout, Harry S. 2006. *Upon the Altar of the Nation: A Moral History of the Civil War.* New York: Viking.

Swanson, James L. 2010. *Bloody Crimes: The Funeral of Abraham Lincoln and the Chase for Jefferson Davis.* New York: Harper Perennial.

Thomas, Emory M. 1979. *The Confederate Nation, 1861–1865.* New York: Harper and Row.

Weigley, Russell F. 2000. *A Great Civil War: A Military and Political History, 1861–1865.* Bloomington: Indiana University Press.

Wheeler, Richard, ed. 1976. *Voices of the Civil War.* Boston: Thomas Y. Crowell.

Widener, Ralph W., Jr. 1982. *Confederate Monuments: Enduring Symbols of the South and the War between the States.* Washington, DC: Andromedia.

Wiley, Bell I. 1943. *The Life of Johnny Reb: The Common Soldier of the Confederacy.* Baton Rouge: Louisiana State University Press.

Wiley, Bell I. 1952. *The Life of Billy Yank: The Common Soldier of the Union.* Baton Rouge: Louisiana State University Press.

Williams, David. 2005. *A People's History of the Civil War: The Struggles for the Meaning of Freedom.* New York: New Press.

Wilson, Douglas L. 1998. *Honors Voice: The Transformation of Abraham Lincoln.* New York: Alfred A. Knopf.

Wolseley, Garnet. 1964. *The American Civil War: An English View.* Charlottesville: University Press of Virginia.

Woodworth, Steven E., ed. 2000. *The Human Tradition in the Civil War and Reconstruction.* Wilmington, DE: SR Books.

Woodworth, Steven E., ed. 2002. *The Loyal, True and Brave: America's Civil War Soldiers.* Wilmington, DE: SR Books.

Wright, Jon H. 1989. *Compendium of the Confederacy: An Annotated Bibliography.* 2 vols. Wilmington, NC: Broadfoot.

Index

About the Author

James R. Hedtke is a professor of history and political science at Cabrini University, where he has taught for 45 years. Dr. Hedtke received his BS from Saint Joseph's University, MA from Villanova University, and PhD from Temple University. His academic interests include the American presidency, terrorism, and the Civil War. He has written over 40 book reviews and is a frequent presenter at regional Civil War roundtables. He is the author of three books: *Lame Duck Presidents: Myth or Reality* (2002), *Civil War Professional Soldiers, Citizen Soldiers, and Native American Soldiers of Genesee County, New York: Ordinary Men of Valor* (2006), and *The Freckleton, England, Air Disaster* (2014). Dr. Hedtke is the father of three daughters and lives in Broomall, Pennsylvania, with his wife, Judy, and grandson, Luke.